Jack Tar's Story

The Autobiographies and Memoirs of
Sailors in Antebellum America

Jack Tar's Story examines the autobiographies and memoirs of ante-bellum American sailors to explore contested meanings of manhood and nationalism in the early republic. It is the first study to use various kinds of institutional sources, including crew lists, ships' logs, and impressment records, to document the stories sailors told. It focuses on how mariner authors remembered/interpreted various events and experiences, including the War of 1812, the Haitian Revolution, South America's wars of independence, British impressment, flogging on the high seas, roistering, and religious conversion.

This book straddles different fields of scholarship and suggests how their concerns intersect or resonate with each other: the history of print culture, the study of autobiographical writing, and the historiography of seafaring life and of masculinity in antebellum America.

Myra C. Glenn is Professor of American History at Elmira College. She is the author of *Campaigns against Corporal Punishment: Prisoners, Sailors, Women, and Children in Antebellum America* and *Thomas K. Beecher: Minister to a Changing America, 1824–1900*. Her work has appeared in numerous professional journals, and she is the recipient of two Fulbright lecture awards.

Jack Tar's Story

The Autobiographies and Memoirs of Sailors in Antebellum America

MYRA C. GLENN

Elmira College

CAMBRIDGE
UNIVERSITY PRESS

CAMBRIDGE UNIVERSITY PRESS
Cambridge, New York, Melbourne, Madrid, Cape Town, Singapore,
São Paulo, Delhi, Dubai, Tokyo, Mexico City

Cambridge University Press
32 Avenue of the Americas, New York, NY 10013-2473, USA

www.cambridge.org
Information on this title: www.cambridge.org/9780521193689

First published 2010

Printed in the United States of America

A catalog record for this publication is available from the British Library.

Library of Congress Cataloging in Publication data
Glenn, Myra C.
   Jack Tar's story : the autobiographies and memoirs of sailors
   in antebellum America / Myra C. Glenn.
      p.   cm.
   Includes bibliographical references and index.
   ISBN 978-0-521-19368-9
   1. Seafaring life – United States – History – 19th century.   2. Sailors – United
   States – Social conditions – 19th century.   3. United States. Navy – Sea
   life – History – 19th century.   4. Sailors' writings, English – United
   States – History – 19th century.   I. Title.
   G540.G46   2010
   387.5092'273–dc22   2010029539

ISBN 978-0-521-19368-9 Hardback

For the next generation: Phoebe, Tyler, Ryan, and Bennett

Contents

Acknowledgments

Many people have helped me during the more than twelve years I have worked on this project. I owe the greatest professional debt to three people. Christopher McKee and Paul Gilje steered me to major sources in maritime history; made incisive, detailed comments on various drafts of this book; and challenged me to become more analytical and focused in my work. Their scholarship has greatly enriched my understanding of seafaring life in antebellum America. Gillian Hughes, a professional researcher in the British National Archives, offered invaluable assistance – she found and photocopied impressment and prisoner-of-war records. Her impeccable research skills and dogged persistence were essential to completing this project.

I also thank Lewis Perry for his helpful comments on an early draft of this book. Charles D'Aniello and the other librarians at the State University of New York in Buffalo unfailingly helped and encouraged me in my work. Commentators at various historical conferences, especially the 2001 Society for Historians of the Early Republic Conference, prodded me to clarify my thinking on multiple issues. Thanks to Joanne Sprott for preparing the index.

Earlier versions of my work appeared in journal articles: "Forging Manhood and Nationhood Together: Sailors' Accounts of Their Exploits, Sufferings, and Resistance in the Antebellum United States," *American Nineteenth Century History* 8(1): 27–49 and "Troubled Manhood in the Early Republic: The Life and Autobiography of Sailor Horace Lane," *Journal of the Early Republic* 26 (Spring

2006): 59–93. I thank both journals for allowing me to use materials from these essays.

The success of my research trips depended on a cadre of dedicated professionals. Charles Johnson and his staff at the U.S. National Archives, Navy & Maritime Division, in Washington, D.C., offered particularly valuable assistance. So too did Rebecca Livingston before her retirement. I also thank the staffs of the following institutions: the U.S. National Archives in New York City; the History and Genealogy Department of the Connecticut State Library; the Library of Congress; the New-York Historical Society; the Massachusetts Archives; the G.W. Blunt White Library; the Boston Public Library; the New York Public Library, especially the Rare Books Division; the New London County Historical Society; the Mystic Historical Society; and the Mystic and Noank Library.

Numerous librarians, archivists, genealogists, and other researchers have tracked down information on the men that I write about. The following were especially helpful: Patrick Ausband and his son Joshua, Sailors' Snug Harbor; Wendy Schnur, Mystic Seaport Museum; Nathaniel Wiltzen, U.S. National Archives in Boston; Jennifer Faux Smith, Massachusetts Archives; Elizabeth Bouvier, Massachusetts Supreme Judicial Court Archives and Records Preservation; and Lynn Calvin, Saratoga County (NYS) Historian's Office.

The staff at Cambridge University Press offered the right mix of professional expertise and encouragement. Research grants from Elmira College and Phi Alpha Theta provided needed financial assistance. I also thank former Academic Dean Bryan Reddick and Dean Peter Viscusi for granting me sabbaticals and spring term leaves. The college's library staff, especially Katie Galvin, also helped me. Colleagues and friends at Elmira College have generously supported me and my scholarship. Particular thanks to Charles Mitchell, Mary Jo Mahoney, and Robert Shephard.

Thanks also to Beth Mattingly and Cynthia Whiteway for their friendship and encouragement. My greatest debt is to my husband David. He has nourished me with his love and support for more than thirty-five years.

List of Abbreviations

RG	Record Group
TNA, PRO:ADM	The National Archives of the United Kingdom, Public Record Office: Admiralty
NA	The United States National Archives and Records Administration

Lane's and Dana's books appeared when the American reading public sought stories about seafaring travels and adventures.
Hundreds of short stories, novellas, and novels churned out tales
about nefarious pirates, dashing naval officers, and beautiful women
on the high seas. James Fenimore Cooper, now best remembered for
his *Leatherstocking Tales*, first became a literary success through
such sea novels as *The Pilot* and *Red Rover*, published respectively
in 1824 and 1827. Herman Melville's sea novels, particularly *Typee*
(1846) and *Omoo* (1847), earned him financial and critical success.[4]

There were also retired sailors who wrote their own works, even
if they received some editorial assistance from friends and publishers. Like Lane, the majority of these men were impecunious hawkers
of ephemeral tales that catered to the public's appetite for adventure
and entertainment. After a career at sea, these men were often too
sick or worn out to earn a decent living.[5] Desperate for money, they
peddled their yarns about adventure on the high seas or wrote exposés detailing abuses committed by arrogant, sadistic officers.[6] Some
also published memoirs and autobiographies. These works were generally longer and more introspective than the exposés, travelogues,
and adventure narratives.[7]

---

[4] Thomas Philbrick, *James Fenimore Cooper and the Development of American Sea Fiction* (Cambridge, MA: Harvard University Press, 1961), discusses these developments.

[5] Although many antebellum ex-seamen achieved a modest competency for them-selves, others lived impoverished lives. For recent studies of what happened to Jack Tar after his seafaring years ended, see Daniel Vickers with Vince Walsh, *Young Men and the Sea: Yankee Seafarers in the Age of Sail* (New Haven, CT: Yale University Press, 2005), 156, 159–60; Vickers, "An Honest Tar: Ashley Bowen of Marblehead," *The New England Quarterly* 69, no. 4 (1996): 531–53; Simon P. Newman, *Embodied History: The Lives of the Poor in Early Philadelphia* (Philadelphia: University of Pennsylvania Press, 2003), 104–24; Billy G. Smith, *The "Lower Sort": Philadelphia's Laboring People, 1750–1800* (Ithaca, NY: Cornell University Press, 1990), 113–15, 142–43, 154–56, 173–75.

[6] Such works were part of a mendicant literature peddled on urban streets. Richardson Wright, *Little Hawkers and Walkers in Early America: Strolling Peddlers, Preachers, Lawyers and Others from the Beginning to the Civil War* (Philadelphia: J.B. Lippincott, Co., 1927) and Ronald J. Zboray, *A Fictive People: Antebellum Economic Development and the American Reading Public* (New York: Oxford University Press, 1993), 37–54.

[7] Louis Kaplan, comp., *A Bibliography of American Autobiographies* (Madison, WI: University of Wisconsin Press, 1962), 362–63, lists seventy autobiographies and memoirs by sailors dealing with the 1800–1850 period.

Who were the retired antebellum mariners who published their memoirs and autobiographies? How did these men remember and interpret their experiences at sea and in port? What common themes, rhetorical strategies, and tropes did they articulate? This book explores these questions by focusing on the self narratives of men who sailed on board American whalers, privateers, merchant and naval vessels during the first half of the nineteenth century.

It views sailor self narratives as a hybrid form of literature, one that straddled different kinds of literary genres. They were partly coming-of-age narratives, didactic reform works, war stories, picaresque rogue tales, captivity narratives, exposés of cruelty and injustice, and conversion narratives.

For as complicated and fractured as some sailor narratives were, they grappled with their authors' quest to achieve manhood and to resist what they saw as threats to their manliness. The concept of manliness was a contested one in antebellum America. Traditional notions of masculinity that prized physical prowess, combativeness, and roistering were increasingly challenged by an evangelical model of manhood that stressed piety, self-restraint, and rejection of the pastimes associated with "rough" masculinity, such as drinking, whoring, and brawling. Irrespective of which model of manhood one subscribed to, however, most antebellum Americans agreed that a "manly" man was one who was brave in battle and defended his rights and freedoms against whoever or whatever threatened them.[8]

A major purpose of this book is to explore sailor autobiographies and memoirs as texts that tell multiple, at times conflicted, stories

---

[8] Numerous works in the historiography of antebellum masculinity, especially working-class masculinity, note these characteristics. See, for example, Bruce Dorsey, *Reforming Men and Women: Gender in the Antebellum City* (Ithaca, NY: Cornell University Press, 2002), esp. 14–28; Gregory L. Kaster, "Labour's True Man: Organized Workingmen and the Language of Manliness in the USA, 1827–1877," *Gender & History* 13, no. 1 (April 2001): 24–64; Michael Kaplan, "World of the B'hoys: Urban Violence and the Political Culture of Antebellum New York City, 1825–1860" (PhD diss., New York University, 1996); Kaplan, "New York City Tavern Violence and the Creation of a Working-Class Male Identity," *Journal of the Early Republic* 15 (Winter 1995): 591–617. See also Amy S. Greenberg, *Manifest Manhood and the Antebellum American Empire* (New York: Cambridge University Press, 2005), esp. 135–69; Greenberg, *Cause for Alarm: The Volunteer Fire Department in the Nineteenth-Century City* (Princeton, NJ: Princeton University Press, 1998), 9, 60–70, 87.

about the contested meanings of manhood in antebellum America. Another goal of this study is to examine how seamen narratives contributed to Americans' sense of nationalism during the 1820–1860 era. In addressing this issue the book builds on the work of Benedict Anderson and other scholars who have explored how print culture helped forge a sense of national identity in the antebellum United States.[9] This monograph argues that sailor authors often intertwined the themes of manhood and nationalism in their life stories.

The majority of the seamen authors discussed in this study fought in the War of 1812. All of the men also served on board American vessels at a time when the young nation was emerging as a major maritime power during the approximate period 1815–1860. Sailors' service on board American men-of-war, merchant vessels, and whalers during this time made possible the transatlantic market economy that enriched the United States while protecting it from Britain and other foreign powers.[10]

In recounting their military exploits and world travels antebellum sailor memoirists and autobiographers were not offering merely adventure yarns. They highlighted the vital role mariners played in making the United States a major power. Their narratives reminded American landsmen that the skeins of sailors' lives were woven into the fabric of their country, even though many of these men were absent for years from the United States.

Even more importantly, these life stories affirmed many Americans' belief that their nation was at the cusp of greatness. They portrayed Jack Tar as the embodiment of an exuberant, even strident, American

[9] Benedict Anderson, *Imagined Communities: Reflections on the Origin and Spread of Nationalism*, rev. ed. (1983; repr., London: Verso, 2006), esp. 37–46; David Waldstreicher, *In the Midst of Perpetual Fetes: The Making of American Nationalism, 1776–1820* (Chapel Hill: University of North Carolina Press, 1997); see also Trish Loughran, *The Republic in Print: Print Culture in the Age of U.S. Nation Building, 1770–1870* (New York: Columbia University Press, 2007).

[10] George C. Daughan, *If By Sea: The Forging of the American Navy – From the American Revolution to the War of 1812* (New York: Basic Books, 2008); Ian W. Toll, *Six Frigates: The Epic History of the Founding of the U.S. Navy* (New York: W.W. Norton & Company, 2006); Benjamin W. Labaree and others, *America and the Sea: A Maritime History* (Mystic, CT: Mystic Seaport Press, 1998), 164–335; Briton Cooper Busch, *"Whaling Will Never Do For Me": The American Whalemen in the Nineteenth Century* (Lexington: University Press of Kentucky, 1994).

nationalism. Seaman narratives also illuminated how antebellum public discourses about nationalism resonated with those about manhood; how at times these discourses intersected, especially when sailors recalled besting the enemies of the United States.[11]

Jack Tar's Story develops the arguments outlined above in five chapters. The first views sailor autobiographies and memoirs as coming-of-age narratives. It analyzes three themes that shaped sailors' recollections of their early lives and quest for manhood by shipping out to sea: escape, freedom, and captivity. The next two chapters focus on sailors' recollections of the international conflicts that roiled their seafaring years during the late eighteenth and early nineteenth centuries. Chapter 2 examines sailor authors' accounts of resisting British impressments and incarceration as prisoners of war, and also their participation in the War of 1812. Chapter 3 explores how mariners depicted the Haitian Revolution and the Latin American wars of independence. Both chapters discuss how attitudes about manhood, tyranny, and patriotism shaped the ways in which sailor authors recounted their experiences in captivity and in combat. In discussing these issues, the third chapter argues that seamen authors contributed to antebellum Americans' sanitized view of their revolution by stressing the shortcomings of the wars of independence in Haiti and Latin America. Chapter 4 examines sailor autobiographies and memoirs as exposés of American cruelty. It explores sailors' discussion of harsh discipline, especially floggings, on board American vessels. This chapter analyzes why sailor authors viewed such punishment as threatening both their manhood and the welfare of the nation. Another vantage point from which to view sailor texts is to see them as conflicted rogue tales and conversion narratives, the subject of chapter 5. It explores how sailor authors depicted the raucous pastimes of the waterfront culture and their ambivalent responses to religious revivals and evangelical reform. Discussion of such issues suggests that many sailor authors straddled conflicting notions of manhood.

---

[11] Historians have begun exploring how sailor doggerel and tattoos also articulated these themes: Dan Hicks, "True Born Columbians: The Promises and Perils of National Identity for American Seafarers of the Early Republican Period" (PhD. diss., The Pennsylvania State University, 2007); Newman, *Embodied History*, esp. 117, 119–21.

It is important at the outset of this book to define key terms and to distinguish *Jack Tar's Story* from earlier historical studies on antebellum maritime life. Although many scholars use the terms autobiography and memoir interchangeably, they refer to different kinds of self narratives. Autobiographies examine authors' entire lives up to the production of their narratives. They offer a "chronology of self."[12] By contrast, memoirs generally focus on a particular experience or time in the author's life. Often they deal with the author's participation in a major historical event.[13] This book will investigate both memoirs and autobiographies.

Although *Jack Tar's Story* builds on the historiography of antebellum maritime life, it differs from this scholarship in several crucial ways. First, this book is not primarily concerned with using sailor narratives to describe the lives of mariners during the Age of Sail. The rich body of work produced by Paul Gilje, Margaret Creighton, and other historians has already done this.[14] Instead this book focuses on sailor narratives themselves to explore how mariner authors remembered, interpreted, their years at sea; how the lens of memory shaped their life stories.

Jack Tar's Story is also distinctive because it is the first study to systematically investigate the veracity of sailor narratives by using a wide variety of institutional records. These include: ships' logs, crew lists, pension files, impressment and prisoner-of-war records from both the American and British navies, census reports, and records

---

[12] Paula S. Fass, "Memoir Problem," *Reviews in American History* 34, no. 1 (March 2006), endnote 5, 122. See also Philippe Lejeune, *On Autobiography*, ed. John Paul Eakin (Minneapolis: University of Minnesota Press, 1989), viii.

[13] Russell Baker and William Knowlton Zinsser, ed., *Inventing the Truth: The Art and Craft of Memoir* (Boston: Houghton, Mifflin, 1987), 21, and Robert F. Sayre, *The Examined Self: Benjamin Franklin, Henry Adams, Henry James* (Princeton, NJ: Princeton University Press, 1964), 6–7.

[14] Paul Gilje, *Liberty on the Waterfront: American Maritime Culture in the Age of Revolution* (Philadelphia: University of Pennsylvania Press, 2004); Margaret S. Creighton, *Rites and Passage: The Experience of American Whaling, 1830– 1870* (Cambridge: Cambridge University Press, 1995); see also Hicks, "True Born Columbians"; Peter Linebaugh and Marcus Rediker, *The Many Headed Hydra: Sailors, Slaves, Commoners and the Hidden History of the Revolutionary Atlantic* (Boston: Beacon Press, 2000); Marcus Rediker, *Between the Devil and the Deep Blue Sea: Merchant Seamen, Pirates, and the Anglo-American Maritime World, 1700–1750* (Cambridge : Cambridge University Press, 1987).

from the Sailors' Snug Harbor, the home for elderly and chronically ill seamen in Staten Island, New York.

By grounding mariners' autobiographical works in historical documentation, *Jack Tar's Story* seeks to complicate and enrich scholars' analysis of these texts. It especially challenges historians to explore the critical difference between what actually happened to antebellum mariners and how they interpreted, presented, that past in their autobiographies and memoirs. This book also cautions historians against accepting at face value self narratives purportedly written by former sailors. This point bears stress since at times historians have cited texts as genuine sailor autobiographies when they were actually works of fiction.

One such work was *A Short Sketch of the Life of Elijah Shaw*, published in 1843 and allegedly written by an ex-mariner who claimed he fought in all four of the United States' naval wars during the late eighteenth and early nineteenth centuries: the Quasi War with France (1798–1801), the wars against the major Barbary States, Tripoli (1802–1805) and Algiers (1815–1816), and the War of 1812 with Great Britain. He also said he experienced captivity in Tripoli and impressment by British press gangs.[15] Shaw's narrative offers a riveting story of combat, heroism, suffering, and narrow escapes from death. But it is the proverbial "too good to be true" tale. Extant naval documents do not list Elijah Shaw as a crew member on the ships he claimed to be on.[16]

---

[15] Elijah Shaw, *A Short Sketch of the Life of Elijah Shaw...*, 3rd ed. (Rochester, NY: Strong & Dawson Printers, 1843). Like many antebellum works, Shaw's text claimed there were earlier editions. But *World Cat* indicates no editions before 1843. For a recent citation of Shaw's narrative as a genuine autobiographical narrative, see Toll, *Six Frigates*, 111 and 368.

[16] Naval records, for example, contradict Shaw's claim that he served as ship's cooper on board the USS *Constellation* when it captured the French frigate *L'Insurgente* on February 9, 1799 (7). His name does not appear on the ship's crew list and a Thomas Kelly is listed as ship's cooper. See *Naval Documents Related to the Quasi-War Between the United States and France...* (Washington, DC: Government Printing Office, 1935), 1:304–16. Shaw claimed he was a carpenter on board the *Philadelphia* when it was captured by Tripoli on October 31, 1803 (16–17). Yet his name does not appear on the crew list and a William Godby is listed as ship's carpenter. See *Naval Documents Related to the United States Wars with Barbary Powers* (Washington, DC: Government Printing Office, 1944), 6:276, 285–86, 484.

A Short Sketch of the Life of Elijah Shaw illustrates what the literary scholar Laura Browder has described as "impersonator autobiographies," texts written by individuals who fabricated their stories.[17] Scholars have yet to determine why such fictional narratives claimed to be genuine autobiographies. No doubt various motives, besides the obvious desire to make money, promoted the writing and publication of such works.

This author leaves the analysis of "impersonator autobiographies" to others. *Jack Tar's Story* examines only those texts which can be documented as genuine autobiographies or memoirs. When determining the validity of these works the author has erred on the side of caution, omitting discussion of texts for which there was insufficient or contradictory historical documentation.

Of course to raise the issue of the authenticity of seamen narratives is to plunge into the thicket of recent controversies concerning the truthfulness of autobiographical writing. Although it is beyond the scope of *Jack Tar's Story* to discuss this controversy in detail, several salient points are pertinent. First, some contemporary scholars charge that all autobiographical narratives are fictional constructs, self-referential works with no meaning outside the text. Not surprisingly, poststructuralists in particular have made this argument. Paul De Man, for example, in a famous 1974 essay entitled "Autobiography as De-facement," declared that autobiographies were a fiction which could not reveal "reliable self-knowledge" since they did not refer to a world outside the text.[18]

Scholars from different fields, especially cognitive psychology, literary studies, and history, have argued persuasively against this view. They have shown that the subjective nature of autobiographies and memoirs does not preclude their ability to refer to a world outside the text. Self narratives, they assert, are not only literary constructs but also historical documents since they are grounded in a referential world, subject to empirical verification. Autobiographies and memoirs, therefore, are inherently interdisciplinary. They straddle both literature and history.[19]

---

[17] Laura Browder, "Fake Autobiographies: A Great American Tradition" http://hnn.us/articles/21679.html (accessed February 13, 2006).

[18] Paul De Man, "Autobiography as De-Facement," *MLN* 94, no.5, Comparative Literature (December 1979), 919–30, esp. 922.

[19] Major theoreticians Philippe Lejeune and John Paul Eakin stress this point. See Lejeune, *On Autobiography*, 22, 119–37, and Eakin's introduction to ibid., ix–x,

Numerous scholars have also stressed that autobiographical works are deeply embedded in the society that produces them. These texts reflect the language, values, and models of self available to the author/protagonist in his particular culture. It is for this reason that one of the leading scholars of American autobiography John Paul Eakin urges students to approach self narratives much as a cultural anthropologist would an artifact.[20] Ultimately autobiographies and memoirs are cultural constructs that illuminate not only the particular life of the author/protagonist but also the society in which they were produced.

In recent years historians have devoted increasing attention to the study of autobiographical works. Ironically the linguistic turn in history has promoted this development. Recognition that all historical documents are what Hayden White calls "fictions of factual representation," has encouraged historians to be less dismissive or suspicious of self narratives.[21] As books by Julie Roy Jeffrey, Alfred Young, and

xxi. See also Eakin's own works, esp. *Living Autobiographically: How We Create Identity in Narrative* (Ithaca, NY: Cornell University Press, 2008), 3–59; *Touching the World: Reference in Autobiography* (Princeton, NJ: Princeton University Press, 1992), 23–31,59,64–67, and *Fictions in Autobiography: Studies in the Art of Self Invention* (Princeton, NJ: Princeton University Press, 1985), 5–7, 181–206. See also James Olney, *Metaphors of Self: The Meaning of Autobiography* (Princeton, NJ: Princeton University Press, 1972), 3–50; George Gusdorf, "Conditions and Limits of Autobiography" and Robert F. Sayre, "Autobiography and the Making of America," both in James Olney, ed., *Autobiography: Essays Theoretical and Critical* (Princeton, NJ: Princeton University Press, 1980), 28–48, 146–68; Roy Pascal, *Design and Truth in Autobiography* (London: Routledge & Kegan Paul, 1960), 61–84, 179–95. Cognitive psychologists argue that simply because autobiographical memories are complex reconstructions rather than snapshots or exact retrievals of the past does not mean that they are fabrications or fictions. In fact they note that autobiographical memories are fundamentally accurate in retelling the gist or core of a person's life story. See Daniel L. Schacter's books, esp. *Searching for Memory: The Brain, the Mind, and the Past* (New York: Basic Books, 1996), 93–95; *Seven Sins of Memory: How the Mind Forgets and Remembers* (Boston: Houghton Mifflin Company, 2001), 5–6; see also Craig R. Barclay, "Schematization of Autobiographical Memory," in David C. Rubin, ed., *Autobiographical Memory* (Cambridge: Cambridge University Press, 1986), 82–84, 95, 97. For historians' discussions of the validity of autobiographical works as historical documents, see the works cited in endnote 22.

[20] Eakin, *Touching the World*, 71–137, 94, 144 and *Living Autobiographically*, 22–31, 100–30.

[21] Hayden White, "Fictions of Factual Representation" in Anna Green and Kathleen Troup, eds., *The Houses of History: A Critical Reader in Twentieth-Century History and Theory* (New York: New York University Press, 1999), 214–229.

other scholars illustrate, studies that place such texts at the center of historical inquiry have become a cottage industry in the profession.[22]

Jack Tar's Story contributes to the rapidly growing historiography of autobiographical narrative. It recognizes that antebellum mariners had multiple agendas when they told their life stories. Eager to attract paying readers in a crowded literary market, they peppered their stories with tales of adventure on the high seas, travel to exotic places, and graphic descriptions of battles, storms, piracy, and impressments. These stories were grounded in fact. Sailors were world travelers, the pioneers of an expansive global frontier. They did suffer horribly from various manmade and natural disasters and they did have all sorts of adventures in exotic places.

Yet if their stories were based on fact, many sailors shaped their narratives to expose various abuses they had suffered, to gain the sympathy of the public, and of course to earn badly needed revenue. No doubt there were times when they padded their life stories, exaggerating or minimizing certain experiences. Like most autobiographies and memoirs, sailors' narratives straddle the boundary between fact and fiction.

In exploring these works *Jack Tar's Story* takes to heart what biographer Vincent Carretta noted about his subject, Olaudah Equiano, the late-eighteenth-century ex-slave, mariner, and autobiographer. Equiano, stated Carretta, had a "double vision" or "dual identity" as he wrote his narrative. Equiano was "speaking both from within

---

[22] Julie Roy Jefrey, *Abolitionists Remember: Antislavery Autobiographies & the Unfinished Work of Emancipation* (Chapel Hill: University of North Carolina Press, 2008); Alfred F.Young, *Masquerade: The Life and Times of Deborah Sampson, Continental Soldier* (New York: Alfred A. Knopf, 2004); Young, *The Shoemaker and the Tea Party: Memory and the American Revolution* (Boston: Beacon Press, 1999). See also David W. Blight, *A Slave No More: Two Men Who Escaped to Freedom, Including their own Narratives of Emancipation* (Orlando, FL: Harcourt Inc., 2007); Sarah J. Purcell, *Sealed With Blood: War, Sacrifice, and Memory in Revolutionary America* (Philadelphia: University of Pennsylvania Press, 2002); Ann Fabian, *The Unvarnished Truth: Personal Narratives in Nineteenth-Century America* (Berkeley: University of California Press, 2000); Mechal Sobel, *Teach Me Dreams :The Search for Self in the Revolutionary Era* (Princeton, NJ: Princeton University Press, 2000); Joyce Appleby, *Inheriting the Revolution: The First Generation of Americans* (Cambridge, MA: Harvard University Press, 2000); Mary Jo Maynes, *Taking the Hard Road: Life Course in French and German Workers' Autobiographies in the Era of Industrialization* (Chapel Hill: University of North Carolina Press, 1995).

and from outside his society," speaking of "past events both as he experienced them at the time and as he reinterpret[ed] them from the perspective of the time in which he [was] recalling them."[23]

Carretta's comments highlight the ways in which sailor memoirs and autobiographies are grist for the historian's mill. These works are crucial historical documents precisely because their authors reinterpreted rather than exactly recollected their past. Study of self narratives offers a window into the values, the mentalités of men whose obscurity has made it difficult for historians to study. But perhaps more importantly, sailor authors revealed, sometimes unintentionally, widespread concerns about manhood and nationalism in antebellum America when they remembered their past.

This fact underscores the need to situate seamen narratives in the cultural context in which they were first published. The kinds of texts former mariners wrote did not become a significant genre of literature in the Western world until the latter part of the eighteenth century. Many scholars of American history point out that autobiographical writing did not become popular in this country until after the American Revolution.[24] Like the novel that emerged during the same period, autobiographical narratives reflected society's increasing recognition of the importance of the individual self. As the historian

---

[23] Vincent Carretta, *Olaudah Equiano The African: Biography of a Self-Made Man* (Athens: University of Georgia Press, 2005), 325.

[24] The following works are especially useful in exploring the emergence of self narratives in the Western world, particularly the United States: Stephen Carl Arch, *After Franklin: The Emergence of Autobiography in Post-Revolutionary America, 1780–1830* (Hanover: University of New Hampshire, 2001); Steven V. Hunsaker, *Autobiography and National Identity in the Americas* (Charlottesville: University of Virginia Press, 1999); Susan Clair Imbarrato, *Declarations of Independency in Eighteenth-Century American Autobiography* (Knoxville: University of Tennessee Press, 1998); Michael Mascuch, *Origins of the Individualist Self: Autobiography and Self Identity in England, 1591–1791* (Stanford, CA: Stanford University Press, 1996); Martin A. Danahay, *A Community of One: Masculine Autobiography and Autonomy in Nineteenth-Century Britain* (Albany: State University of New York Press, 1993); Lawrence Buel, "Autobiography in the American Renaissance" in John Paul Eakin, ed., *American Autobiography: Retrospect and Prospect* (Madison: University of Wisconsin Press, 1991), 47–69. Earlier studies remain important, such as James M. Cox, *Recovering Literature's Lost Ground : Essays in American Autobiography* (Baton Rouge: Louisiana State University Press, 1989), 11–32; Sayre, *Examined Self*; Albert E. Stone, "Autobiography and American Culture," *American Studies: An International Newsletter* 12 (Winter 1972): 22–38.

Mechal Sobel has noted, the few self narratives that did appear before the late eighteenth century were often tales of repetitive events over which individuals seemed to have little or no control. Events just "happened" to the authors. There was little sense of the narrator developing a notion of self as he or she recalled past occurrences.[25]

By the late eighteenth century, however, autobiographers and memoirists were no longer portraying themselves as passively enduring events but seeking to shape them. Of course Benjamin Franklin's now classic autobiography, its first English edition appearing in 1793, illustrated this shift. During the antebellum period popular biographies and life narratives of self-made men testified to Americans' growing belief in transforming one's life to overcome obstacles and achieve success.[26]

Autobiographies, memoirs, and biographies appeared in a fiercely competitive and rapidly changing literary market. Revolutions in printing techniques, the spread of literacy, especially in the North, and the emergence of a mass consumer culture promoted both the democratization and commercialization of literature. Although these developments began in the late eighteenth century, they accelerated during the antebellum era. No longer the preserve of educated elites, the literary marketplace produced increasingly diverse texts in an effort to attract a wide audience. Penny presses, mammoth weeklies, novels, exposés, and fashion magazines competed for the attention of working-class and especially middle-class readers.[27]

The democratization of American literature popularized the life stories of ordinary men and women. Although biographies of the rich and famous continued to sell, so, too, did narratives by or about

[25] Sobel, *Teach Me Dreams*, 19.

[26] Louis P. Masur, ed., *The Autobiography of Benjamin Franklin, with Related Documents*, 2nd ed. (Boston: Bedford/St. Martin's Press, 2003), 14–19; Scott E. Caspar, *Constructing American Lives: Culture in Nineteenth-Century America* (Chapel Hill: University of North Carolina Press, 1999), 6–7, 88–106.

[27] Ronald J. Zboray and Mary Saracino Zboray, *Literary Dollars and Social Sense: A People's History of the Mass Market Book* (New York: Routledge, 2005); Isabelle Lehuu, *Carnival on the Page: Popular Print Media in Antebellum America* (Chapel Hill: University of North Carolina Press, 2000); Zboray, *Fictive People*; William J. Gilmore, *Reading Becomes a Necessity of Life: Material and Cultural Life in Rural New England, 1780–1835* (Knoxville: University of Tennessee Press, 1989); Cathy N. Davidson, *Revolution and the Word: The Rise of the Novel in America* (New York: Oxford University Press, 1986), 3–79.

artisans, farmers, slaves, soldiers, criminals, beggars, alcoholics, and other nonprivileged people. Recent historical and literary scholarship has highlighted how revolutionary such self-narratives were. People who were traditionally silenced or excluded from public discourse now contributed to it. They used their autobiographies to assert a public voice for themselves and to articulate notions of self that could challenge established hierarchies of power.[28]

Sailor narratives appeared in the context of these broader cultural developments. Although a minority of sailor narratives appeared before 1815, most seamen authors, including those who served in the American Revolution, published their works after this period. Andrew Sherburne's popular memoir detailing his seafaring life and imprisonment by the British during the revolution, for example, did not appear until 1828.[29] Significantly, Louis Kaplan in *A Bibliography of American Autobiographies* lists almost fifty sailor narratives published during the 1815–1860 period, compared to only three published before 1815.[30]

This book focuses on the autobiographies and memoirs of American sailors published during the 1815–1860 period.[31] It pays particular

---

[28] Carretta, *Olaudah Equiano The African*; Fabian, *The Unvarnished Truth*; Sobel, *Teach Me Dreams*; Ronald Hoffman, Mechal Sobel, and Fredrika J. Teute, eds., *Through a Glass Darkly: Reflections on Personal Identity in Early America* (Chapel Hill: University of North Carolina Press, 1997); William L. Andrews, *To Tell a Free Story: The First Century of Afro-American Autobiography, 1760–1865* (Urbana: University of Illinois Press, 1986).

[29] Andrew Sherburne, *Memoirs of Andrew Sherburne: A Pensioner of the Navy of the Revolution. Written by Himself* (1828; repr., Honolulu: University Press of the Pacific Honolulu, 2004).

[30] Kaplan, *Bibliography of American Autobiographies*, 362–63, lists fourteen sailor memoirs dealing with the period before 1800. Yet eleven of these were published after 1815. The two earliest works cited, John Ashmead's *Voyages ... Between the Years 1758 and 1782* and John Benson's *A Short Account of the Voyages, Travels and Adventures*, list no dates of publication. *A Narrative of Joshua Davis, An American Citizen, Who Was Pressed and Served on Board Six Ships of the British Navy ...* appeared in 1811. See Kaplan, *Bibliography of American Autobiographies*, 12, 24, 77. Twenty-two of the seventy sailor narratives Kaplan cites for the 1800–1850 period were published in the late nineteenth and early twentieth centuries. Many of these later texts were the diaries and logbooks of long dead mariners, often published at the behest of their descendants.

[31] *Jack Tar's Story* will examine one book published after the Civil War – Roland Gould's 1867 memoir. This work warrants discussion since Gould was an antebellum seaman and tackled many of the same issues explored in earlier mariner narratives.

attention to over twenty-five narratives that are especially rich and
detailed works (see the appendix for a list of these books). This study
compares these texts to other autobiographical works. It particularly
explores the resonance between sailor and Barbary captivity narratives. It also briefly compares the life stories of mariners who fought in
the War of 1812 with those who served in the American Revolution.

Jack Tar's Story primarily investigates works by Anglo-American
mariners who were either native-born or naturalized citizens of the
United States. On the face of it such a focus seems unjustifiably
restrictive. The first half of the nineteenth century was a period when
growing numbers of men from different countries served on board
American vessels. The historian Christopher McKee, for example,
has documented that almost half of the enlisted men on the New York
station in 1808 were foreign nationals, the majority of them from the
British Isles.[32] A number of antebellum native-born American mariners stressed that they sailed with men who came from all over the
world.[33]

Yet most foreign-born sailors who served on board American vessels did not publish autobiographical narratives available to the antebellum English-speaking world. Not surprisingly, the few who did
originated from Great Britain (the Englishman Samuel Leech) or its
dominions (the Canadian-born Ned Myers) and became American
citizens as young men. The case of Nicholas Peter Isaacs is the exception that proves the rule. Although born in Norway, Isaacs was sent
to live with an uncle in London when he was six years old and as a
sailor made Mystic, Connecticut, his home port (5–7, 73).

This book studies the narratives of mostly white sailors since black
mariners produced relatively few autobiographical works during the
late eighteenth and first half of the nineteenth centuries. Olaudah
Equiano's richly detailed 1789 autobiography discussing his seafaring
years in the Atlantic world remains a notable exception.[34] No doubt
various factors contributed to the paucity of self narratives by African

---

[32] Christopher Mc Kee, "Foreign Seamen in the U.S. Navy: A Census of 1808,"
William and Mary Quarterly, 3rd ser., 42, no. 3 (1985): 383–93.
[33] Dana, *Two Years Before the Mast*, 470; Browne, *Etchings of a Whaling Cruise*, 43;
Caswell, *Sketch of the Adventures*, 6.
[34] Robert J. Allison, ed., *The Interesting Narrative of the Life of Olaudah Equiano.
Written by Himself, with Related Documents*, 2nd ed. (Boston: Bedford/St.
Martin's Press, 2007). See also Caretta, *Equiano the African*, 303–29. W. Jeffrey
Bolster, *Black Jacks: African American Seamen in the Age of Sail* (Cambridge,

American sailors, especially during the antebellum period – the significantly lower rates of literacy for black mariners in comparison to their white counterparts,[35] the fact that the minority of literate African American male writers focused on producing slave narratives or works detailing their conversion to evangelical Christianity and subsequent ministries. Significantly Kaplan's *Bibliography of American Autobiographies* lists numerous autobiographies by antebellum black clergymen and former slaves published during the 1800–1850 period. Yet he cites only one narrative by an African American mariner during this period, *Sketch of the Life and Travels of Joseph Deane*.[36]

Unfortunately this thirty-five-page work offers only a tantalizingly brief sketch of Deane's seafaring career as a steward on board merchant vessels. Much of the narrative concentrates on Deane's career as a barber. Since Deane often omitted to cite the names of the ships on which he sailed or his dates of service, it is particularly difficult to corroborate his seafaring life.[37]

Another example of an antebellum black mariner memoir is the one by Paul Cuffe, the son and namesake of a leader in the African American Massachusetts community during the late eighteenth and early nineteenth centuries. Although Cuffe's memoir is only twenty-one pages, it offers a fascinating glimpse of its author's thirty years at sea, especially his journey to post revolutionary Haiti.[38] Chapter 3 will compare this work with those by white mariners to explore how the prism of race shaped sailor authors' views of the Haitian Revolution.

MA: Harvard University Press, 1997), 37, states that mariners wrote the first six autobiographies of blacks published in English before 1800. Yet most of these works are better categorized as slave narratives or other kinds of autobiographies since they offer only relatively brief discussions of seafaring lives (248, endnote 56).

[35] On differences in literacy between white and black sailors in the early republic, see Lee Soltow and Edward Stevens, *The Rise of Literacy and the Common School in the United States: A Socioeconomic Analysis to 1870* (Chicago: University of Chicago Press, 1981), 50–51; Dye, "Early American Merchant Seafarers," 340–43.

[36] Kaplan, *Bibliography of American Autobiographies*, 354, 78.

[37] Joseph Deane, *Sketch of the Life and Travels of Joseph Deane. Written by Himself*, 3rd ed. (Lancaster, PA: Pearsol & Geist, 1857).

[38] Paul Cuffe, *Narrative of the Life and Adventures of Paul Cuffe, A Pequot Indian, During Thirty Years Spent at Sea, and in Travelling in Foreign Lands* (Vernon, NY: Printed by Horace N. Bill, 1839). On Cuffe's father and family, see Thomas D. Lamont, *Rise to Be a People: A Biography of Paul Cuffe* (Urbana: University of Illinois Press, 1986).

Jack Tar's Story recognizes that concerns about race and slavery significantly shaped the narratives of antebellum white mariners. It explores how these men's fears of becoming enslaved and emasculated haunted their recollections of seafaring life. These fears were especially evident when white seamen authors discussed the issues of British impressment and wartime imprisonment, capture by the Barbary States, revolutionary upheavals in Haiti and South America, and flogging on the high seas.

Class and gender as well as racial issues will merit discussion. This book focuses on the memoirs and autobiographies written by men who came from working-class backgrounds and who discussed in detail their years as mariners on board different kinds of vessels during the Age of Sail. Yet it also utilizes narratives written by "gentlemen sailors," men who came from relatively privileged families and for whom seafaring was an interlude in a professional life on land.[39] Despite their obvious differences, both groups of mariner authors explored common themes in their self narratives. Both shared concerns about asserting their manhood and national identity as Americans.

But class differences often did shape how sailor authors interpreted their experiences and those of their crew mates. Chapter 1 investigates this issue when it compares how "gentlemen sailors" and mariners from impoverished families portrayed their decision to go to sea. Chapters 4 and 5 explore how the dimension of class shaped seamen writers' discussion of the practices of flogging, drinking, and religion.

Exploring the issue of gender construction is central to this study. Recent scholarship has noted how the personal narratives of women were much more conscious than those of men in examining how the "dynamics of gender" affected their lives.[40] This study explores how constructions of masculinity affected the personal narratives of antebellum sailors. As Margaret Creighton and Lisa Norling have

[39] Hugh McKeever Egan uses the phrase "gentlemen sailors" to describe seamen from middle- or upper-class families in "Gentlemen-Sailors: The First-Person Sea Narratives of Dana, Cooper, and Melville" (PhD diss., University of Iowa, 1983).

[40] Personal Narratives Group, ed. *Interpreting Women's Lives: Feminist Theory and Personal Narratives* (Bloomington: Indiana University Press, 1989), 4–5. See also Maynes, *Taking the Hard Road*, 8, 32–33, 148–50, 196–98; Estelle Jelinek, ed., *Women's Autobiography* (Bloomington: Indiana University, 1980).

stressed, sailors were "gendered beings" who both reflected and helped to shape their society's views of masculinity.[41] This study will explore in particular how antebellum sailor writers used their narratives to assert their rights as men in a world that often seemed to be conspiring against their manhood.

What kinds of men were these authors? Were they typical or representative sailors? Did they receive extensive help in writing their narratives? How did they seek to establish credibility with their readers? Did their books often find a large audience? Discussion of these questions begins to reveal both the men who authored sailor narratives as well as the process by which they produced their works.

Perhaps the most difficult question to investigate is the last. Unfortunately it is impossible to determine how many people bought or read the antebellum narratives of former mariners. But many obviously did find an audience. Publishers regularly printed these texts and a number of them went though several editions. After its initial publication in 1843, Leech's *Thirty Years from Home* was regularly published by both Boston and London presses during the 1840s and 1850s.[42] *Ned Myers* had thirteen different reprints and editions, mostly before 1860.[43] Lesser known works were also regularly reprinted. Jacob Hazen's *Five Years Before the Mast*, for example, first printed in 1854 by the Philadelphia publisher Willis P. Hazard was reissued in 1856, 1860, and enjoyed numerous additional reprints throughout the latter half of the nineteenth century.[44] These developments suggest that some sailor self narratives sold briskly, even if they were not as popular as Dana's *Two Years Before the Mast*. They sold

[41] Lisa Norling, *Captain Ahab Had a Wife: New England Women & the Whalefishery, 1720–1870* (Chapel Hill: University of North Carolina Press, 2000), 1–2, 48; Creighton, *Rites & Passages*, 5–6 ; Creighton and Norling, eds., *Iron Men, Wooden Women: Gender and Seafaring in the Atlantic World, 1700–1920* (Baltimore, MD: Johns Hopkins University Press, 1996); Creighton, "American Mariners and the Rites of Manhood, 1830–1870," in Colin Howell and Richard Twomey, eds., *Jack Tar in History: Essays in the History of Maritime Life and Labor* (Frederickton, NB: Acadiensis, 1991), 143–63.

[42] Michael J. Crawford in his introduction to the 1999 Naval Institute Press edition of Leech's book notes that it was printed in London in 1845 and 1851 and regularly reprinted in the United States during the nineteenth century (xv). See also *World Cat* for a listing of the different editions of Leech's book.

[43] *Ned Myers*, xvi, and *World Cat*.

[44] See *World Cat* for the different reprints and editions of Hazen's book.

enough to encourage many former sailors to write their works and to find presses willing to publish them.

Even works which did not do well commercially, however, still merit the historian's attention. Philippe Lejeune, one of the leading theoreticians in the field of autobiographical studies, cogently argues this point while discussing his study of obscure nineteenth-century French merchant autobiographies. Such works warrant analysis because they illuminate the "social history of discourse" of the culture that produced them as well as the lives of relatively unknown authors.[45]

This book will examine sailor narratives that enjoyed popularity during the antebellum period as well as those that sold poorly and quickly sank into obscurity. It does not claim that sailor authors were representative American mariners during the Age of Sail. Then as now, most people, let alone nonprivileged ones, did not publish narratives of their lives. But memoirs and autobiographies need not be written by typical individuals to illuminate the values and experiences of their particular group. The recent historiography of the autobiographical narratives of slaves, artisans, and other working-class people underscores this point.[46]

Discussion of antebellum sailor narratives also raises the issue of editorial intrusion. Did retired sailors write their own stories? If not, does this invalidate their autobiographies and memoirs as a historical source? Similar questions have bedeviled historians who use the self narratives of other working-class people, including slaves.[47] Of course it is virtually impossible to determine with certainty exactly how much help, if any, individual sailor authors had in writing their narratives. That many retired mariners received assistance in editing, even writing, their texts is probable, especially since many of them had limited schooling.[48]

[45] Lejeune, *On Autobiography*, 171.

[46] See, for example, Blight, *A Slave No More*; Carretta, *Equiano The African*, 270–329; Ameland, *Flight of Icarus*, 201–24; Young, *Masquerade*; Young, *The Shoemaker and the Tea Party*.

[47] Jean Fagin Yellin did a particularly good job in documenting that former slave Harriet Jacobs authored her autobiography *Incidents in the Life of a Slave Girl Written by Herself*, and not her editor Lydia Maria Child. See Yellin's edition of this book (Cambridge, MA: Harvard University Press, 1987), esp. vii, xiii–xxxiv. See also Yellin, *Harriet Jacobs: A Life* (New York: Basic Civitas Books, 2004), xv–xxi, 119–36.

[48] There is no consensus on how literate antebellum mariners were. Literary scholars, utilizing sources such as shipboard library records, assert that sailors had an above

In some cases, sailor authors noted at the beginning of their texts that they received help with writing. Nicholas Peter Isaacs, for example, declared that he profited from the assistance of a man identified only as the editor of Leech's *Thirty Years From Home* to produce his own autobiography *Twenty Years Before the Mast* (1845). In the preface this unnamed editor admitted revising Isaac's manuscript to provide "grammatical accuracy and perspicuity." Yet he quickly added: "No attempt has been made to work up his [Isaac's] adventures."[49]

Of course the most famous example of an antebellum sailor author relying on another writer to produce his book is the collaboration between Ned Myers and James Fenimore Cooper. The two served together on board the merchant vessel the *Stirling* during its 1806–1807 voyage to the Mediterranean and elsewhere. Cooper was only seventeen years old at the start of the voyage, a youth from a prominent upstate New York family whose college scrapes and fighting had gotten him expelled from Yale University and who now hoped to prepare for a career as a naval officer. In 1806 Myers was a thirteen-year-old cabin boy beginning his life as a merchant sailor. He came from an unstable, hardscrabble family and had little schooling.

Despite their different backgrounds, the two youths became friends during their voyage. Cooper also rescued Myers from drowning when the latter fell overboard while the *Stirling* was docked in London. In 1843, after Myers wrote to Cooper, the two men renewed their friendship. By then Cooper was a successful novelist, living on his family's Cooperstown estate. Myers was an impoverished and crippled ex-sailor with many stories to tell about his seafaring years. He lived

average degree of literacy among working-class men. See, for example, Hester Blum, *The View from the Masthead: Maritime Imagination and Antebellum American Sea Narratives* (Chapel Hill: University of North Carolina Press, 2008), 19–45, and Harry S. Skallerup, *Books Afloat and Ashore* (New York: Archon Books, 1974), 203–18. Most historians who use institutional records, such as seamen protection certificates, argue that most mariners had trouble reading and writing. Simon Newman, "Reading the Bodies of Early American Seafarers," *William & Mary Quarterly*, 3rd ser., 55, no. 1 (January 1998), 65–66, estimates that almost 80 percent of sailors were "barely literate." Ira Dye argues that most sailors could write their names on protection certificates but "with some difficulty." See Dye, "Seafarers of 1812 – A Profile," *Prologue: The Journal of the National Archives* 5, no. 1 (Spring 1973), 8. Dye, "Early American Merchant Seafarers," *Proceedings of the American Philosophical Society* 120, no. 5 (October 1976), 340–43, notes that the most literate sailors were whites from the urban Northeast. In ibid, 357–59, he estimates that 57 percent of white seamen were functionally literate.

49 Issacs, *Twenty Years Before the Mast*, title page, preface, and 199.

five months in Cooper's home and the two collaborated on producing Myers's narrative, first published in 1843.

Scholars continue to debate how much help and what kind Cooper offered to Myers in writing his narrative. Did Cooper mostly transcribe Myers's words or did he use them to create a genuinely collaborative work, one that reflected as much Cooper's as Myers's words? The fact that Cooper conceded that "in a few instances he has interposed his own greater knowledge of the world" in narrating Ned Myers's story suggests that the latter was the case.[50]

Historians must be especially cautious in using self narratives which may have been heavily edited or redacted. Yet as the rich historiography of antebellum slave narratives shows, historians can use autobiographical works edited/revised by others, provided they remain aware of how both the protagonist and his/her editor may have shaped the narration of the life story.[51]

Significantly most sailor authors stressed that they were the creators or authors of their autobiographical works. Even those writers who conceded that they had the help of others in preparing their narratives still emphasized that they were the authors of these texts. Ned Myers, for example, stated that although he and Cooper worked together on his autobiography, it is "literally my own story, logged by my old shipmate" (278). Similarly, Nicholas Peter Isaacs stressed that he wrote his autobiography himself and merely received editorial assistance (title page and 199).

Some mariners made a point of noting that they wrote their autobiographies or memoirs without help from others. Horace Lane wanted his readers to know that he not only authored his autobiography but also marketed it. He wrote "candidly and sincerely" about his life and used what little money he had to finish his book and to get it printed (vi, 219). Lane also stressed that he authored his exposé of

---

[50] Blum, *View from the Masthead*, 71–106; Blum, "Before and After the Mast: James Fenimore Cooper and Ned Myers," in *Pirates, Jack Tar, and Memory: New Directions in American Maritime History*, eds., Paul A. Gilje and William Pencak (Mystic, CT: Mystic Seaport, 2007), 115–34; William S. Dudley's introduction to the 1989 Naval Institute Press edition of *Ned Myers*, vii–xix; Egan, "Gentlemen-Sailors," 136–78.

[51] Andrews, *To Tell a Free Story*, and Dickson D. Bruce Jr., *The Origins of African American Literature, 1680–1865* (Charlottesville: University Press of Virginia, 2001).

prison conditions in Auburn and Sing Sing, published in 1835 (209). Both works were published for him by a press in Skaneateles, New York, the Luther A. Pratt Company, with money that Lane probably scrounged from family and friends and also earned by selling cheap song books and jewelry.[52] Like other impoverished authors, Lane became an itinerant book peddler, hawking his writings on the streets of New York City, Philadelphia, and other cities.

The question of how nonprivileged folk, including sailors, achieved enough literacy to write their own narratives warrants extensive study. While exploring this issue, historians need to remember that years at sea did not disqualify a man from achieving a fairly high level of literacy, enough so that he could author his own memoir or autobiography. In fact a life spent at sea, much like one spent in prison, may have encouraged literacy among men who initially had little schooling. Reading became especially important for sailors who served on whalers and other merchant vessels in the early nineteenth century. This activity was one of the few acceptable pastimes they had on often monotonous voyages that lasted for months, sometimes years.[53] In Lane's case, confinement for five years in Auburn and Sing Sing prisons, as well as sailing on long sea voyages, gave him the opportunity to hone his reading and writing skills as well as the determination to tell his story.[54]

Significantly a number of sailor authors noted that their literacy skills enabled them to help their crew mates in several ways. Leech, for example, recalled that he often acted as a kind of "scribe" for

---

[52] See the title pages of Lane's *Wandering Boy* and his *Five Years in State's Prison; Or, Interesting Truths, Showing the Manner of Discipline in the State's Prisons at Sing Sing and Auburn ...*, 7th ed. (New York: Luther Pratt & Son, 1835). Although various editions are given for the latter book, they all refer to the same 1835 text. See Carol Rinderknecht, comp., *A Checklist of American Imprints for 1835* (Metuchen, NJ: The Scarecrow Press, 1985), 245. Lane boasted that he sold eleven thousand copies of his pamphlet (see *Wandering Boy*, 211) but this is unlikely, especially since the exposé did not seem to be reprinted and Lane remained impoverished. The *Wandering Boy*, 217–19, describes Lane's peddling and traveling to Kentucky to get money from an uncle to publish his autobiography.

[53] Skallerup *Books Afloat and Ashore*, 203–18. See also Zboray, *Fictive People*, 14, and Zboray, "Reading in America and the Ironies of Technological Innovation" in Cathy N. Davidson, ed., *Reading in America: Literature and Social History* (Baltimore, MD: Johns Hopkins University Press, 1989), 180–200.

[54] Lane, *Wandering Boy*, vi, 199, 209–10. Lane noted his reading repeatedly the Bible and evangelical reform literature while in Auburn Prison. See 191–92.

shipmates who could neither read nor write. He read and wrote their letters and also helped them get through long voyages by reading books obtained from officers (64). Jacob Hazen noted that he was appointed schoolmaster on board a school ship and assigned the task of keeping the logbook on another vessel, since the master's mate lacked the "penmanship and mathematics" to fulfill this duty.[55] When shipmates on board the *Preble* wanted to protest the Navy's failure to discharge them after their years of service ended, they unanimously elected Hazen to write a letter to the Secretary of the Navy protesting this injustice, a task he ably fulfilled (192–93).[56]

Like other working-class people who published self narratives in antebellum America, many sailor autobiographers and memoirists prefaced their works with testimonials by "respectable" men of their communities to establish their credibility. Leech, for example, prefaced his autobiography with testimonials from numerous ministers, a headmaster of a private academy, and Erastus Corning, a prominent New York businessman and politician, testifying to his integrity and truthfulness (xxv – vi). In the sixteenth American edition to Leech's book, published in 1857 with the revised title of *A Voice from the Main Deck: Being a Record of the Thirty Years Adventures of Samuel Leech*, Richard Henry Dana wrote a preface stressing that Leech "rigidly adhered to the truth" in his narrative (xxi – ii). Similarly, Isaacs offered testimonials from four New York City pastors, including one who edited the *Christian Advocate and Journal*. All depicted him as a man of "known Christian character and veracity" ("Testimonials," frontispiece).

Such testimonials underscore the major challenge that faces historians who utilize autobiographical narratives: to what extent do such texts accurately portray the lives of their subject/authors? *Jack Tar's Story* investigates this question by comparing the stories told in sailor narratives with those presented in various official documents. This book ultimately views mariners' autobiographies and memoirs as both historical documents and literary texts. It offers another vantage point

---

[55] Hazen, *Five Years Before the Mast*, 226, 232, 240, 290.
[56] Ibid, 226, 240, 290, 192–93. See also Jacob Hazen to Secretary of the Navy James K. Paulding, 21 October 1840, "Miscellaneous Letters Received by the Secretary of the Navy, 1801–84," National Archives Microfilm Publications, Microcopy No. 124, Roll 175, No. 91, RG 45, NA, Washington, DC.

from which to view the autobiographical works of nonprivileged people, including soldiers, slaves, recovering alcoholics, and criminals. It suggests resonances among these seemingly disparate narratives. Study of sailors' autobiographical works also offers another perspective from which to view the evangelical reform literature to "uplift" not only sailors but other groups of men in antebellum America. Sailor narratives, therefore, offer historians a wide angle lens from which to view multiple but connected discourses about different groups of nonprivileged men in the early republic.

This book straddles different fields of scholarship and suggests how their concerns intersect or resonate with each other: the history of print culture, the study of autobiography and memoir, and the historiographies of seafaring life and of masculinity in antebellum America. It ultimately views sailor autobiographies and memoirs as a kind of archaeological site with multiple, at times conflicted meanings, to be sifted, interpreted by historians. It takes to heart the historian Luisa Passerini's observation that "all autobiographical memory is true; it is up to the interpreter to discover in which sense, where, for which purpose."[57] Perhaps the best place to begin analyzing antebellum sailors' life stories is to explore them as coming-of-age narratives, works which recalled their authors' youthful efforts to become men by shipping out to sea.

[57] Luisa Passerini, "Women's Personal Narratives: Myths, Experience, and Emotions," in Personal Narratives Group, *Interpreting Women's Lives*, 197.

I

Stories of Escape, Freedom, and Captivity

Seamen Authors Recall Their Early Years

In 1849 Herman Melville published *Redburn*, one of his most popular novels. It offered a revealing glimpse into why many antebellum youths went to sea and how it transformed them. *Redburn* told the story of a provincial, naïve boy who shipped on board a packet bound for Liverpool. As his first name suggested, Wellingborough Redburn was well born, "a gentleman's son." Yet the death of his father caused his genteel family to slip into poverty. Like so many actual youths in antebellum America, Redburn shipped out to sea to escape a difficult life on land. The world, he said, was "bitter cold as December, and bleak as its blasts..." Although only a boy Redburn described himself as already "a misanthrope...with the warm soul of me flogged out by adversity."

Redburn was running away from much more than hard times and despair when he became a sailor. His description of the parting scene with his mother and three sisters suggested the eagerness with which he fled a feminized domesticity: "So I broke loose from their arms, and not daring to look behind, ran away as fast as I could..." Redburn's older brother, so ill that he could barely walk with him to the dock, was a cautionary example of what happened to males who did not leave home and strike out on their own.[1]

---

[1] Herman Melville, *Redburn, His First Voyage. Being the Sailor-boy Confessions and Reminiscences of the Son-of-a Gentleman, in the Merchant Service* (1986; rpr., New York: Penguin Classics, 1849), 52–53.

Redburn's four-month stint as a sailor toughened him both men-
tally and physically. It also exposed him to a wider world, especially
during his travels to Liverpool and London. In short, the seafaring life
transformed him from a "green recruit" into a seasoned man. By the
time Redburn returned home he had entered "the stout time of manhood, when the gristle has become bone." He could now "stand up
and fight" for himself and his family.[2]

Redburn was an autobiographical novel, based on Melville's first
seafaring voyage. In 1839 he shipped on board a merchant vessel
for a three-month journey to Liverpool. Like his alter ego Redburn,
Melville was a fatherless youth who sought to help his financially
straitened family and to escape from the domination of his mother,
a widow plagued by depression and other illnesses. Failure to secure
good employment on land led Melville to resume his life as a mariner.
In January 1841 he shipped on board a whaler for four years.[3]

A seafaring life offered Melville a needed respite from the land
life he found constraining and depressing. Perhaps his most memo-
rable fictional persona, *Moby Dick*'s narrator Ishmael, best articulated Melville's association of the sea with regeneration and freedom.
Ishmael said he chose the maritime life to resist "a damp, drizzly
November in [his] soul," one that tempted him to harm himself or
others. Going to sea, asserted Ishmael, was his "substitute for pistol
and ball." It was also a way to escape the kind of constricted, stifling life that Ishmael saw so many men leading on land. "Landsmen"
were often "pent up in lath and plaster – tied to counters, nailed to
benches, clinched to desks."[4]

Although hardly a typical sailor, Melville articulated concerns that
seamen authors discussed when they remembered their boyhoods and
their decision to become mariners. Like *Redburn*, many sailor autobiographies and memoirs described how their authors' going to sea
enabled them to come into their own manhood. Dana's *Two Years
Before the Mast* was the most successful of such books. Yet other

---

[2] Ibid., 53.

[3] Andrew Delbanco, *Melville: His World and Work* (New York: Alfred A. Knopf,
2005): 26–38; Herschel Parker, *Herman Melville. A Biography*, 2 vols. (Baltimore,
MD: Johns Hopkins University Press, 1996), 1:143–51; 636–41.

[4] Herman Melville, *Moby-Dick, or the Whale* (1851; repr., New York: Penguin
Classics, 1992), 3–4.

sailor works became stories of failed manhood. Perhaps that is why autobiographies like Lane's *The Wandering Boy* failed to attract a wide audience.

Whether produced by a successful Harvard educated lawyer like Dana or a pauper like Lane, sailor narratives offered similar reasons as to why their writers first went to sea. They stressed that maritime life provided a needed escape from their lives. Class differences, however, played a pivotal role in determining how "gentlemen sailors" like Dana and career mariners like Lane depicted the hardships and constraints they faced on land. These differences also shaped what each group of writers meant when they said that they went to sea in search of a manly independence.

Chapter 1 discusses the above issues by viewing antebellum sailor autobiographies and memoirs as coming-of-age narratives. It highlights a major shift in how mariner authors depicted their early seafaring years. They often began their works by stressing how their first voyages promised and initially delivered a sense of personal liberation and empowerment. Yet such accounts quickly gave way to bitter recollections of hardships endured at sea. Many sailor autobiographies and memoirs became captivity narratives that depicted their authors' growing sense of oppression. These men graphically depicted how grueling work, cruel officers, and harsh weather destroyed their hopes of achieving manly independence and instead ensnared them in a harsh, demeaning life

Exploring the different layers of meanings that sailor authors created when they remembered their early seafaring years requires identifying the men who produced such works. This is not difficult to do for well known authors like Dana. But many sailor autobiographers and memoirists were obscure men for whom there is little available historical documentation. Of course those who produced full-scale autobiographies discussing their lives before and after their seafaring years usually provided more biographical information than memoirists. Those who served in the United States Navy often had pension records and land bounty grant applications that also help the historian explore their lives. By piecing together information gleaned from sailors' own writings as well as from other sources, including pension, probate, and census records, this chapter offers biographical snapshots of sailor authors whose especially rich narratives form the basis for this book. Integrating this material into an analysis of seamen's autobiographical works illuminates the complex relationship between a mariner's actual life and his narrative about that life.

The memoirs of Richard Henry Dana and Charles Nordhoff offer particularly revealing discussions of why youths from relatively privileged homes decided to go to sea. Both men came from families with enough funds and stability to provide them with education and the opportunity to establish themselves as professionals. Dana came from the most privileged background. As noted earlier, his family was one of the most distinguished in the early nineteenth-century United States. Although the Danas had suffered financial reverses by the early 1830s, they still enjoyed an affluent life and could afford to send their son to Harvard College. In August 1834 Richard shipped out on board the *Pilgrim*, a brig bound for California to deal in the hide trade. After his return home in 1836, he resumed his privileged life as a Boston Brahmin and enjoyed a successful, multifaceted career as lawyer, author, public speaker, and legislator before his death in 1882.[5]

Born in August 1830 in Prussia, Nordhoff emigrated with his family to Ohio when he was five years old. Although he attended the preparatory program of Woodward College in Cincinnati, Nordhoff decided to leave school at age thirteen and begin an apprenticeship in a Cincinnati printing firm. Yet he soon became restless and when he was fifteen years old he shipped out from Philadelphia on board the USS *Columbus* as a "first-class boy." For nine years Nordhoff sailed the high seas, mostly as a whaleman and merchant mariner, before retiring at the age of twenty-three to pursue a career in journalism. He enjoyed a long and successful career in his profession, working as a newspaper correspondent for various papers and later serving as editor of Harper & Brothers and the New York *Evening Post*. Nordhoff also authored various books, including three major memoirs based on his seafaring years, published in a three volume set entitled *Nine Years a Sailor*, before his death in 1901.[6]

[5] Thomas Philbrick's introduction to Richard Henry Dana, Jr., *Two Years Before the Mast*, 9–11, 14–15; *American National Biography Online*, s.v. "Dana, Richard Henry, Jr." (By Robert L. Gale), http://www.anb.org/articles/16/16–02681-article.html (accessed July 5, 2006).

[6] John B. Hattendorf's introduction to Nordhoff, *Man-of-War Life*, xviii, 11–12; *Dictionary of American Biography*, s.v. "Nordhoff, Charles"; see also *The National Cyclopedia of American Biography*, 11:226. Unless noted otherwise, all quotes from Nordhoff are from his memoir cited above.

Nordhoff and Dana were men who enjoyed primarily professional careers on land. Their educations enabled them to produce memoirs about their lives at sea that helped them launch successful literary careers. Ironically, however, both men began their memoirs by recalling how as youths they sought to leave their lives on land. Ostensibly they became sailors to escape failing health. Nordhoff recollected that illness made it impossible for him to continue his apprenticeship as a printer (11). Dana noted that he shipped out in hope that a "long absence from books and study" would "cure" the "weakness of [his] eyes," a condition that had already forced him to take a leave from Harvard (40).

Yet a closer reading of these men's memoirs as well as other writings suggests that Dana and Nordhoff sought to flee a life they found increasingly stifling. When he left his apprenticeship Nordhoff was at sixes and sevens, living at home and unable to establish his independence as a man by earning his own living. A "book-worm," he read about sea travel and soon became obsessed with going to sea. "Sleeping or waking," he recalled, "I thought of nothing but the sea, ships, sailors, and the wonders of foreign lands" (11–12). Nordhoff ran away to Philadelphia and sought but failed to secure a berth for himself on board an outgoing vessel. Although family and friends tried to dissuade him from shipping out, Nordhoff persisted in his quest and finally got on board the USS *Columbus* when he was fifteen years old (22). Significantly Nordhoff recalled that "from the very first breath of salt air I had inhaled, I had felt myself gaining health and strength" (87).

Dana sought not only adventure and good health but also freedom from the cloying restraints of genteel Boston society and collegial life when he became a sailor. Before he went to sea, Dana's life had been one of rebellion and failure. He had been suspended from Harvard as a sophomore for participating in a student rebellion. Far from being upset by this, Dana reveled in his temporary freedom and returned to Harvard only reluctantly. He recalled that he went back to his studies "as a slave whipped to his dungeon." Poor eyesight soon forced Dana to return home and he felt himself to be a "useless, pitied and dissatisfied creature." Seven years after he decided to join the *Pilgrim*, Dana noted that he did this as much to "escape from the depressing situation of inactivity and dependence at home" as to "cure my eyes" and to satisfy his "love of adventure."[7]

Dana's comments bring to mind Melville's remark about a seafaring voyage ending the "damp, drizzly November in my soul" and reinvigorating him. For young men like Dana and Melville the sea offered an escape, even if only a temporary one, from a respectable but stifling life. At sea, far away from the strictures of his genteel parents and Harvard college officials, Dana could become physically strong and self reliant. In other words, he could become a man.

A closer look at Dana's writings, including his letters to family and friends, fleshes out these points. Significantly Dana repeatedly escaped from his respectable life in his later years by visiting the rough waterfront haunts of sailors or by going on long sea voyages. The latter activity particularly reinvigorated Dana, offering him a needed respite from both his familial and professional responsibilities in Boston. During his voyage home after a trip to England in 1856, Dana enthusiastically declared in his journal:

What is like the sea for healthfulness, vigor and joy! And to me beyond all this, the infinite delight of freedom ... the certainty that there is nothing I can do. No matter how many strings you have left flying, no matter what ... you ought to do, you banish and forget them all in the knowledge that miles of blue water ... makes them impossible. To me this is an unspeakable delight.[8]

Of course when Dana was a youthful sailor and not a first-class passenger he had to work while the ship was at sea as well as in port. Yet even when he was a busy mariner on board the *Pilgrim* Dana still stressed how the seafaring life braced him, making him feel free, independent, and hearty. As he wrote to his brother Ned during the *Pilgrim*'s voyage: "I feel I have done my duty in coming to sea; I can

---

[7] For quotes see Philbrick's introduction to Dana's *Two Years Before the Mast*, 10. For original sources, see Dana's letters to his aunt and brother Ned while he was at sea, reprinted in James Allison, ed., "Five Dana Letters," *The American Neptune: A Quarterly Journal of Maritime History* 13, no.3 (July 1953):162–63,166–67; see also Dana's "An Autobiographical Sketch – 1815–1844," in Robert F. Lucid, ed., *The Journal of Richard Henry Dana, Jr.*(Cambridge, MA: The Belknap Press of Harvard University Press, 1968),1:26–27.

[8] Charles Francis Adams, *Richard Henry Dana: A Biography* (1890; repr., Detroit, MI : Gail Research Co., 1968), 1: 361–62.

truly say that I am, at heart, lighter and happier...I am now independent...and capable of taking care of myself if necessary."[9]

But it was *Two Years Before the Mast* that best captured the trans-
formative power of the seafaring life. Dana proudly noted that when
he returned to Boston after his two-year stint as a sailor, a man who
had last seen him as a puny, sickly undergraduate was astonished at
meeting Dana again. He was now a picture of "health and strength,"
a "'rough alley' looking fellow, with duck trousers and red shirt, long
hair, face burnt as black as an Indian's" (458).

Dana's comments resonated with antebellum Americans increasingly concerned about the nation's youth becoming sickly, weak, and
effeminate. Popular songs derided effeminate upper-class dandies
whose late hours and decadent life sapped both their manly strength
and virtue. Audiences in New York's Tremont Theatre, for example,
heard the popular actor Henry J. Finn sing "Adam and Eve," one of
whose stanzas declared:

> The dandies now look slim and pale,
> Once they look'd hearty, fresh, and hale;
> Their voices sound like a squeaking fiddle,
> And they're small as a wasp around the middle!
> Singing, Heigho, I grieve, I grieve, for the good old days of
> Adam and Eve.[10]

Popular plays, such as Anna Cora Mowatt's "Fashion," counter
posed effeminate drawing room fops with "True Man," the arche-
typal farmer noted for his physical rigor and stoic virtue.[11] Reformers
regularly urged strenuous physical exercise and Spartan diets as a way
to toughen up urban, middle-class youths.[12] Boxing and other con-
tact sports began to attract young men from the middle and upper
classes as a way to stave off anxieties about becoming effeminate in a
genteel society.[13] The antebellum years also saw Americans becoming

---

[9] Richard Henry Dana to Edmund T. Dana, 20 March 1835, in Allison, ed., "Five
Dana Letters," *American Neptune*, 166.

[10] David Grimsted, ed., *Notions of the Americans, 1820–1860* (New York: George
Braziller, 1970), 148–49.

[11] Ibid., 161–96.

[12] Robert H. Abzug, *Cosmos Crumbling: American Reform and the Religious
Imagination* (New York: Oxford University Press, 1994), 116–24,163–82.

[13] Elliott J. Gorn, *The Manly Art: Bare-Knuckle Prize Fighting in America* (Ithaca,
NY: Cornell University Press, 1986). See also Jackson Lears, *No Place of
Grace: Antimodernism and the Transformation of American Culture, 1880–1920*
(New York: Pantheon Books, 1981), 103–39.

obsessively concerned about the practice of masturbation. Numerous ministers, physicians, and reformers argued that the "solitary vice" would sap the vital force needed for manly physical vigor and the procreation of healthy children.[14]

That sailors had the reputation of being an especially hardy, tough group of men made their fraternity especially attractive for many young males. Gaining entrance into the manly brotherhood of mariners was especially crucial for youths who feared that an increasingly sedentary life on land was weakening them. Initiation into this brotherhood could alleviate a youth's fear of emasculation, of being a puny, overgrown boy rather than a hardy, robust man. These anxieties may have been especially acute among youths who felt smothered by an increasingly genteel and feminized domesticity. [15]

Significantly Nordhoff described veteran seamen as "hearty," "hale," "brawny," "stout," "rough looking" (152, 68). He contrasted the "puny" seasick green hands such as himself, youths who still had the "*hay-seed* sticking to their collars," with the manly confidence of a veteran sailor, who "walked with head erect…with an easy, rolling gait"(68, 78). Such comments of course resonated with those of Dana when he stressed how going to sea transformed him from a sickly youth into a "rough alley" sailor. They also remind readers of how Melville juxtaposed Redburn's healthy constitution with the sickly one of his brother who remained trapped in a household of women.

Some seamen authors from privileged backgrounds admitted that they shipped out to sea to escape moral rather than physical degeneracy. They became mariners in hopes of exchanging a life of frivolity and dissipation for the discipline required on long, demanding sea voyages. Nathaniel Ames (1796–1835) was one such man. Like Dana, Ames was a Harvard student before he became a sailor in 1815. He also came from a distinguished Massachusetts family, noted for its scientists, physicians, mathematicians, and political leaders. His grandfather and uncle produced one of the nation's leading almanacs while his father Fisher Ames was a distinguished Federalist politician.[16]

[14] Ben Barker-Benfield, "The Spermatic Economy: A Nineteenth Century View of Sexuality," *Feminist Studies* 1, no. 1 (Summer 1972): 45–74.

[15] Ann Douglass, *The Feminization of American Culture* (New York: Alfred A. Knopf, 1977), esp. 289–329.

[16] Warren S. Walker, "A Note on Nathaniel Ames," *American Literature* 26, no. 2 (May 1954): 239–41; Ames, *Mariner's Sketches*, 259–70, esp.263–66; see also Hans-Joachim Land and Benjamin Lease, "The Authorship of Symzonia: The Case

In his 1830 memoir entitled *A Mariner's Sketches* Nathaniel Ames recalled frittering away much of his three years at college. Somewhat sheepishly he admitted being penalized repeatedly for various escapades and poor academic performance. Ames also remembered that he acquired "a great reputation for rolling nine-pins" at a nearby hotel (269). He probably had himself in mind when he recounted how "the pleasures and gaieties" of nearby Boston enabled Harvard students to indulge in their "oppressive tendency to dissipation" (259).

Ames became the black sheep of his family, especially after he left Harvard without a degree. He was probably suspended from the college for failing grades since he noted spending six months studying with a clergyman in hopes of improving his mastery of arithmetic and other subjects. Yet Ames was soon distracted from his studies. He dryly recalled becoming well known for "snaring partridges and attending balls, singing-schools, and huskings." Ames seemed almost jocular when he concluded recollections of his early life by noting that he shipped out to sea once the War of 1812 ended and he was in no danger of being shot or captured by the British (269–70).

Ames's difficult life after his Harvard years belies the jaunty tone he affected in his memoir. He was a sailor for over ten years before he settled in Providence, Rhode Island. Prosperity and family stability eluded him. A lifelong bachelor, Ames tried numerous ways to earn a living. According to the Providence city directory of 1828, he was a commission merchant. He also published essays about his seafaring years in *The Manufacturer's and Farmer's Journal* of Providence. Ames expanded his essays into two memoirs, *A Mariner's Sketches* (1830) and *Nautical Reminiscences* (1832). A fictional work *An Old Sailor's Yarns* was published posthumously in 1835. Although Dana praised *A Mariner's Sketches* and Melville used this text as a source for several of his books, Ames's works did not sell. Debtor's prison marred his last years.[17]

Ames's failure to prosper after his seafaring career ended is in stark contrast to the success that Dana and Nordhoff enjoyed in their post-maritime lives. Despite the different trajectories their lives

for Nathaniel Ames," *The New England Quarterly* 48, no. 2 (June 1975) : 251–52; Samuel Eliot Morison, "Squire Ames and Doctor Ames," *The New England Quarterly* 1, no. 1 (January 1928) : 5–31.

17 Ibid.

took, each of these sailor authors used their narratives to articulate anxieties about an enervating life on land. Escaping such a life and embracing one associated with a hardy, robust, disciplined masculinity was why they shipped out to sea. This was true even for Nathaniel Ames, despite his cavalier tone in describing his decision to become a mariner. Significantly Ames praised sailors as generous, brave, loyal men (239–40). This depiction of Jack Tar of course was the opposite of how Ames portrayed the dissipated, spoiled youth at Harvard, including his younger self. Like Dana, Ames went to sea to escape a privileged yet unsatisfying life and to belong to a fraternity of men he admired.

Youths who came from families like those of Ames and Dana generally did not become mariners. Most of the men who formed the backbone of antebellum America's merchant and naval vessels were from working-class families where poverty and limited schooling handicapped the young.[18] Not surprisingly, this background characterized the majority of antebellum sailor autobiographers and memoirists. Many of these men spent a significant part of their working lives on the high seas. They were often dogged by poverty, illness, and family losses throughout their lives. Some succumbed to alcoholism. Even those who managed to achieve a modest competency for themselves and their families still had to struggle for many years to achieve this much.

Discussion of the lives of four sailor authors who left particularly rich self narratives, Horace Lane, James Wordon, Samuel Leech, and Samuel F. Holbrook, illustrates these points. Lane's childhood, for example, was marred by poverty, instability, mistreatment, and bad luck. He was born in February 1789 in Lanesborough, Massachusetts, and spent his childhood in Stillwater, New York, a small village located on the west bank of the Hudson River. Postrevolutionary Stillwater and the surrounding environs were at the cusp of the market revolution

---

[18] Simon P. Newman, *Embodied History: The Lives of the Poor in Early Philadelphia* (Philadelphia: University of Pennsylvania Press, 2003), esp. 110–11; see also Daniel Vickers with Vince Walsh, *Young Men and the Sea: Yankee Seafarers in the Age of Sail* (New Haven, CT: Yale University Press, 2005), 204–10; Margaret S. Creighton, *Rites & Passages: The Experience of American Whaling, 1830–1870* (Cambridge: Cambridge University Press, 1995), 46–51; Ira Dye, "Early American Merchant Seafarers," *Proceedings of the American Philosophical Society* 120, no. 5 (October 1976): 338.

which would soon transform the antebellum Northeast.[19] Seeking to prosper in an increasingly commercial economy, Lane's father Asa stopped being a farmer and started a rafting business, transporting lumber on the Hudson River. Yet Asa Lane did not prosper. Although the reason for this remains unclear, he may have been a spendthrift. His son Horace ruefully declared that his father's "lack of discretion, in choosing his company, baffled all his efforts to accumulate property..." (7).

In April 1795 Horace Lane's life changed dramatically when his mother died after a short illness. Unable to care for his son and two other children, Asa Lane apprenticed them out to different families. Horace had bitter memories of being placed with an "avaricious farmer and cobbler" who mistreated him (10). A number of other apprenticeships followed, including ones to a country storekeeper and a clothier. Discontented and eager for adventure, Lane ran away when he was eight and a half years old. Like Huckleberry Finn, Lane used the river to escape. He sailed on a raft to Troy where he met a man who took him on board a sloop loaded with lumber and bound for New York City. Asa Lane, however, tracked down his son and made him return to Stillwater. Yet Horace's wanderlust persisted and he

---

[19] Lane, *Wandering Boy*, 7–19; "Petition of Horace Lane for Pension on account of his Naval Services to the United States," Jan. 17, 1855, RG 233, Records of the House of Representatives, 33rd Congress, Committee on Invalid Pensions: Petitions and Memorials (HR 33A-G 9.1), NA, Washington, DC. See also Myra C. Glenn, "Troubled Manhood in the Early Republic: The Life and Autobiography of Sailor Horace Lane," *Journal of the Early Republic* 26 (Spring 2006): 59–93. On the late-eighteenth- and early-nineteenth-century Hudson River Valley area, especially Saratoga County where Stillwater is located, see *A Gazeteer of the State of New York* ... (Albany, NY: J. Disturnell, 1842), 359–63, 386; *Our County and Its People: A Descriptive and Biographical Record of Saratoga County, New York* (n.p.: The Boston History Co., Pub., 1899), 84–89, 145–46; Nathaniel Bartlett Sylvester, *History of Saratoga County, New York, With Illustrations and Biographical Sketches of Some of Its Prominent Men and Pioneers* (Philadelphia, PA: Everts & Ensign, 1878). For discussion of how the market economy transformed the Hudson Valley area, see Martin Bruegel, *Farm, Shop, Landing: The Rise of a Market Society in the Hudson Valley, 1780–1860* (Durham, NC: Duke University Press, 2002). Stillwater was then part of Albany County and the 1790 census shows Asa Lane and his family living there. See *Heads of Families at the First Census of the United States Taken in the Year 1790, New York* (Baltimore, MD: Genealogical Pub., Co., 1966), 50. Asa Lane's name did appear once in the "Minutes of the Board of Supervisors of Saratoga County" (Saratoga County Historian's Office, Ballston Spa, New York). In 1799 the Board noted the county owed Lane and other men money for "assisting a constable."

sought passage on various vessels. In July of 1799 Horace Lane finally shipped out on the USS *Connecticut* as a "ship's boy." He was a little over ten years old and his career as an ordinary sailor had begun. It would last for over a quarter of a century.[20]

Alcoholism ruined Lane's adult life. As he sadly recounted in *The Wandering Boy*, delirium tremens, destitution, and failed romantic relationships became his lot (161–82). By the mid-1820s Lane's seafaring career was pretty much over. Although he worked briefly on the docks in Troy, New York, and married, stability and prosperity eluded him. As his drinking worsened, Lane became a burglar. In May 1827 he began serving a three-year sentence at the Auburn Penitentiary for grand larceny. Shortly after his release, Lane resumed his drinking and thieving. In December 1830 he began a two-year sentence at Sing Sing.[21]

Horace Lane tried to reform after his release from Sing Sing. But both his pension application and records from the Sailors' Snug Harbor document his downward spiral. Towards the end of his life Lane was alone, ill, and destitute. He also seems to have been an

[20] The muster roll of the *Connecticut* confirms that Lane did serve as a "boy" from July 2, 1799 to November 7, 1800. See *Naval Documents Related to the Quasi-War Between the United States and France. Naval Operations from August 1799 to December 1799*, 7 vols. (Washington, DC: Government Printing Office, 1936), 4:7. See also Lane, *Wandering Boy*, 19.

[21] Lane, *Wandering Boy*, 190–97; Lane, *Five Years in State's Prison; Or, Interesting Truths, Showing the Manner of Discipline in the State's Prisons at Sing Sing and Auburn* ... (New York: Luther Pratt & Son, 1835), 6–9. See also "State of Connecticut vs. Horace Lane," New London County, Superior Court Files, 1711–1891, Box 49, RG 3, Connecticut State Library, History and Genealogy Unit, Hartford, CT. Lane's case appears in the Saratoga County Court records and related proceedings. The "[Saratoga County Court of] Oyer & Terminer – Minutes, July 1791–December 1842" notes that Horace Lane pleaded guilty to the charge of grand larceny on May 30,1827, and he was sentenced to three years of hard labor in Auburn. Although Lane stated that he arrived in Sing Sing on December 12, 1830, his name does not appear on the convict list. But he probably used an alias, since he noted that the authorities would have sentenced him to at least ten years if they had known he was an "old offender" (*Wandering Boy*, 196–97). Significantly, one Adam Lane, sentenced on October 5, 1830, and serving a two-year sentence for grand larceny, does appear in the Sing Sing list of convicts. It is quite possible that Adam and Horace Lane were the same person. See "Annual Report of the Inspectors of the State Prison at Mount Pleasant," *Documents of the Senate of the State of New York*, vol. 1, no. 13, 1834, 57th session, document L, "List of Convicts Discharged...from the 30th of September, 1832 to the 30th of September, 1833" (Albany, NY: E. Croswell, Printer to the State, 1834).

obstreperous man. During the early to mid-1840s Lane was expelled twice from the Sailors' Snug Harbor for "breaking the rules" and using abusive language toward both the superintendent and his fellow mates.[22] Destitution forced Lane to seek a pension for his naval service but since he was not disabled in the line of duty he did not receive one. But Congress in April 1855 did grant Lane a bounty of land in the West. Yet this did not make him solvent. When he died in June 1866 at the age of seventy-seven, Lane left a total of only $4.85.[23]

Unlike Lane, James Wordon, a sailor for over twenty-eight years, was not an alcoholic. Yet he led a hard life. Born in 1812 in Groton, Connecticut, Wordon never even mentioned his father in his 1855 autobiography. He did stress that after his mother died when he was nine years old, he became "friendless and homeless" (3). Wordon lived with different people and sometimes on the streets before he shipped out on board a brig bound for Jamaica in 1824. Major illnesses sometimes incapacitated him for months while he was a merchant sailor. In 1825, for example, Wordon became ill with yellow fever while in the Caribbean. With obvious bitterness he recollected that "the Captain, disliking the trouble of me, had me put into an out-house, where I remained for five days, without being visited by any one" (5). That Wordon was only thirteen years old in 1825 made him particularly vulnerable to ill usage. He survived because a "Creole gentleman" took pity on him and got him into a hospital where he stayed for three months. Additional bouts of illness weakened Wordon's constitution. He remembered being so sick with "palsy" while on board the *Constitution* in the early 1840s that he almost died and never became "a well man" after that (34).

Despite his poor health, Wordon tried to make a new life for himself on land after his discharge from the Navy in November 1841.[24]

---

22 See the following records of the Sailors' Snug Harbor, Sealevel, NC: "Register of Pensioners," vol. 1 (Aug. 1, 1833–Nov.28, 1854), 73, for quote; "Register of Inmates Admitted to Sailors' Snug Harbor", vol. 1 (1833–1894), 14.

23 Unindexed bounty land warrants for War of 1812 veterans are found in the NA, Washington, DC. Lane's file is in Can. No. 1045, Bundle No. 65; The Sailors' Snug Harbor, "Register of Pensioners," 73, and "Record of Deaths and Burials" (1834–1908), 46.

24 Naval records state Wordon was discharged from the service on November 15, 1841. See Pension Application Files, Miscellaneous Service, Old Wars Series, "James Worden [sic]," File No. 1685, RG 15, NA, Washington, DC.

He married the sister of his shipmate, moved to Norfolk, opened a boarding house, and started a family. For the next five years Wordon and his young family lived in different places. He ran several boarding houses and also worked as a laborer. But luck was against him. His wife and three of his children died of illness, the little money he had went for doctor bills and funeral costs. After sending a surviving son to live with an uncle, Wordon "knocked about Norfolk" and the surrounding towns for several months before returning to his hometown Groton and then to Mystic, Connecticut (34–35).

Although Wordon initially stayed with family members in the Groton area, the deaths of his brother and sister left him increasingly alone. In his memoir Wordon recalled that for several years he had to stay intermittently in the poor house, presumably the one in New London (35). In January 1854 Wordon got a break – he received a navy invalid pension for becoming disabled while in the line of duty. Naval records show that he was retroactively awarded $3.00 a month from November 1841 to January 1853 and then received $6.00 a month afterward.[25] Although this money offered Wordon badly needed assistance, poverty and isolation dogged him. Wordon's health also deteriorated. As he sorrowfully noted: "I was all the time sick, without anything to encourage me" (35). Most of his pension money went to pay for doctors.

Wordon became a wanderer. Repeatedly he petitioned the Navy to send his pension to different places, including Hartford, New York City, Albany, and Washington, DC.[26] There are no records to be found in Mystic, Groton, or New London on Wordon. Like many impoverished transients, he vanishes from the historical record.

Samuel Leech and Samuel Holbrook are case studies of men who achieved prosperity and stability after their seafaring years ended. Leech, who served six years on board British and American men-of-war, was born in 1797 in Wanstead, England. His parents were servants to the British nobility. Leech's father died when he was three years old and his mother, unable to take care of her son, sent him to live first with one aunt and then another. Leech recalled being beaten by some of his relatives for the slightest offense. Eager to escape his

[25] Ibid. See also Wordon, *Life and Adventures*, 35.
[26] Wordon's requests appear in notarized letters and are found in his pension application file (see endnote 24).

difficult life, Leech shipped on board the British man-of-war, the *Macedonian*, in July 1810. He was thirteen years old. Naval records confirm that Leech, then a powder boy, was captured by American forces after the *Macedonian*'s defeat in October 1812. He later served on board several American naval and merchant vessels.[27]

By 1817 Leech's seafaring career was over and he was making a painful transition to life in his adopted country. In his memoir he recalled tramping to different Connecticut towns in search of work (178). At one point an armorer's mate from the *Macedonian*, living in Mansfield, got Leech a job at his brother-in-law's clothing shop. Leech also earned money by braiding straw hats, doing farm work, and other manual labor. He became a Methodist and married a fellow church member (180–82, 193).

Leech took other steps to establish himself in his new country. In September 1835 he became a citizen of the United States.[28] He also became a storekeeper, opening several shops, first in Mansfield and Somers, Connecticut, and later in Wilbraham, Massachusetts (192–93). By the time Leech died in January 1848, he had amassed an estate of over $3,500. Although by no mean a wealthy man, Leech had achieved a measure of prosperity. The inventory of his estate listed not only a wide variety of dry goods and furniture but also books, suggesting that Leech was a man who enjoyed reading and had enough money to create his own library.[29]

Samuel Holbrook is an example of another retired sailor who became modestly prosperous in his later years. Born in New York City in July 1793, Holbrook moved with his family to Worcester and later Roxbury, Massachusetts, in 1798. According to Holbrook, several business partners fleeced his father and the latter had to scrounge for a living in New York. For a while Holbrook lived with his paternal

---

[27] Leech, *A Voice from the Main Deck*, 1–13. On the *Macedonian*'s defeat and capture, see ibid., 83–90. The "List of Officers, Seamen, and Marines, Prisoners from Frigate *Macedonian*, October 26, 1812" lists Leech as a prisoner (No. 45). See "Naval Records Collection of Naval Records & Library, Subject File, 1775–1910," RG 45, NA, Washington, DC.

[28] See the Hampden County Supreme Judicial Court Record Book, September 1835 session, p. 217, docket #42, Supreme Judicial Court Archives and Records Preservation, Boston, Massachusetts (SJCA).

[29] Hampden County Probate Court, estate of Samuel Leech, Case No. 6804, 1848, SJCA.

grandfather in Boston and attended schools where he and other schoolchildren were beaten or subject to other harsh punishment. Holbrook admitted that he was expelled from school after he beat a teacher who falsely accused him of putting a dead rat on his desk and then started hitting him. Returning to New York to live with his now financially straitened family, Holbrook ran with a gang and fought with different groups of boys. When he was fourteen in 1807 he went to sea as a cabin boy, cook, and steward (11–28).

In 1808 Holbrook apprenticed himself to a shipwright. In 1814 he joined the United States Navy as a carpenter's mate. While serving as ship's carpenter on board the *Macedonian* in 1820, Holbrook permanently injured his left foot. Although he returned briefly to naval service in 1862, his lame foot cut short his seafaring career.[30] Despite his disability and bitterness over the meager government pension he got, Holbrook nevertheless achieved some success. Shortly after his discharge from the *Macedonian* he moved to Boston, joined the Methodist Episcopal Church, married, and with his savings became a shipwright (350–55). The Boston City Directory shows that Holbrook owned his own house and shipwright business by the early 1850s.[31] When he died on June 8, 1885, he left a personal estate of $3,000.[32]

These four biographical sketches underscore how difficult life was for most ex-sailors, including those who managed to earn a decent living for themselves and their families. Not surprisingly, most seamen authors stressed that they went to sea to escape a dead-end life on land, one characterized by destitution, grueling labor, punitive discipline, and little if any family ties. This pattern of course was evident in the narratives of Horace Lane, James Wordon, Samuel Leech, and Samuel Holbrook.

But numerous other sailor authors offered similarly grim portraits of their early years. The Canadian-born Ned Myers, for example,

---

[30] Holbrook received a government pension for becoming disabled. See the "Invalid Navy Pensioners. List Complete to November 17, 1848," Records of the Veterans Administration and "Pension Application Files. Miscellaneous Service. Old War Series," File No. 762, RG 15, NA, Washington, DC.

[31] *The Boston Directory, for the Year 1852. Embracing the City Record…and Business Directory …* (Boston: George Adams, 1852), 129 and 145.

[32] "Samuel F. Holbrook," No 73967, *Suffolk County Probate Record Books*, vol. 572, p. 152, Massachusetts Archives, Boston, Massachusetts. See also vol. 574, p. 376, ibid.

recalled that he ran away to sea at the age of fifteen to escape the floggings he endured at the hands of several families with whom he lived in Nova Scotia and elsewhere when he was a boy. Significantly Myers stated that he had only vague memories of his father, a British soldier, and could not remember his mother at all (6–17). In his 1831 memoir David Bunnell, a sailor for over twenty-three years, remembered a similarly fractured family life. Born in 1793 in Cheshire, Connecticut, Bunnell lost his father, a sailor, when he was two years old. His mother remarried and when her second husband died, she began leading a peripatetic life, living briefly in different towns with son David. At one point she bound him out to a stonecutter in New York City who was a "tyrant." Bunnell noted that his mother moved on and "left [him] as it were alone." He did not see her again for almost twenty-four years (5–6). Roland Gould, another career sailor born in 1817 in Charlestown, Massachusetts, recalled living a wandering life after his father died and the family became impoverished. By the time he shipped out to sea at the age of fifteen, stated Gould, he had lived in numerous towns and cities, including Boston. He had worked at various jobs, including driving a milk cart, tending ten pin alleys, manufacturing saddles and trunks, and learning carpentry, a trade to which he returned after his seafaring career ended (14–23).

The difficult lives of most seamen authors offer a needed context for interpreting their narratives. Such works were often a form of mendicant literature. Many sailor authors admitted that they desperately needed money when they published their narratives. Lane, for example, ended *The Wandering Boy* on a plaintive note, declaring that he had spent his last three cents on a candle so that he could finish his work (219). Other seaman authors stressed that they were ill or disabled as well as destitute. As noted earlier, Wordon pointedly noted that his health was "bad" and that he spent most of his money on doctors (35). Gould emphasized that he was blind and in "pecuniary embarrassment" (preface). Bunnell asserted that his health was "wrecked" and he looked to the "patronage and generosity of [his] countrymen" for assistance (preface). Such comments made readers painfully aware of how badly these writers needed money.

Seamen authors sought to tug at the reader's heart strings as well as purse. A graphic description of harsh, unstable childhoods was one way to snag readers' sympathies. Such descriptions were also an effective strategy to mitigate the author's later failure in life or to make his modest success as an adult seem all the more impressive. Yet recollections of difficult childhoods were not just rhetorical devices or strategies. They also were a way for seamen authors to bear witness, to show readers, especially those from comfortable homes, how instability, poverty, and cruelty marred the childhoods of young boys and caused them to go to sea at a young age.

It is important to recognize that these writers did not describe atypical childhoods when they depicted their harsh, early lives. As the historiography of childhood has shown, numerous children and youths led hardscrabble lives in the early republic, lives dogged by poverty, illness, death, corporal punishment, and instability.[33] Perhaps it was because their childhoods were not all that unusual among the working poor that seamen authors often described their early woes in a matter-of-fact way.

Occasionally such an author did express anger about growing up without much stability or nurturing. This was the case with Jacob Hazen, a man from Muncy, Pennsylvania, who served for five years on board whalers and American men-of-war, and spent his later years as a shoemaker. Hazen recalled that he came from "humble parentage" and at the age of five was "placed out to earn my own living among strangers." Although he periodically returned home as a child, Hazen with obvious bitterness recalled that his parents left him to grow up "pretty much after my own fashion." Perhaps in a slap at Dana and other "gentlemen sailors," Hazen stated that unlike youths "reared in wealth and nurtured in luxury," the impoverished boy who had grown up "like a wild sapling of the forest," had few "tender associations of family" and therefore felt "little or few regrets" about leaving their homes or their country. As if to hammer his point home, Hazen added that when he left for the sea the only childhood memories he had were of the "cold frown of the master, and the shrill scolding voice of the mistress" (13–16, 58). It was significant what he omitted – he recalled no memories, not even bad ones, of either of his parents.

[33] Steven Mintz, *Huck's Raft: A History of American Childhood* (Cambridge, MA: Harvard University Press, 2004), 133–53; Jacqueline Renier, *From Virtue to Character: American Childhood, 1775–1850* (New York: Twayne Pub., 1996), 125–50.

For working-class youths like Hazen a seafaring career provided not only an escape from a harsh, rootless life on land but also a chance to earn a decent living and achieve some measure of manly independence. In fact a seafaring life even offered antebellum young males from modest circumstances the opportunity to become masters of merchant vessels or whalers.[34]

Hazen stressed in his autobiography that shipping out to sea was the "best remedy for hard times," at least for "poor boys" like him. He illustrated his point by describing the circumstances that forced him to become a mariner. When the Panic of 1837 hit Philadelphia Hazen lost his job as a journeyman shoemaker. Unable to find work he became morose as well as destitute: "Discouraged, disheartened, and moneyless – a boarding bill accumulating from day to day, with no prospect of ever being able to discharge it – I felt most wretchedly dejected" (16–17). It was only then, recalled Hazen, that he got the "wild idea" of joining a whaling expedition, even though he had "never before had any inclination for a sea-faring life." Going to sea, he admitted, was an act of desperation, a way to flee from his failed life and make a fresh start for himself, perhaps "to hit upon some plan to make a fortune" through whaling (18).

Irrespective of what kind of life they left on land, whether privileged or desperate, sailor autobiographers and memoirists stressed that being at sea was initially a liberating experience for them. They recalled feeling free, independent, and healthy, when they began sailing the high seas. Hazen, for example, stated: "I felt as wild and joyous as a bird released from its cage, to soar aloft in the free and open atmosphere" (58). Bunnell felt a similar exhilaration when he began a transatlantic voyage: "I felt my glory. I could please and feed my rambling disposition. I was young, and had the whole world before me.... I was my own master, and determined to remain so.... I was like a young bear ... (45).

Bunnell and Hazen echoed Dana and Nordhoff when they stressed how independent and rejuvenated they felt at sea. Yet recollections of feeling free and joyful assume a particular resonance when uttered by men from impoverished backgrounds. Their blighted early lives seemed to doom them to a marginal, rootless existence. Before going

---

[34] Vickers & Walsh, *Young Men and the Sea*, 118–23, 203–04.

to sea these men were in a kind of prison, one forged by destitution, instability, loneliness, and despair. It was therefore poignant when they remembered how happy they felt when first at sea. The analogies they used – Hazen comparing himself to a bird released from its cage or Bunnell recalling that he felt like a young bear with the whole world before him – dramatized their sense of liberation and optimism as they began their seafaring life.

But seamen authors were quick to remind their readers that their hopes for a better life were soon destroyed. They detailed a litany of maritime grievances and ultimately portrayed a seafaring career as a kind of imprisonment. In Bunnell's case imprisonment was not merely a metaphor but a grim reality. The British impressed him and later incarcerated him as a prisoner of war in Dartmoor Prison between December 1814 and July 1815.[35] Since Hazen was a sailor during the late 1830s and early 1840s he never suffered these experiences.[36] Nevertheless he stressed in his memoir that he regretted his decision to become a mariner (92–93). Hazen offered a grim inventory of the numerous difficulties he endured while at sea, including harsh discipline, bad food, and grueling work. He recalled that he was overjoyed when his term of service in the U.S. Navy ended and he could regain his "personal independence" (393).

A seafaring life meant the loss not the attainment of manly freedom and independence for many youths. Sailor authors bitterly noted how their initial hopes for a better, freer life at sea quickly gave way to disillusionment and even despair. Their narratives graphically depicted how maritime life enmeshed them in an oppressive web of hardships and injustices. Some of these writers ruefully recalled that this became painfully evident during their maiden voyage.

[35] Bunnell, *Travels and Adventures*, 56. Bunnell states that he was impressed on board the British ship *Grenada* (46). The muster books of the HMS *Grenada* show a David Bunhill being impressed on board this ship on November 28, 1808 (TNA, PRO: ADM 37/339). Bunnell discusses his incarceration in Dartmoor Prison in ibid., 137–40. Bunnell's name appears on the General Entry Books, Prisoners of War, Americans, Dartmouth, 1814–1815, TNA, PRO: ADM 103/90.

[36] Naval records confirm Hazen's military service. The "Muster Roll of the USS *Columbus*," vol. 480, No. 1279, Box 37, RG 217, NA, Washington, DC, for example, shows him coming on board on December 1, 1840, and being discharged on January 11, 1842. The logbook of the *Fairfield* shows that a number of men from the *Columbus*, including Hazen, were received on board on May 27, 1841. For logbook see "Records of the Bureau of Naval Personnel ... Logs of US Naval Ships, 1801–1915", vol. 14, RG 24, NA, Washington, DC.

Horace Lane's account of his experiences as a "ship's boy" on board the *Connecticut* in the late 1790s vividly illustrated this point. Seasickness made Lane yearn for dry land. Officers slapped and cursed him when he was late with their breakfast or accidentally broke dishes. His crew mates could also be a problem. The ritual of the Captain Neptune ceremony designed to initiate sailors making their first voyage was much more than rough play. Lane thought he was "a gone chicken" as he experienced this initiation. It took him three hours to clean himself after his mates lathered his face "with tar and hen manure, and scraped [it] with an iron hoop" (20–24).

Yet these difficulties paled in comparison to the major challenge that Lane faced, combat. He began his seafaring career during the United States' undeclared naval war with France which was fought mostly in the West Indies between 1798 and 1800.[37] The twenty-four-gun *Connecticut* was one of the fastest ships in the Navy, capturing a number of French privateers during her sixteen-month cruise.[38] Lane was one of the powder boys who kept the gun crews supplied with ammunition. But as he sheepishly admitted, the onset of battle paralyzed him. Only a slap on the head and a reproach from a shipmate waiting for his powder snapped Lane out of his terror (23).

A seafaring life promised much more than it delivered for impoverished youths like Lane and Hazen. But was this also true for the minority of "gentlemen sailors," many of whom made only one sea voyage? Exploration of this question inevitably brings to mind Dana's description of his first and only voyage as a mariner. As noted earlier, his joy and exuberance at being at sea was a prominent theme in his famous memoir. Yet Dana was ultimately very ambivalent about maritime life. Scholars have noted that *Two Years Before the Mast*, which began as a story of liberation and adventure, became a captivity narrative.[39] While in California curing hides as a member of the *Pilgrim*

---

[37] Michael A. Palmer, *Stoddert's War: Naval Operations During the Quasi-War with France, 1798–1801* (Columbia: University of South Carolina, 1987); Howard P. Nash, Jr., *The Forgotten Wars: The Role of the U.S. Navy in the Quasi War with France and the Barbary Wars, 1798–1805* (South Brunswick, NJ: A.S. Barnes, 1968).

[38] On the *Connecticut*, see Howard I. Chapelle, *The History of the American Sailing Navy: The Ships and their Development* (New York: Bonanza Books, 1949), 145; Palmer, *Stoddert's War*, 149.

[39] Philbrick's introduction to Dana, *Two Years Before the Mast*, 25–29 & Egan, "Gentlemen Sailors," 87–89. See also Bryan Charles Siniche, "'The Test of Salt

crew, Dana jumped at the chance to return home on board the *Alert* and not extend his seafaring by several years. He believed that if he was a sailor for longer than two years he would remain one for the rest of his life. This prospect frightened Dana who ultimately sought only a temporary escape, not a permanent exile from his privileged Boston life (239, 349). Dana veered into melodrama as he described his confrontation with his captain who insisted he remain on board the *Pilgrim*: "No court of star chamber could proceed more summarily with a poor devil...[He was] condemning me to a punishment worse than a Botany Bay exile, and to a fate which would alter the whole current of my future life" (349). Fortunately another man volunteered to take Dana's place on board the *Pilgrim* and he returned home on board the *Alert*. Dana recalled he felt "like one who had just sprung from an iron trap which was closing upon him" (353).

Nordhoff also recalled being disillusioned with a seafaring life and seeking to escape it. For him as for Dana, this life became a kind of imprisonment or captivity. Nordhoff's 1857 memoir *Whaling and Fishing* particularly articulated his regrets about becoming a mariner. Bitterly this former sailor recalled how naïve and reckless he had been when he first shipped out to sea with "a light heart." The harsh realities of whaling, groused Nordhoff, soon exposed as a sham "the thick mist of romance" he initially associated with seafaring.

The prospect of remaining a sailor "alarmed" Nordhoff as much as it did Dana. By the time he turned twenty one, Nordhoff remembered, he realized that he had "no returns" to show for his grueling labors as a seaman and was in fact "losing ground," "lessening [his] chances of ever returning to a better life." The belief that he had "wasted," "thrown away," years of his life as a mariner troubled him. So too did the fact that he was increasingly "acting" and "thinking" like a "genuine, irredeemable sailor." Nordhoff recalled that his stock taking made him resolve to start a new life on land (345, 349–50).

Of course Nordhoff's and Dana's fears about being mariners for life highlighted their status as "gentlemen sailors." Yet their memoirs articulated concerns that other seamen authors expressed about maritime life. Irrespective of their class background and length of

Water': Literature of the Sea and Social Class in Antebellum America" (PhD diss., University of North Carolina at Chapel Hill, 2006), 98–100.

maritime service, sailor autobiographers and memoirists stressed that a mariner's life was often grueling, dangerous, and unremunerative.

These writers also emphasized how unfree a sailor was. Repeatedly they recalled being at the mercy of men and forces beyond their control when they were at sea. Lane of course did this when he remembered how various events, such as naval battle and Captain Neptune's ceremony, bewildered, even terrified, him. Seamen authors like Lane conveyed how maritime life often overwhelmed and demoralized them when they recounted enduring numerous hardships at sea. Their narratives revealed, perhaps inadvertently, how powerless they had been when they navigated the high seas.

Concerns about manhood reverberated throughout this discussion. In antebellum America a male was manly if he exerted agency, control, over his life and successfully defended his freedom.[40] Popular autobiographies of self-made men underscored this belief. Both the narratives of Benjamin Franklin and Frederick Douglass, for example, trumpeted each man's ability to emancipate himself from subordination to others. Franklin recalled first doing this when as an apprentice printer he defied the authority of his employer who was also his older brother. Throughout his autobiography Franklin noted how he bested a series of powerful men to achieve both financial and political independence.[41] In his autobiography Douglass detailed his defiance of slaveholders and attainment of freedom.[42]

The autobiographies and memoirs of seamen authors constructed a very different kind of narrative when they described being buffeted by numerous developments that denied them manly agency and independence. Of course former sailors noted how they were subject to the ravages of nature and war. But what galled them was being subject to men who abused, humiliated them. Even many years after their seafaring days had ended, seamen authors remained indignant over the mistreatment they had suffered at the hands of shipmates and especially officers. These writers used their texts to publicize their

---

[40] Bruce Dorsey, *Reforming Men and Women: Gender in the Antebellum City* (Ithaca, NY: Cornell University Press, 2002), 14–28, offers a recent, succinct discussion of this issue.

[41] Louis P. Masur, ed., *The Autobiography of Benjamin Franklin, with Related Documents*, 2nd ed. (Boston: Bedford/St Martin's Press, 2003).

[42] David W. Blight, ed., *Narrative of the Life of Frederick Douglass, an American Slave, Written by Himself...*, 2nd ed. (Boston: Bedford/St Martin's Press, 2003).

sufferings and excoriate those who inflicted it. Perhaps more importantly such works also revealed their authors' belief that the abuses
they endured as mariners had imperiled their manhood.

Ben-Ezra Stiles Ely graphically illustrated these points in his 1849
memoir. Descended from a long and distinguished line of Presbyterian
ministers, Ely went to sea after ill health and expulsion from a preparatory academy whetted his desire to see the world. His reading of
Dana's memoir and other seafaring literature stoked Ely's "restless,
excitement-loving disposition" (xxvi). In November 1844 he joined
the whaling vessel the *Emigrant* for a twenty-seven-month journey.
After this trip ended Ely tried his hand at numerous other jobs until
his death in 1910. He was a lawyer, gold miner, boarding house man-
ager, bartender, California state legislator, and finally, a minister. But
he never again became a mariner.[43]

Ely's memoir revealed why he did not return to seafaring. Like
Dana's more famous work, Ely's quickly becomes a captivity narrative, detailing a litany of sufferings, including seasickness, putrid food,
grueling, odorous work, and homesickness. But what most rankled
Ely was the misbehavior of his captain, a man the crew list identified
as James Shearman (148). Ely's portrayal of this officer adumbrates
Harriet Beecher Stowe's depiction of the slaveholder Simon Legree
in *Uncle Tom's Cabin*. The commander of the *Emigrant* was allegedly a lecherous, drunken, sadistic bully. Ely elaborated by itemizing
Shearman's faults: he was "abominably profane in speech," made "las-
civious remarks" about women, including his own mother and sister,
tortured the ship's pet animals, and defied the *Emigrant*'s temperance
pledge by guzzling liquor he smuggled on board (13, 15, 41, 67). This
person, avowed Ely, was "the most foul-mouthed and degraded man
I ever knew" (15).

Ely described Shearman in ways that resonated with middle-class
readers. The *Emigrant*'s commanding officer personified the antith-
esis of what constituted respectable manhood in antebellum America.
Significantly Ely mocked Shearman's manliness. It was "our manly
captain," he sneered, who tormented the cook's pet pig and almost
whipped to death the ship's cat. Ely sarcastically concluded that such

---

[43] Curtis Dahl draws on Ely's manuscript autobiography, owned by one of the latter's
descendants, to discuss his life. See Dahl's introduction to Ely, *"There She Blows,"*
xiii–xxxiii. For confirmation of Ely's service on board the *Emigrant*, see 148–49.

actions were "an honourable employment, truly, for one who considered himself a man ..." (41).

Ely's choice of words is revealing. According to him, Shearman may
have considered himself a man but in fact he was not. As Ely repeatedly insisted, this officer was an undisciplined brute. What clinched
this belief for Ely was his former captain's mistreatment of the crew.
Ely claimed that Shearman had regularly cursed, threatened, over-
worked, and starved the men under his command. He had allegedly
treated sailors "like dogs" (15–16).

This last comment underscored Ely's belief that he and his shipmates had been stripped of their manly independence and dignity
while on board the *Emigrant*. Their captain, fumed Ely, had tried
to degrade them to the level of beasts. There was bitter irony in this
accusation. A commander who was allegedly brutish and unmanly
had sought to debase males noted for their manliness to the level of
animals.

Ely was obviously a deeply embittered man when he castigated his
former captain. Yet he undermined his own case against Shearman
when he conceded that this officer had not flogged one man during the
over two-year-long voyage (41). Claims that Shearman "torture[d]"
his crew (41), that he treated them "like dogs," smacked of hyperbole.
So, too, did Ely's contention that most officers were like Shearman.
They were "incarnate devils" who brutalized sailors (14, 85, 119).

Ely's blanket condemnation of officers might well have reflected
the resentment a "gentlemen sailor" felt when forced to take orders
from men he saw as beneath him in social status. Significantly Ely
noted that he was regularly "ordered about deck like a dog, at the
beck and call of men" who were his "inferiors" (40).

But Ely's diatribe against Shearman and other officers was not only
rooted in class resentment. It also reflected his concerns about manliness. When Ely remembered his voyage on board the *Emigrant* what
he stressed was how this trip endangered rather than furthered his
youthful bid to achieve manhood. He noted that he disliked his brief
stint as acting steward since it entailed doing work gendered feminine.
"It humbled my pride not a little to wash dishes and make bread,"
recalled Ely, and he yearned to be "a sailor bold and free" (65).

To be "a sailor bold and free," to achieve manly independence –
this is what Ely and numerous other youths sought when they went

to sea. But Ely's memoir suggests that this hope remained unrealized. Instead of gaining freedom and independence, he asserted, mariners often found themselves at the mercy of men who abused and humiliated them; who treated them like animals. And not just any animal, stressed Ely, but one noted for its domestication, for its dependence on a master.

The fact that Shearman may not have been as abusive and domineering as Ely claimed is beside the point. What is important is how Ely remembered, interpreted, his time at sea. For him it was a time when he felt debased, emasculated. The memory of this gnawed at Ely. It led his memoir to become a bitter exposé.

Sailor authors used their narratives to voice their profound disenchantment with seafaring life. Their works sought to unmask the romantic notions that many of their middle-class readers had about this life. Perhaps Dana put it best when he ruefully noted how the veil of illusions which the "witchery of the sea" spun quickly "falls off" and sailors soon see their new lives in its "true light," one of "work and hardship" (462–63). In bitter hindsight most sailor authors believed that their decision to set out to sea had ensnared them in a new kind of captivity, one perhaps more oppressive than the difficult lives they had sought to escape on land.

Yet if on one level seamen narratives were captivity narratives, on another they were stories about resistance to oppression. Chapter 4 will discuss in detail how sailor autobiographers and memoirists recounted their opposition against cruel, tyrannical officers, especially those who regularly flogged their men. But oppression came in many forms when a youth shipped out to sea during the late eighteenth and first half of the nineteenth centuries. As David Bunnell's life story illustrated, many American sailors were subjected to British impressment and incarceration as prisoners of war. As they recalled these experiences and resistance to the British, sailor authors articulated crucial issues. In particular their narratives explored how notions of manhood and nationalism intersected in antebellum America and helped lead the nation to war in 1812.

Manhood, Nationalism, and Sailor Narratives of British Captivity and the War of 1812

James M'Lean had an especially difficult time of it as a sailor in the late eighteenth and early nineteenth centuries. Born in Hartford County, Connecticut, he shipped off to sea when he was only ten years old in the mid-1790s. In December 1797 M'Lean was impressed by the British man-of-war *Madras* in Grenada.[1] He quickly learned that producing a seaman protection certificate carried no muster with the British. Captain John Dilkes dismissed M'Lean's document, claiming: "I could get one, if I was in America, for half a crown as good as that." When he insisted that he was an American citizen, M'Lean was called a "*Scotch rascal*" and threatened with the lash (168–69). Although he escaped almost a year later, M'Lean was soon impressed again. British naval records corroborate what his narrative detailed: a repeated pattern of impressments and escapes.[2] Often the

---

[1] M'Lean, *Seventeen Years' History*. Reprinted in Daniel E. Williams, ed, *Liberty's Captives: Narratives of Confinement in the Print Culture of the Early Republic* (Athens: University of Georgia Press, 2006), 164–79. Although M'Lean says he was impressed in March 1798 (168), the muster book of the HMS *Madras* lists him entering from Grenada on December 21, 1797 (TNA, PRO: ADM 36/13036).

[2] M'Lean, *Seventeen Years' History*, esp. 169–74. The muster books and other records of various British ships confirm M'Lean's claims that he was impressed on these ships during the approximate times he gave. For example, M'Lean's name, spelled McClane, appears on the list of impressed sailors on board the *Tonnant*. He is no. 201, entry on May 19, 1799 at Lisbon (TNA, PRO: ADM 36/12668). M'Lean/McLane's name is also listed in the *Windsor Castle*'s muster book. He is listed as no. 125, a "prest" man transferred from the *Cambridge* and appearing on August 16, 1799 (TNA, PRO: ADM 36/14075). The supernumerary list of the *Pique* confirms M'Lean's claim that he was impressed at the Falmouth Rendezvous on January 8,

British treated M'Lean harshly, seeming to single him out for punishment because he was an American. He recalled, for example, how once when he was hauling a buoy rope a lieutenant criticized his work and hit him. "[He] knocked out two of my teeth, and cut my face shockingly, and caused much effusion of blood, saying at the same time 'you are one of the Scoth Yankees;' to which I replied, no I am a true born American; with that, he said, 'no reply, you rascal! Go to your duty.'"(172). Finally in October 1813 M'Lean made it back home after an absence of over seventeen years.

M'Lean's narrative illustrated not only how American sailors suffered when impressed by the British but also how they stood up to their captors. Deeply held beliefs about manliness, honor, patriotism, and tyranny formed the cultural template upon which M'Lean and other sailor authors mapped out their life stories. In fact these men highlighted two intertwined themes in their life narratives: the patriotic defense of the nation's sovereignty and honor and the assertion of the manhood and rights of American sailors. Yet at times such works also implicitly rebuked American landsmen, including the nation's leaders. They suggested that the country failed to protect those men who risked their lives to promote the nation's overseas interests and defend its shores. Discussion of the narratives of sailor veterans of the American Revolution and the War of 1812 fleshes out these points.

M'Lean's text, which appeared in 1814, was at the cusp of a new subgenre of literature: the memoirs and autobiographies of sailors who had fought against the British. These works came in two overlapping stages. Starting in the late 1780s but especially during the first two decades of the nineteenth century, memoirs and autobiographies by Revolutionary War veterans became a staple of the American literary

1801 (TNA, PRO: ADM 36/15324). He said this occurred on January 18, 1801 (170). M'Lean says he was then transferred to the *Toudryant*. The ship's actual name was the *Foudroyant*. Its muster book shows M'Lean/Mc Lane was transferred from the *Pique* on March 1, 1801(TNA, PRO:ADM 36/14947). M'Lean remembered the date as March 6, 1801 (170). Captain John Clarke Searle's log of the *Foudroyant* shows that M'Lean suffered twenty-four lashes for disobedience of orders on February 5, 1802 (TNA, PRO: ADM 51/1395). M'Lean noted this incident in his narrative (171). On M'Lean's desertions see the following: the *Madras* pay book indicates he left the ship at Chatham on September 30, 1798 (TNA, PRO: ADM 35/1114). The *Raisonable*'s pay book confirms that M'Lean deserted on May 13, 1805 while the ship was in Plymouth (TNA, PRO: ADM 35/3052). See also M'Lean, 172–73.

War of 1812. To understand more fully the context in which such narratives appeared discussion of the events leading to the War of 1812 is in order.

The wars waged between Britain and France during the 1793 and 1815 period threatened both the lives and liberties of American sailors. Both nations violated the young republic's rights to trade as a neutral nation, harassing American ships and confiscating American cargo. Yet by the early 1800s it was the British who were the worst offender of American maritime rights. The Royal Navy's dominance of the high seas enabled Britain to enforce the Orders-in-Council, British restrictions on neutral trade with Continental Europe. Impressment was another flashpoint between the Americans and the British. Pressing American sailors into British service had long been a standard practice, one resented by Americans even before the Revolutionary War began. In fact one reason why American sailors had played such a prominent role in the anti-British riots protesting the Stamp Act of 1765 was because they resented the British press gangs which trawled American seaports.[8]

War with France in 1793 forced the British Royal Navy to resort increasingly to the practice of impressment to fill its voracious need for sailors. The historian Donald Hickey estimates that the British probably got fifty percent of their sailors during the Napoleonic Wars through this kind of coercion. Although the majority of impressed mariners were British citizens, a significant minority were Americans. Refusing to recognize the right of British men to become naturalized American citizens, the Royal Navy impressed such men found on board American vessels. British press gangs also impressed native-born American citizens from merchant ships. Historians estimate that almost ten thousand Americans were impressed by the British between 1796 and 1812, with approximately seven thousand forced into service between 1803 and 1812.[9]

---

[8] Paul A. Gilje, *Rioting in America* (Bloomington: Indiana University Press, 1996), 30–33; Gilje, *The Road to Mobocracy: Popular Disorder in New York City, 1763–1834* (Chapel Hill: University of North Carolina Press, 1987), 23–24, 32, 65, 178–79; Jesse Lemisch, *Jack Tar vs John Bull: The Role of New York's Seamen in Precipitating the Revolution* (New York: Garland Pub., Inc.,1997), and Lemisch, "Jack Tar in the Streets: Merchant Seamen in the Politics of Revolutionary America," *William and Mary Quarterly*, 3rd ser., 25 (1968): 371–407.

[9] Donald R. Hickey, *Don't Give Up the Ship: Myths of the War of 1812* (Urbana: University of Illinois Press, 2006), 19; James Fulton Zimmerman,

Impressment enraged Americans. Incidents such as the HMS *Leopard*'s attack of the United States frigate the *Chesapeake* off the coast of Virginia in June 1807 stoked American anger. Although the Royal Navy tried to justify its actions by arguing that the *Chesapeake*'s commander had refused to return four recent British deserters, Americans were furious by what they saw as an unprovoked attack on their country and sailors.

Britain's actions incited angry protests throughout the United States. Not surprisingly, protests were most heated in Norfolk after the shot-up *Chesapeake* limped into port. A mob of angry Americans destroyed supplies recently sold to the British. A town resolution urged citizens to wear mourning clothes for the "martyrs" of the *Chesapeake*. When one of the wounded men died, a crowd of over four thousand paraded his body through the streets of Norfolk and demanded revenge for British insults against American sovereignty.[10]

Although many issues, such as British violations of the United States' territorial waters and right to trade, led Congress to declare war against Great Britain in June 1812, that of impressment struck a particularly resonant chord with the American public.[11] Significantly when President James Madison delivered his war message to Congress on June 1, 1812, he listed Britain's impressment of American sailors as the first cause for war. This was not simply a rhetorical strategy to rally the nation to war but also reflected the deep anger many Americans, including the president and members of Congress, felt about the impressment of their sailors. By the 1820s most Americans believed that the War of 1812 occurred to defend "free trade and sailors' rights," a belief shared by many contemporary historians.[12]

Impressment of American Seamen (New York: Longmans, Green & Co., 1925), 259–75, esp. 267.

[10] Ian W. Toll, *Six Frigates: The Epic History of the Founding of the U.S. Navy* (New York: W.W. Norton &Company, 2006), 294–302; Spencer C. Tucker and Frank T. Reuter, *Injured Honor: The Chesapeake-Leopard Affair, June 22, 1807* (Annapolis, MD: Naval Institute Press, 1996), 1–17, 101–07.

[11] On the causes of the War of 1812, see: Donald R. Hickey, *War of 1812: A Forgotten Conflict* (Urbana: University of Illinois Press, 1989), esp. 44; Reginald Horsman, *The Causes of the War of 1812* (New York: A.S. Barnes & Company, 1962).

[12] For discussions of how the cry of "free trade and sailors' rights" promoted public support for the war, see Paul A. Gilje, "Free Trade and Sailors Rights: Commerce and Common Folk" (Keynote address, annual meeting of the Society for Historians of the Early American Republic, Springfield, IL, July 16–19, 2009), esp. 1; Gilje, *The Making of the American Republic, 1763–1815* (Upper Saddle River, NJ: Pearson

Ironically the war left unresolved the major issues over which it began, including that of impressment. The Treaty of Ghent, signed on December 24, 1814, basically returned to the status quo antebellum.[13] Although the United States won some major victories, it also suffered numerous defeats, especially when it attacked British Canada. The end of this conflict resulted not so much from American military successes but rather from the fact that the British viewed it as a distraction from finally defeating Napoleon's armies in Europe and establishing a new European order at the Congress of Vienna.[14]

Yet the War of 1812 was a milestone for the United States, not so much for what it accomplished militarily but, rather, for how Americans remembered it. Soon after the fighting ended, many Americans began to mythologize this war. They depicted it as a triumph for the United States, one that vindicated the nation's honor as well as protected its territorial sovereignty. This portrait of the War of 1812 helped allay Americans' anxieties that the nation was failing to live up to the high standards set by the Revolutionary generation, that it was becoming corrupt, divided, weak. Significantly the War of 1812 quickly became known as "The Second War of Independence."[15]

The ways in which antebellum Americans remembered the War of 1812 also helped to nurture an exuberant sense of nationalism. As Benedict Anderson has observed, nationalism ultimately depends on people imagining themselves as part of a wider community with shared traits and goals.[16] Various developments contributed to an

Prentice Hall, 2006), 276, 293; Gilje, *Liberty on the Waterfront: American Maritime Culture in the Age of Revolution* (Philadelphia: University of Pennsylvania Press, 2004), 169–75; Hickey, *Don't Give Up the Ship*, 39; Hickey, *War of 1812*, 26–27.

[13] The war itself formally ended on February 16, 1815, when President James Madison ratified the treaty after unanimous Senate approval. See Hickey, *Don't Give Up the Ship*, 344.

[14] Other historians have viewed the War of 1812 as a sideshow for the British. See, for example, Gilje, *Making of the American Republic*, 300–01; Horsman, *Causes of the War of 1812*, 263–67.

[15] Dan Hicks, "Broadsides on Land and Sea: A Cultural Reading of the Naval Engagements in the War of 1812," in *Pirates, Jack Tar, and Memory*, eds., Gilje and Pencak, 135–41; Hicks, "True Born Columbians: The Promises and Perils of National Identity for American Seafarers of the Early Republican Period" (PhD diss., The Pennsylvania State University, 2007), 145–206; Steven Watts, *Republic Reborn: War and the Making of Liberal America, 1790–1820* (Baltimore, MD: The Johns Hopkins University Press, 1987), 276–89.

[16] Benedict Anderson, *Imagined Communities: Reflections on the Origin and Spread of Nationalism*, rev. ed. (London: Verso, 2006). Numerous historians have

American sense of nationalism in the years after the War of 1812. Certainly one of these major developments was the creation of a public memory about the two wars Americans fought against the British. The "mystic chords of memory" that Abraham Lincoln hoped would preserve the Union were tragically not strong enough to avert Civil War in 1861. Nevertheless they did play a pivotal role in forging a sense of national identity during the late eighteenth and especially the first half of the nineteenth centuries.[17]

At the crux of antebellum Americans' public memory was their celebration and mythologizing of the American Revolution. Numerous scholars have documented different aspects of this process. These included: popular hagiographic biographies of revolutionary leaders,[18] the recognition of obscure, elderly men who fought in the Revolution as national heroes,[19] annual celebrations of the Fourth of July and other events commemorating the Revolution,[20] and the spread of a national print discourse and iconography glorifying the revolutionary principles of liberty, equality, and civic virtue.[21]

argued that the War of 1812 promoted a sense of exuberant, even strident, nationalism in the United States. For recent examples of this, see the works by Hicks; Gilje, *The Making of the American Republic*, 303–04; Daniel Walker Howe, *What Hath God Wrought: The Transformation of America, 1815–1848* (New York: Oxford University Press, 2007), 71; Sean Wilentz, *The Rise of American Democracy: Jefferson to Lincoln* (New York: W.W. Norton & Company, 2005), 175–78.

[17] Michael Kammen's scholarship is central to understanding the role of public memory in creating Americans' sense of national identity in the first half of the nineteenth century. See esp. *Mystic Chords of Memory: The Transformation of Tradition in American Culture* (New York: Vintage Books, 1993; first published in 1991 by Alfred A. Knopf, Inc.), 3–90; *A Season of Youth: The American Revolution and the Historical Imagination* (New York: Alfred A. Knopf, 1978). I have also profited from reading an excerpt of Paul Gilje's section on "nationalism" from his forthcoming encyclopedia of American concepts. Paul Gilje, e-mail message to author, January 23, 2008.

[18] Scott E. Caspar, *Constructing American Lives: Biography & Culture in Nineteenth-Century America* (Chapel Hill: University of North Carolina Press, 1999), 19–76.

[19] Young, *The Shoemaker and the Tea Party.*

[20] David Waldstreicher, *In the Midst of Perpetual Fetes: The Making of American Nationalism, 1776–1820* (Chapel Hill: University of North Carolina Press, 1997); Len Travers, *Celebrating the Fourth: Independence Day and the Rites of Nationalism in the Early Republic* (Amherst: University of Massachusetts Press, 1997).

[21] Ibid.; Gilje, "Nationalism." Kammen, *Season of Youth*, 186–220, argues that although antebellum Americans glorified the Revolution they often minimized its radical aspects. I discuss this latter issue in the next chapter.

Antebellum Americans remembered and mythologized the War of 1812 in ways that resonated with their interpretation of the Revolution. Depictions of the War of 1812 as a heroic second struggle for independence underscored this point. Americans' celebration of the War of 1812, much like their celebration of the Revolution, reaffirmed their sense of national identity, of belonging to that "imagined community" known as the United States.

Great Britain of course was the foil used to hone Americans' allegiance to their newly established republic. The nationalism of the postwar years went hand in hand with Anglophobia. Various British actions, particularly impressment of American sailors, the abuse of American prisoners of war, especially in notorious Dartmoor Prison, the burning of Washington, DC, and the atrocities committed against American civilians by British soldiers and their Indian allies, fomented a widespread hatred of Britain in the United States.[22]

The War of 1812 put American sailors at the center of the public discourse regarding British tyranny. These men came to symbolize the nation. When Britain abused these men, stripped them of their independence and rights, the United States was humiliated as well as they. American seamen who resisted British abuses, especially when they defeated in battle her far superior navy, vindicated their nation's honor as well as their own. They also gave proof of their bravery, toughness, and martial prowess, qualities long associated with manliness.

Much was demanded of American mariners in the early republic. Perhaps veterans of the naval war of 1812 best knew this. Sailors who published life narratives recognized how crucial it was to portray their resistance as well as their sufferings at the hands of the British. Their works often echoed those of American Revolutionary War sailors when they offered bitter, graphic recollections of captivity by the British, either as impressed sailors or incarcerated prisoners of war. Yet the narratives of sailor authors who fought in the "Second War of Independence" also differed from those who fought in the earlier war against the British. The former offered more pointed, detailed

---

[22] Hickey, *Don't Give Up the Ship*, 310–12; Hickey, *War of 1812*, 300–09; Ira Dye, "American Maritime Prisoners of War, 1812–1815," in *Ships, Seafaring and Society: Essays in Maritime History*, ed. Timothy J. Runyan (Detroit, MI: Wayne State University Press, 1987), 293–320.

depictions of how their authors helped defeat the vaunted Royal Navy in battle. Such accounts were perhaps the best way to reassure the nation that Jack Tar remained a "true born American," no matter how many hardships he endured.

Who were the sailor authors who experienced or witnessed the War of 1812? How did they remember/interpret their impressment and incarceration as prisoners of war? How did they portray the major naval battles in which they and their shipmates fought? How did their narratives contribute to the mythology of the War of 1812? How did these texts associate Jack Tar with manhood and nationalism? Exploration of these questions offers another angle of vision from which to study antebellum sailor memoirs and autobiographies.

Chapter 2 begins discussion of these questions by focusing on the memoirs of Joshua Penny and James Durand, published respectively in 1815 and 1817.[23] They were the earliest autobiographical narratives produced by sailors who experienced the War of 1812.[24] Penny and Durand fueled the Anglophobia then rampant in the United States, especially when they detailed their sufferings as impressed British seamen before and during the war. Yet neither man was content to recount their anguish. Penny and Durand also noted their defiance of the British and loyalty to the United States.

Their narratives are rousing tales of captivity, endurance, and resistance. Like all autobiographical works, however, they are complicated texts that at times distort or obscure crucial aspects of their authors' lives. It is therefore crucial to document the stories Penny and Durand told. Only then can the reader distinguish between what these men experienced during their seafaring years and how they later portrayed these experiences in their memoirs.

Separating fact from fiction, myth from reality, is always a daunting task. This is particularly the case in autobiographical writing when narrators/subjects reinterpret their past through the prism of memory and sometimes misrepresent their earlier lives. Analysis of

---

[23] This study relies on the revised and enlarged edition of Durand's book, published in 1820. See the appendix for further details on Durand's book.

[24] Besides Durand's book, Louis Kaplan, comp., *A Bibliography of American Autobiographies* (Madison: University of Wisconsin Press, 1962), 367, lists eleven seamen autobiographies and memoirs dealing with the naval war of 1812. But they were published after 1817.

the memoirs of Penny and Durand and of naval records that corroborate or refute their recollections illuminates how antebellum seamen authors did this.

Joshua Penny's narrative offered a scorching indictment of the British, particularly their navy. Penny claimed he was impressed in Jamaica in 1794 and spent most of the next eleven years either in the British Navy or as a deserter on the run (205).[25] For him a British naval vessel was "a Pandora's box – a nefarious floating dungeon, freighting calamities to every part of this lower world" (214).

What Penny found most objectionable about British captivity was not the arduous labor or harsh discipline but, rather, the lack of freedom. He repeatedly depicted impressment as a form of enslavement and portrayed British press gangs as "man-stealers" who "mocked" liberty by "enslav[ing]" free men (209, 205). Significantly Penny ended his memoir with an undated reprint of a poem entitled "The Kidnapped Seamen." It deplored the plight of impressed sailors who had been "seized by ruffians on the ocean," chained, whipped, and "forced to render [their] devotion to relentless tyrant's sway" (237).[26]

Of course such language evoked the plight of enslaved Africans. During the antebellum era growing numbers of Americans believed that slavery promoted a figurative if not literal emasculation. The condition of slavery denied enslaved males the very qualities associated with manliness in the late eighteenth and first half of the nineteenth centuries. A male who was a slave was degraded, dishonored, since he lacked any independence or freedom. A slave's subservience to his

[25] British naval records confirm that Penny did serve on a number of Royal Navy ships. The muster book of the *Alligator*, for example, shows a Jos[ua] Penn from Long Island entering service on July 5, 1794, from Port Royal, Jamaica and being discharged on February 13, 1795, to join the *Stately*. The muster book of the *Stately* confirms that Penn/Penny came on board from the *Alligator* on February 14, 1795 (TNA, PRO: ADM 36/11245 and 36/12112).Like many mariners who deserted ships and feared recapture, Penny used an alias, Jonas Inglesburg. See his *Life and Adventures*, esp. 211, 214, 218. The muster book of the *Sceptre* lists Jonas Ingleburg from Long Island as entering the ship on December 17, 1797 (TNA, PRO: ADM 36/13055) and the muster book of the *Sphynx* lists Ingleberg as no. 133 in the supernumeraries list, entering on September 29, 1798 (TNA, PRO: ADM 36/14941). The *Raisonable* lists Ingleberg as a twenty-seven-year-old American, entering as no. 1679 on January 10, 1799 (TNA, PRO: ADM 36/12245).

[26] Hicks, "True Born Columbians,"191–93, discusses this poem while exploring how sailor doggerel associated impressment with enslavement.

master made him powerless to protect either himself or his family. The image of the slave became the counterpoint to that of a manly man in antebellum America. In fact the counter position of "manly freedom" with "slavish dependence" was central in forging a "grammar of manhood" in the early republic.[27]

Fears of enslavement and emasculation haunted antebellum white men. Significantly such fears characterized disparate kinds of discourses and reform movements during the late colonial and early national periods. Revolutionary-era pamphlets repeatedly urged American men to defend their manhood by fighting the alleged British conspiracy to enslave them.[28] Temperance advocates railed against alcohol in much the same ways that abolitionists attacked the institution of slavery. Alcohol allegedly enslaved, unmanned, men who drank by denying them any control over their bodies.[29] Labor activists mobilized white working-class men against the prospect of "wage slavery";[30] while businessmen sought to preserve their manly independence by avoiding bankruptcy and "debt slavery."[31]

Penny drew on a wellspring of meaning when he depicted impressed sailors as slaves. He also capitalized on the public's revulsion against the capture and enslavement of American mariners by the Barbary States, especially Algiers and Tripoli. Between 1785 and 1815 over thirty-five ships and over seven hundred American sailors

[27] Mark E. Kann, *A Republic of Men: The American Founders, Gendered Language and Patriarchal Politics* (New York: New York University Press, 1998), 5–51; Orlando Patterson, *Slavery and Social Death: A Comparative Study* (Cambridge, MA: Harvard University Press, 1982), 77–101.

[28] Bertram Wyatt-Brown, *The Shaping of American Culture: Honor, Grace, and War, 1760s–1880s* (Chapel Hill: University of North Carolina Press, 2001), 31–35, especially explores this theme.

[29] Elaine Frantz Parsons, *Manhood Lost: Fallen Drunkards and Redeeming Women in the Nineteenth-Century United States* (Baltimore, MD: Johns Hopkins University Press, 2003); Bruce Dorsey, *Reforming Men and Women: Gender in the Antebellum City* (Ithaca, NY: Cornell University Press, 2002), 113–31, 136, 194.

[30] Gregory L. Kaster, "Labour's True Man: Organized Workingmen and the Language of Manliness in the U.S.A., 1827–1877," *Gender & History* 13 (April 2001): 24–64; David Roediger, *The Wages of Whiteness: Race and the Making of the American Working-Class*, rev. ed. (1991; repr. London: Verso, 1999), 13, 65–92.

[31] Scott A. Sandage, *Born Losers: A History of Failure in America* (Cambridge, MA: Harvard University Press, 2005), 194; see also Toby Ditz, "Shipwrecked; Or, Masculinity Imperiled: Mercantile Representations of Failure and the Gendered Self in Eighteenth-Century Philadelphia," *Journal of American History*, 81 (June 1994), 51–80.

were captured by these countries, especially by their corsairs.[32] This continued until an American naval force led by Stephen Decatur in 1815 defeated Algiers and compelled it and other Barbary States to end their depredations against American ships and the enslavement of her sailors.[33]

During the late eighteenth and first half of the nineteenth centuries the Barbary Captivity narrative became a popular genre of American literature. Plays, novels, broadsides, and newspaper accounts competed with memoirs purportedly written by the survivors of captivity. Some works hawked as memoirs were complete fabrications, while others were genuine. Yet irrespective of whether they were fictional or factual accounts, Barbary captivity narratives offered graphic, sometimes lurid, accounts of what their subjects suffered.[34]

These works had a profound impact on American culture. They fueled the growing public revulsion against all kinds of slavery, including that of African Americans in the antebellum South. Abraham Lincoln's antislavery sentiments, for example, were nurtured by his youthful reading of Connecticut sea captain James Riley's harrowing account of his 1815 enslavement by North African corsairs. Riley's book *Sufferings in Africa*, first published in 1817, went through numerous editions and sold over a million copies.[35] But the most

---

[32] Robert J. Allison, *The Crescent Obscured: The United States and the Muslim World, 1776–1815* (New York: Oxford University Press, 1995), 110.

[33] Frederick C. Leiner, *The End of Barbary Terror: America's 1815 War Against the Pirates of North Africa* (New York: Oxford University Press, 2006); Frank Lambert, *The Barbary Wars: American Independence in the Atlantic World* (New York: Hill & Wang, 2005); Robert J. Allison, *Stephen Decatur: American Naval Hero, 1779–1820* (Amherst: University of Massachusetts Press, 2005), 163–68.

[34] Lawrence A. Peskin, *Captives and Countrymen: Barbary Slavery and the American Public, 1785–1816* (Baltimore, MD: Johns Hopkins University Press, 2009), 7–49, 163–86; Hester Blum, *The View from the Masthead: Maritime Imagination and Antebellum American Sea Narratives* (Chapel Hill: University of North Carolina Press, 2008), 46–70; Blum, "Pirated Tars, Piratical Texts: Barbary Captivity and American Sea Narratives," *Early American Studies* 1, no. 2 (Fall 2003): 133–55; Robert J. Allison, "Sailing to Algiers: American Sailors Encounter the Muslim World," *The American Neptune* 57, no.1 (1997): 5–17. For excerpts from Barbary captivity narratives, see Daniel E. Williams, ed., *Liberty's Captives: Narratives of Confinement in the Print Culture of the Early Republic* (Athens: University of Georgia Press, 2006), 105–30, 270–83; Paul Baepler, ed., *White Slaves, African Masters* (Chicago: University of Chicago Press, 1999).

[35] Gordon H. Evans, ed., *Sufferings in Africa: Captain Riley's Narrative ...* (1817; repr., New York: The Lyons Press, 2000), esp. vi–vii; Allison, *Crescent Obscured*, 207–25.

immediate impact of Barbary Captivity narratives was to mobilize public outrage against what many Americans regarded as piracy and to spur the creation of the United States Navy to fight the Barbary Coast nations.[36]

Not surprisingly, antebellum sailor narratives regularly invoked the specter of captivity and enslavement at the hands of "barbarous" North African corsairs as well as other Muslim captors. Durand, for example, recalled seeing captured Christians serving as galley slaves on board Turkish men-of-war. Chained to their oars, they were severely beaten for the slightest infraction. As for the Algerines, Durand stated that they were "wholly destitute of humanity" and sold any captured Christian to the highest bidder at the slave markets (28–29). Samuel Holbrook's anger was palpable as he described the cruelties Algerines had inflicted over the years on captured American sailors. He was delighted when French forces defeated Algiers, that "abominable place," in 1830 (177–81).[37]

Narratives by or about Americans captured by corsairs offer another vantage point from which to view American sailors' denunciation of British impressment. The association of impressment with enslavement resonated with Americans outraged over Jack Tar's captivity by corsairs. What made recollections of impressment particularly powerful was that this time it was not an alien, non-Christian society that allegedly enslaved America's fighting men but, rather, Great Britain, the nation regarded as the most advanced Christian and European society in the world.

The trope of enslavement was a powerful and pervasive one in the early republic. Antebellum seamen authors recognized that it was also a double-edged sword. Describing impressed sailors as "enslaved" not only dramatized their sufferings but also risked portraying them as subjugated and therefore emasculated. Sailor authors went out of their way to convince fellow Americans that the latter was not true. Impressed sailors, they repeatedly asserted, were still manly, brave mariners who resisted British oppression.

[36] Peskin, *Captives and Countrymen*, 111–33; Lambert, *Barbary Wars*; Leiner, *End of Barbary Terror*; Allison, *Crescent Obscured*, 127–51.

[37] Albert Hourani, *A History of the Arab Peoples* (Cambridge, MA: The Belknap Press of Harvard University Press, 1991), 263, 269–70, notes that the French conquest of Algiers began in 1830 but culminated in 1847 with the defeat and exile of the resistance leader Abd al-Qadir.

The memoirs of Penny and Durand offered vivid accounts of sea-men doing this, even when impressed in the British Navy. According to Penny, he defied British authority whenever possible. Shortly after he and the other forty Americans captured in Jamaica by the HMS *Alligator* arrived in England, recalled Penny, he refused "to sign up for his majesty's bounty." Penny claimed that he was singled out and pressured to join since he had received medical care and extra food when he became deliriously ill with fever. But he adamantly refused "his majesty's bounty," saying that not even "a chest full of guineas and a lieutenant's commission" could tempt him to sign up. Denounced as a "d_____d yankee rebellious rascal," Penny preferred ill treatment rather than volunteer for British service (206–07).

Penny's memoir also detailed the severe punishments he alleg-edly endured in the Royal Navy to protect his fellow Americans. He emphasized, for example, that he suffered twelve lashes on board the HMS *Sphynx* because he refused to divulge information about several "Yankees" who had recently deserted. The pain was so excruciating, Penny recalled, that "my senses left me" after only "three strokes of the *cat.*" Yet Penny said he preferred to receive his full dozen lashes rather than volunteer information about his shipmates' whereabouts (215–16).

Penny stressed that he also resisted the British by deserting. He recalled, for example, feigning illness while on board the HMS *Sceptre* and running away when hospitalized near Cape Town, South Africa. After his desertion he allegedly lived for fourteen months as a hermit in the wilderness of Table Mountain before managing to work his way back home to Long Island in 1805 (217–26). Penny stressed that he preferred to live with the "ferocious animals" on Table Mountain rather than with the "more savage English" (221). In fact he resolved to die in this wilderness rather than return to British service. It was better "to become a breakfast for a lion, sooner than be taken to another floating dungeon," or British ship (218).

The Life and Adventures of James Durand provided a similar por-trait of resistance to the British. Durand admitted that when he began his allegedly seven years of impressment, he was in anguish (47).[38]

---

[38] British naval records show that a James During, an American from New Haven (Durand's birthplace), served on the British men-of-war cited by Durand. Occasionally there are slight discrepancies in dates of service. Durand, for example,

"Despair so completely seized my mind," recalled Durand, that he contemplated suicide and "almost" lost "his reason" (49). Yet not his will to resist the British. Durand noted that he refused to fight against his fellow Americans even though it led to severe punishment and almost execution. At one point, stressed Durand, he and several other impressed American sailors who would not fight against their nation had halters placed on their necks and were given one last opportunity to fight before being hanged. When they still refused to fight, they were put in irons and fed "maggoty bread and water" until they finally complied (49 and 76).

The "grammar of manhood" in antebellum America required both Durand and Penny to highlight their resistance to British authority. Yet naval records suggest that each man exaggerated their actual defiance of British officers. Impressment on a British man-of-war, especially during wartime, left men little choice but to obey a command or face draconian punishment, including death.

Significantly British naval records do not indicate that Durand was punished for refusing to do his duty. They also list him as a volunteer rather than an impressed sailor. The muster book of the HMS *Narcissus*, for example, showed him coming on board as a volunteer on August 21, 1808.[39] The British may well have pressured Durand into joining their navy. Impressed sailors faced a stark choice: either enter as a volunteer and get a bounty or remain impressed and therefore receive no compensation for their services.[40]

When faced with such a decision Penny also volunteered for duty, just as Durand did. This was the case after he arrived at the major naval port in Spithead. The muster book of the HMS *Stately* shows him signing up as a volunteer and entitled to a bounty of five pounds.

---

stated that he was impressed on board the HMS *Narcissus* on August 21, 1809 (49). The muster book of the *Narcissus* shows During/Durand entering service on August 21, 1808 (TNA, PRO: ADM 37/2438). Durand stated that he was sent from the *Narcissus* to the *St. Salvadore* on March 7, 1812 (63–64). The muster book of the *Narcissus* confirms this, although it calls the ship the *Salvadore*. According to Durand, he boarded the *Pactolus* on January 11, 1814 (73). The muster book of this ship shows him under the name of During as joining the ship on January 18, 1814 (TNA, PRO: ADM 37/5392).

39 Ibid.
40 Michael Lewis, *A Social History of the Navy, 1793–1815* (London: George Allen & Unwin LTD, 1960), 137.

It is impossible to know what motivated Penny to do this. But it is quite plausible that he decided to make the best of a bad situation when he was in Britain. Like many other American sailors, Penny may have volunteered for duty in hopes of getting better treatment and pay. One thing is certain: Penny ran on September 10, 1795, even though he lost his bounty and any wages due him after almost seven months of service.[41]

Penny's memoir also offered a skewed interpretation of his flogging on board the *Sphynx*. The captain's log of this ship confirms that Penny was flogged for disobedience of orders on November 14, 1798. This punishment, however, occurred over a week *before* the American shipmates Penny claimed he was protecting deserted.[42] In other words, Penny did not suffer the lash because he was protecting Americans who had escaped their British captors.

What is one to make of the discrepancies between Penny's and Durand's accounts of their seafaring years and those offered in the logbooks of the ships on which they sailed? The inaccuracies in these men's stories make it tempting to dismiss their narratives as mostly fabricated yarns, tall tales concocted by ex-mariners seeking money and sympathy. But that would ignore the fact that the main parts of their accounts are grounded in historically verifiable evidence.

One can never know with certainty if Penny and Durand misremembered their past or misrepresented it. The way in which these men told their stories, however, underscores a crucial point about all memoirs and autobiographies: these texts are often constructed by their authors to forge a public persona for themselves, one that enhances their credibility and reputation. Joshua Penny and James Durand were neither the first nor the last memoirists to do this. Like other antebellum seamen authors, they recalled their years in the Royal Navy in ways that highlighted their loyalty to their fellow American mariners and their resistance to the British. This did not make the memoirs of Penny and Durand a fabrication. But it did illustrate how particularly

---

[41] See TNA, PRO: ADM 36/12112. Penny claimed he was impressed into the *Stately*'s service after being on the *Alligator* (206–07).

[42] The log of Captain Thomas Alexander of the *Sphynx* records that Jonas Ingleberg (Joshua Penny) received twelve lashes on November 14, 1798, but that James Hall and George Roberts did not desert until November 22, 1798 (TNA, PRO: ADM 51/1236).

subjective a life story is when told by an author who is both the subject and narrator.

Even if Penny and Durand stretched the truth, their books articulated grievances endured by many American sailors during the late eighteenth and early nineteenth centuries, especially that of impressment. The memoirs of these men, published so soon after the War of 1812 ended, helped to forge a larger narrative, one expanded on by later seamen authors. Penny and Durand portrayed themselves and their fellow tars as proud, brave men who defended their own independence as well as that of their fledgling nation against British imperial might.

This was especially evident when Penny stressed how he jumped at the opportunity to attack the British when he returned to Long Island. His memoir proudly recounted his participation in a plot to torpedo the *Ramillies*, the flagship of the British Commodore Thomas Hardy, anchored near Long Island during the War of 1812. This plot reflected Americans' growing desperation to end the British blockade of New York and other major seaports, especially as the nation suffered increasing economic losses and civilians in the Chesapeake area endured attacks from Rear Admiral George Cockburn's forces. In March 1813 Congress authorized the use of "torpedoes, submarine instruments, or any other destructive machines ... to sink or destroy British vessels." Any American who succeeded in this task would receive a generous federal bounty.[43]

No doubt the prospect of such a bounty must have appealed to Penny whose modest livelihood as a sailor making runs along the coast and sometimes to the West Indies was now endangered by the British blockade. Yet in his memoir Penny stressed that what motivated him to join the torpedo plot was the desire for revenge rather than money. He snapped up "the first opportunity of doing mischief to those who had so long tortured me" (226).

Unfortunately the plot was discovered and on August 20, 1813, British troops surrounded Penny's home and took him prisoner, an event he described with gusto in his memoir. Seized while he and his wife and three young children slept in bed, Penny was almost murdered by a lieutenant from the *Ramillies*: "He presented a pistol to my

[43] Toll, *Six Frigates*, 421–22.

nose, and attempted to shoot me. I never saw more fire issue from a lock in my life – it flew into my eyes – it rolled on the floor; but as luck would have it, missed fire!" (228–29).

Penny was unrepentant about his actions, even though he recalled being imprisoned for over nine months (236). His only regret was that he failed to blow up the *Ramillies*, thereby "terrifying John Bull and avenging" himself as well as his nation (236). Increasingly shrill in his rhetoric, Penny fulminated against the "hypocritical whining" of the British. Why, he wondered, did the British denounce the "NOVEL mode of using torpedoes," when they used much worse forms of warfare. "Infernal monsters" like Cockburn attacked American women and children "indiscriminately"; the British were "invading Goths and Vandals" who should be driven from American "sacred soil" by any means possible (234).

Despite his hyperbolic denunciation of the British, Penny offered an accurate account of his role in the torpedo plot. Naval records confirm that he was incarcerated in Melville Prison near Halifax for nine months as punishment for his role in the attempted attack against the *Ramillies*.[44] Penny's kidnapping from his home and subsequent imprisonment became a minor cause célèbre in the New York area. Several newspapers described his seizure and urged retaliation. Major Benjamin Case, the commander of United States troops at Sag Harbor, demanded Penny's release and even President James Madison in a September 6, 1813, letter to Secretary of the Navy William Jones declared that "putting him [Penny] in Irons...should be instantly retaliated...." But the British held firm. As Hardy noted in an August 23, 1813, response to Case, Penny was justifiably detained as a prisoner of war since he participated in a planned act of war.[45]

---

[44] Both British and American naval records confirm Penny's story. See "Halifax Registers of American Prisoners of War" (TNA, PRO: ADM 103/167). See also "Pension Application Files. War of 1812. Death or Disability," File No. 4687, RG 15, NA, Washington, DC. The muster book of the *Ramillies* (TNA, PRO: ADM 37/4110) lists Penny being taken prisoner on August 23, 1813.

[45] Penny, *Life and Adventures*, 231–34, reprinted letters from Major Benjamin Case and Captain Thomas Hardy as well as an undated editorial in the *Long Island Star*. The correspondence between Case and Hardy is also found in William S. Dudley, ed., *The Naval War of 1812: A Documentary History* (Washington, DC.: Naval Historical Center, 1985), 2: 245–47. See also the "Case of Joshua Penny," *Long Island Star*, September 8, 1813, 1.

Penny never got the satisfaction of defeating the Royal Navy in battle. But sailor authors who were combat veterans of the War of 1812 did. Their recollections of victories at sea echoed the poem Penny cited, "The Kidnapped Seaman," when it urged sailors, the "sons of freedom," to "arm for battle" and "avenge" the sufferings of their impressed maritime brethren (237).

Seamen memoirists and autobiographers who published their narratives during the 1830s and 1840s fleshed out the interpretive framework that Durand and especially Penny erected when they discussed how American seamen resisted John Bull. Many noted their impressment into the British Navy. Yet these writers spent less time detailing what they suffered as impressed men than did Penny and Durand. Instead they emphasized how after their desertion from British ships they joined the United States Navy and bested the Royal Navy in sea battles.

Such recollections served several crucial purposes. First, they helped to validate the manliness of Jack Tar by offering vivid accounts of seamen's bravery and determination in confronting a formidable enemy. Of course stories about defeating the Royal Navy both reflected and contributed to the exuberant nationalism that characterized the United States during the antebellum era.

The autobiographies of David Bunnell and Horace Lane richly illustrated these themes. Each offered riveting accounts of combat. Bunnell graphically described his participation in the Battle of Lake Erie in September 1813, a critical battle that enabled the United States to gain control over the Northwest. Bunnell noted the "awful silence" right before battle, the horror of seeing human bodies blown apart, and the deck of his ship, the *Lawrence*, turning into "one continued gore of blood and carnage." At one point, he recollected, a man's "brains flew so thick in my face, that I was for some time blinded ..." Bunnell himself was wounded, losing much of his hearing for over a year. Yet he did not regret his participation in battle. In fact Bunnell reveled in the American victory, declaring: "What a glorious day to my country [*sic*] ..." He happily added that the English commodore's ship looked like "a slaughter house."[46]

---

[46] Bunnell, *Travels and Adventures*, 113–118. Bunnell's description of the Battle of Lake Erie is consistent with historians' account of this battle: David Curtis Skaggs and Gerard T. Altoff, *A Signal Victory: The Lake Erie Campaign, 1812–1813*

Horace Lane was also boastful as he recalled fighting the British while serving on board the *General Armstrong*. In the summer of 1814 this American privateer inflicted heavy casualties on three British men-of-war in the Port of Fayal in the Azores. This battle helped delay the British ships' arrival to New Orleans and facilitated Andrew Jackson's legendary victory there.[47] In his autobiography as well as in an 1840s broadside and 1855 pension application Lane stressed the heavy casualties that the *General Armstrong* inflicted on the British, men who had tried to make him a "slave" in their navy.[48]

Lane's comments reflected the fact that he had been impressed several times by British men-of-war between 1801 and 1811.[49] As noted earlier, Bunnell had also suffered impressment and incarceration as an American prisoner of war in Dartmoor Prisoner between December 1814 and July 1815.[50] Neither man, however, wanted their fellow Americans to view them primarily as victims of British oppression, as captives or slaves. When they related their successes in combat, when they crowed over British casualties, Bunnell and Lane

(Annapolis, MD: Naval Institute Press, 1997), 118–48 and Hickey, *Don't Give Up the Ship*, 124–31. Bunnell received an invalid's pension for his naval service: "War of 1812 Navy Invalid Application File of David C. Bunnell," No. 216, RG 15, NA, Washington, DC. See also Records of the Veteran Administration, "Pension Claims...Relating to Navy and Privateer Service and the Navy and Privateer Pension Funds, 1800–1900," box no. 1, entry 34, RG 15, NA, Washington, DC.

[47] Jack Sweetman, *American Naval History: An Illustrated Chronology of the U.S. Navy and Marine Corps, 1775–Present* (Annapolis, MD: Naval Institute Press, 1984), 36; Robert J. Hanks, "Sea Fight at Fayal," *Proceedings of the United States Naval Institute* 93, no. 11 (1967), 157–60.

[48] Lane, *Wandering Boy*, 118–19; "Yankee Boy that Went to Sea from 99 to 43" (John Hay Library, Brown University, Providence, RI); "Petition of Horace Lane on Account of his Naval Service to the U.S.," January 17, 1855, RG 233, Records of the House of Representatives, 33rd Congress, Committee on Invalid Pensions: Petitions and Memorials (HR 33 A-G 9.1), NA, Washington, DC.

[49] For discussion of his impressments, see Lane, *Wandering Boy*, 36, 78–86, 111–12. Government records corroborate that Lane suffered impressment. "A return or list of American seamen and citizens who have been impressed" in American State Papers, Foreign Relations, *Documents, Legislative and Executive of the Congress of the United States...* (Washington, DC: Gales & Seaton, 1832), 3: 66, for example, notes Lane's impressment on board the *Cormorant*.

[50] Bunnell, *Travels and Adventures*, 56. Bunnell states that he was impressed on board the British ship *Grenada* (46). The muster books of the HMS *Grenada* show a David Bunhill being impressed on board this ship on November 28, 1808 (TNA, PRO: ADM 37/339). Bunnell discusses his incarceration in Dartmoor Prison in ibid, 137–40. Bunnell's name appears on the General Entry Books, Prisoners of War, Americans, Dartmouth, 1814–1815, TNA, PRO: ADM 103/90.

highlighted a crucial point: they and other American sailors, despite suffering impressments and other hardships, remained proud, brave, determined warriors, capable of defeating the world's leading navy.

Seamen authors, especially combat veterans, ultimately integrated their stories of fighting the British into a powerful national narrative about defending their own and their country's liberty and honor. As they twinned together these themes, sailor memoirists and autobiographers forged an image of Jack Tar as the embodiment as well as defender of the nation.

This was particularly apparent in the 1846 memoir of Moses Smith, entitled *Naval Scenes in the Last War*. A longtime resident of Quincy, Massachusetts, Smith served four years in the United States Navy, three of them on board the *John Adams* and the *Constitution*.[51] In his text Smith displayed great pride in his naval service as well as hatred of the British. He offered a litany of British cruelties, including impressments of Americans. Smith recalled, for example, how an impressed American escaped his British captors by coming on board the *Adams* when it was docked at Annapolis shortly before the war began. In an effort to resist recapture, the sailor stood on deck and in full view of the crew cut off the fingers of his right hand with an axe, screaming: "Now let the English take me, if they want me." Smith praised this man's heroism. He also bitterly noted that the British dragooned the crippled sailor back into their service, an act which American officers were then powerless to stop (7).

Ignoring the fact that many foreigners served on United States vessels, Smith claimed that they were mostly manned with American-born sailors. These men were "hardy tars" with "stout heart[s]," "truly American hearts," and therefore "could not brook anything which looked like insult or reproach to our nation's honor." They were glad when war was declared. It finally gave them an opportunity to gain "honor in heroic fight."[52]

[51] Moses Smith's widow Cecilia Smith successfully petitioned for a pension based on her husband's naval service. The claim was approved January 13, 1879. See the "Service Pension Application, War of 1812," Widow's Claim No. 23.280, Pension Files, RG 15, NA, Washington DC.

[52] Smith, *Naval Scenes in the Late War*, 7, 11, 17, 23–26. Christopher McKee, "Foreign Seamen in the United States Navy: A Census of 1808" *William and Mary Quarterly* 42, no. 3 (1985): 383–93, documents that almost half of the enlisted men on the New York station in 1808 were foreign nationals, the majority of them from the British Isles.

Of course nowhere was honor and heroism more evident than when Smith described his service on board the *Constitution*, rated forty-four guns, and probably the most famous of the six frigates built in the late 1790s that established the United States Navy. Ironically the heroism of the *Constitution*'s crew was particularly evident when their ship made a daring escape from the enemy. This incident occurred in mid-July 1812 when the *Constitution* was near the New Jersey coast and stumbled upon a British squadron of five men-of-war. Facing overwhelming odds, Captain Isaac Hull knew that the key to his ship's survival was to outrun his pursuers and live to fight another day. In a three-day chase that quickly became legendary, the *Constitution* evaded its pursuers and fled to the relative safety of the high seas.[53]

Smith's account of the crew's actions during this chase enhanced the *Constitution*'s reputation for boldness and bravery. He stressed the determination of both the captain and his crew. Hull, he said, "coolly surveyed the scene" and ordered the hoisting of the American flag when he saw the British men-of-war closing in. Hull also went on the attack:

He clapped the fire to my gun, NO.1, and such a barking as sounded over the sea! It was worth hearing. No sooner had our iron dog opened his mouth in this manner, than the whole enemy opened the whole of theirs. Every one of the ships fired directly towards us. Those nearest kept up their firing for some time; but of course not a shot reached us then, at the distance we were. (26)

Smith also noted the resolve of the crew to fight to the death, to "go down like men," rather than be captured. Convinced that "the well-known and honored frigate *Constitution* was to be the theatre for a naval action that should cover the Republic either with living disgrace or glory," her crew determined to die bravely rather than live and suffer the humiliation of capture and imprisonment. "A more resolute set of men never smelt salt water," proudly asserted Smith (26–27).

On August 19, 1812, the *Constitution*, fitted with fifty six guns, achieved a noted military victory when it captured the British frigate,

53 Tyrone G. Martin, *A Most Fortunate Ship: A Narrative History of Old Ironsides*, rev. ed. (1997; repr., Annapolis, MD: Naval Institute Press, 2003), 143–51; Linda M. Maloney, *The Captain from Connecticut: The Life and Naval Times of Isaac Hull* (Boston: Northeastern University Press, 1986), 171–77.

the *Guerriere*, rated thirty eight guns, mounted forty nine.[54] Even years after the event Smith's pride at this victory was palpable: "Amid the dying and the dead, the crash of timbers, the flying of splinters and falling of spars, the American heart poured out its patriotism with long and loud cheers. The effect was always electrical, throughout all the struggle for our rights" (32).

"The struggle for our rights" – this phrase recurred in Smith's memoir as it did in so many other narratives by antebellum sailors. Early on in his text Smith stressed that American sailors were free proud men who went to battle against the best navy in the world to defend their rights as well as the nation's. For Smith the two set of rights were inseparable. American sailors, he declared, "felt a real interest in their country's welfare" and fought not from "compulsion or gain" but because they loved the United States. Yet these men, stressed Smith, also fought to vindicate the rights of American sailors: "When they struck, therefore, they struck as freemen fighting for their rights, and every blow told hard upon the quailing enemy" (24).

The reality was more complicated than Smith's words suggested. American sailors fought not only for love of country but also because their survival was at stake. Defeat meant capture as prisoners of war. Mercenary motives, particularly the opportunity to earn prize money by seizing enemy vessels, also came into play when American mariners fought the British.[55] But seamen authors generally elided the complexity of sailors' motives as they constructed narratives that stressed the patriotism and valor of Jack Tar.

Crafting such narratives was especially important for sailor authors who were naturalized Americans. They used their works to legitimize a new American identity and to gain the sympathy as well as money of their adopted countrymen. To achieve these goals, they often glossed over whatever allegiances they still had to their birth country as well as the difficulties encountered in becoming an American.

It is peculiarly fitting that *Ned Myers; Or, A Life Before the Mast*, edited by James Fenimore Cooper, one of the pioneers in forging a distinctly American literary canon, should highlight this point. Myers

[54] Maloney, *The Captain from Connecticut*, 185–91(191 lists the number of guns for each ship); Toll, *Six Frigates*, 346–54; Martin, *A Most Fortunate Ship*, 155–62.

[55] Gilje, *The Making of the American Republic*, 292, discusses sailors' motives.

sought to compensate for his Quebec birthplace by stressing his allegiance to the United States. Repeatedly Myers hammered away at this point: "I was born...in the English territory, it is true; but America was, and ever has been, the country of my choice" (113); "I do not believe America had a truer heart, in her service, than mine" (115). Myers also made it a point of noting his emphatic refusal to join the Royal Navy, even though the British repeatedly pressured him to do this when he was an American prisoner of war in Halifax, Nova Scotia: "I did not like England, and I did like America. My birth in Quebec was a thing I could not help; but having chosen to serve under the American flag, and having done so for years, I did not choose to go over to the enemy" (117).

Like other seamen authors Myers may have padded his part when he recalled his sufferings at the hands of the British and refusal to serve in their navy. According to the Halifax Prisoner of War Register Myers was a prisoner of war for a little under two months and not the almost two years he claimed in his narrative.[56] At times Myers undercut his own claims of resolutely refusing to cooperate with the British. He conceded, for example, that he and other prisoners agreed to work on several transport vessels that supplied British men-of-war. They did this to get badly needed food and clothing. Aware that his voluntary labor on board any British vessel might undermine his professions of loyalty to the United States, Myers asserted that he and the other prisoners plotted to mutiny and take control of the ships on which they worked but each time were discovered and punished (105–06, 110–11).

Eager to prove his allegiance to his adopted country, Myers detailed how he fought and suffered for the United States during the War of 1812. Pension records confirm the major parts of his story. Enlisting in the United States Navy in 1812, Myers was one of only sixteen out of one hundred sailors to survive the destruction of the ten-gun schooner the *Scourge* when it capsized during a storm on Lake

---

[56] William Dudley outlines Myers's life story in his edition of Cooper, ed., *Ned Myers*, vii–xix. See *Ned Myers*, 120 and 136, for discussion of his length of imprisonment. The Halifax Prisoner of War Register lists Edward Myers, No. 6201 (TNA, Pro: ADM 103/168) and shows him being received from the HMS *Saturn* on May 25, 1814, and discharged on July 11, 1814 (Myers claimed he was freed in March 1815).

Ontario on August 8, 1813. Although hurt in this tragedy, Myers was soon back in the war. He was wounded in action while on board the schooner *Julia* on August 10, 1814, as it fought the British on Lake Ontario.[57] But despite almost dying from multiple wounds, Myers assured his readers in his 1843 narrative that he never regretted his service in the United States Navy. "God bless the flag," he resolutely declared (213).

Two other naturalized Americans, Nicholas Peter Isaacs and Samuel Leech, also used their narratives to highlight their allegiance to their adopted country. Isaacs railed against the British policy of impressment just as American-born sailors did. A British press gang, he fumed, was "that most hateful of all gangs" and its use by the Royal Navy was a "disgrace" (77, 90). Isaacs had good reason to be angry. He suffered several British impressments. The muster roll book of the HMS *Cherub* listed him as a "prest" seaman from Norway who came on board October 28, 1808, and deserted on November 6.[58] The British again impressed him when they captured the American privateer on which he sailed, the *Rolla*, in January 1813.[59]

In his autobiography Isaacs took pains to assure his American readers that he remained loyal to the United States when he was a "prest" man. He adamantly refused, he stressed, to serve in the Royal Navy, even though the British threatened him with "severe punishments" and then used "kindness and flattery" and the promise of "speedy promotion" as incentives (81). Repeatedly he demanded to be accorded prisoner-of-war status. When an impressed Dane tried to convince Isaacs to "fight for England," he recalled sternly rebuking the man: "if he was disposed to join with the enemies of his country, I was not, and ... the mere fact of my being impressed, could not, and should not change my sense of duty to my country" (82). Isaacs also described how he foiled his British captors by deserting from the *Cherub*. He escaped by swimming in shark infested waters when this

---

[57] *Ned Myers*, 77–100; "Pension Application Files. War of 1812. Death or Disability," File No. 1109 – Edward Myers..." (1814), RG 24, NA, Washington, DC.

[58] Muster book, HMS *Cherub*, TNA, PRO: ADM 37/1555.

[59] Isaacs was one of the prisoners listed in the January/February 1813 muster book of the HMS *Maidstone*, TNA, PRO: ADM 37/4347. Later he was discharged to the HMS *Belvidera* (for muster book see ibid., 37/3528).

ship was anchored near St. Thomas. Apparently his hatred of British impressment outweighed his fear of shark attacks (82–86).

Isaacs's impressment on board the *Belvidera* did not end so dramatically. He and other captured Americans were paroled and allowed to return to the United States with the proviso that they would not participate in attacks against the British.[60] Isaacs stressed that he violated the terms of his parole when he volunteered for duty on board the American sloop the *Hero*. It went hunting for the aptly named vessel the *Fox*, a former American sloop captured and refitted by the British, which now preyed on American vessels near Mystic, Connecticut, where Isaacs lived. His autobiography offered a gripping description of how he and his mates on board the *Hero* prepared for battle against the *Fox*. They "beat to their quarters to the tune of 'Yankee Doodle'." They then fought hard against the *Fox*, captured her and brought her back "in triumph" to Mystic (148–50).

Isaacs repeatedly stressed his identification with the United States and his sense of himself as an American. When the English rejected his claim that he was an American, he pointedly countered: "I feel myself to be one" (132). He "excused" himself from the conditions of his parole, he declared, because the depredations of the *Fox* in the Mystic area "concerned my home, and my immediate friends" (147). Isaacs's choice of words was telling. Mystic was now his home and the United States was his country and he made clear he was prepared to fight and die for both.

Since he was born an Englishman, Samuel Leech had to go to particular lengths to show his patriotic devotion to America. In fact Leech began his seafaring career as a British sailor and fought the Americans in one of the most noted naval battles of the War of 1812. On October 25, 1812, the fifty-six-gun ship, the *United States*, commanded by Stephen Decatur, and the forty-nine-gun British man-of-war, the *Macedonian*, commanded by John Carden, squared off in the North Atlantic.[61] Leech vividly described the battle which left the

[60] Isaacs, *Twenty Years Before the Mast*, 138–39; muster book of the HMS *Belvidera*, ibid.

[61] For recent accounts of this battle, see Allison, *Stephen Decatur*, 115–20; Toll, *Six Frigates*, 360–70. Although the *United States* was rated a forty-four-gun frigate, it carried an additional twelve guns for this battle. Similarly the *Macedonian* was rated a thirty-eight-gun frigate but it carried an additional eleven guns. See Hickey, *Don't Give Up the Ship*, 100 and 332. Howard I. Chapelle, *The History of the*

Macedonian in tatters, with much of its crew dead or wounded. As a powder boy supplying the men of the fifth gun on the main deck with gunpowder, Leech witnessed at close quarters the carnage on board the *Macedonian*. He described the agony of wounded shipmates, men groaning without arms and legs, and gore swamping the decks.[62]

By 1843 Leech's recollections of these gruesome events were filtered through the prism of his new American life. Significantly Leech credited the American victory not only to the *United States*' superior military power but also because its sailors fought voluntarily for their nation and in defense of the cherished principles of "free trade and sailors' rights." By contrast, stressed Leech, "many" of the British seamen on board the *Macedonian* were "in the service against their will." They "sympathized with the great principle[s] for which the American nation so nobly contended" and also with the impressed Americans on board the *Macedonian* (97).

Leech portrayed the *United States* as a magnanimous victor as well as worthy adversary. American sailors, he recalled, quickly won over the survivors of the *Macedonian* by readily sharing their supplies. Glossing over the carnage that he himself so graphically described, Leech quickly shifted gears in his narrative to stress the conviviality and solidarity that allegedly united the recent enemies. He also stressed that he quickly identified with his American captors:

I soon felt myself perfectly at home with the American seamen; so much so, that I chose to mess with them. My shipmates also participated in similar feelings in both ships. All idea that we had been trying to shoot each other's brains so shortly before, seemed forgotten. We eat [sic] together, drank together, joked, sung, laughed, told yarns; in short, a perfect union of ideas, feelings, and purposes, seemed to exist among all hands. (95)

But Leech reserved his highest praise for the victorious and popular commander of the *United States*. Stephen Decatur "showed himself

---

American Sailing Navy; Their Ships and Development (New York: W.W. Norton & Company, Inc., 1949), 500, 556, 252, 546.

[62] Leech, *A Voice from the Main Deck*, 82–87. Both British and American records confirm that Leech served on board the *Macedonian*. Leech's name appears in the muster book of the HMS *Macedonian* as a "boy." He began his service on July 16, 1810 (TNA, PRO: ADM 37/3615). See also "List of Officers, Seamen, and Marines. Prisoners from Frigate *Macedonian*, October 26, 1812" (Leech's name appears as No. 45), in "Naval Records Collection of Naval Records & Library, Subject File, 1775–1910," RG 45, NA, Washington, DC.

to be a gentleman as well as a hero" in his generous treatment of the defeated British officers and crew of the *Macedonian*. By contrast, Leech depicted the commander of the *Macedonian* as a cruel and imperious officer (51). That Captain Carden forced impressed American sailors to fight against their countrymen, declared Leech, was a "fact…more disgraceful to the captain…than even the loss of his ship. It was a gross and a palpable violation of the rights of man" (81).

Leech was preaching to the choir when he made such comments. Of course his indictment of the British Navy helped to rationalize his desertion from the *Macedonian* shortly after its capture and arrival in New York (100–02). It also reassured his American audience that he was no longer an enemy but rather a compatriot.

Seamen authors, whether naturalized or native-born Americans, used their autobiographical works to showcase their loyalty to the United States and their resistance to the British. Significantly even those writers who seemed to veer away from this dominant narrative ended up contributing to it. Josiah Cobb was one such memoirist. Towards the end of the War of 1812 he joined an American privateer which was soon captured by the British. On December 28, 1814, he was sent to Dartmoor Prison. The prison register described him as a stout nineteen-year-old youth from Massachusetts with a dark, oval face.[63]

In his 1841 narrative Cobb described his five months in captivity. He detailed the grueling conditions for which Dartmoor was infamous, including hunger, disease, and beatings. Cobb also used his memoir to identify those whom he blamed for the prisoners' plight. Like many former inmates of Dartmoor, Cobb was angry at the American agent Reuben Beasley for his failure to provide adequately for the prisoners. He approvingly noted when prisoners hung Beasley in effigy, blaming him for failing to provide adequately for the prisoners of war and letting them suffer destitution.[64]

Yet Cobb reserved most of his anger for the British. He excoriated Dartmoor's commanding officer Captain Thomas G. Shortland for allegedly murdering seven American prisoners and wounding

---

[63] See "Prisoner-of-War Register for Dartmouth, Number 6234 – Josiah Cobb," TNA, PRO: ADM 103/91.

[64] Cobb, *Green Hand's First Cruise*, 2: 190–93.

many others when they gathered in the prison yard on April 6, 1815. Although Shortland was exonerated of this charge and a British-American commission showed that some prisoners were rowdy and taunting the soldiers to fire, Americans quickly viewed this incident as a "massacre," one made all the more terrible by the fact that the peace treaty had been signed almost four months before.[65]

Together with similar accounts by other survivors of this event,[66] Cobb's memoir stoked his countrymen's anger at what happened in Dartmoor on April 6, 1815. Over twenty five years after the event, Cobb remained incensed at what he saw as mass murder committed by the British against defenseless American prisoners.

Cobb's book offered a graphic, stinging indictment of Dartmoor Prison. Yet like earlier works that described the sufferings of impressed sailors, it ran the risk of undermining Jack Tar's reputation for manliness and independence. As Cobb hammered away at what American prisoners of war endured, as he depicted the alleged massacre of some of these inmates on April 6, 1815, he promoted an image of Jack Tar as a victim, unable to defend himself, much less his nation.

But like other seamen authors, Cobb did not want his readers to view American sailors, even those subject to the terrible conditions at Dartmoor, as mere victims. He stressed that most of these men retained their spunk, patriotism, and therefore manliness. Most remained defiant against the British and steadfastly loyal to the United States. To illustrate his point Cobb recounted how prisoners administered rough justice to the allegedly few Americans who collaborated with the British. One night, recalled Cobb, two Americans who had bragged about their service in the British Navy were seized by other inmates and the word "traitor" was stamped on their foreheads and the initials "T" and "R" carved into their cheeks. Cobb praised the "patriotism" of the prisoners who did this and noted with satisfaction that one marked man died from infection when he tried to cut the letters from his face (250–51).

[65] Ibid., 196–221. Hicks, "True Born Columbians," 207–54, and Gilje, *Liberty on the Waterfront*, 187–91, offer recent discussions of the alleged massacre.
[66] See, for example, Joseph Bates, *The Autobiography of Elder Joseph Bates; Embracing a Long Life on Shipboard* ... (Battle Creek, MI: Steam Press of the Seventh-Day Adventist Publishing Association,1868), 77–82.

Cobb ended his memoir by asserting that his time at Dartmoor had made a man out of him. Prison was not a "humiliation" but "the proudest period of his existence." The months of "roughing hardships sent the boy further into manhood," he declared, "than the like number of years would have done in the sober routine of still life" (319). Such comments of course sought to reassure Americans that their sailors were strong, proud men, even when incarcerated under dreadful conditions.

The narratives of sailors who experienced the War of 1812 helped to forge a national myth, one that blended into an almost seamless web belief in the virility and patriotism of its men with faith in the virtue, strength, and resilience of the nation. Yet by the mid-1850s the power of this myth was waning. The passage of time made the War of 1812 an increasingly distant memory. Americans turned inward to focus on problems within their nation's borders, especially the growing sectional tensions between the North and South. Significantly the popularity of American sea fiction declined in the 1850s.[67] Of course the deaths of many mariners who had served in the War of 1812 meant that there were fewer firsthand accounts of this conflict being published.

These developments made the appearance of Samuel Holbrook's autobiography in 1857 noteworthy. Holbrook did not fight the British during the War of 1812 but he commemorated the mariners who did.[68] In doing this he sought to revitalize the public's fading historical memory of the United States' second war with Great Britain. He urged his fellow Americans to not forget the sacrifices made and the victories won by its seamen during this conflict.

Holbrook began his discussion of the naval war of 1812–1814 by echoing a theme articulated by earlier seamen authors, especially combat veterans of this conflict: Jack Tar's valor and competency played a critical role in preserving the sovereignty and honor of the United States when it was a fragile, new republic. Holbrook's pride was obvious as he recollected how America's "raw recruits" and its "Lilliputian Navy" managed to hold its own against the "well disciplined and hardy" British forces, the "heroes" of Trafalgar. But "WE

[67] Thomas Philbrick, *James Fenimore Cooper and the Development of American Sea Fiction* (Cambridge, MA: Harvard University Press, 1961), 260–61.
[68] Chapter 1 discusses Holbrook's life and naval career.

DID," he exclaimed, because "our cause was a just one, the contest was for the honor of our country, and for our national rights" (63).

Belief in a code of honor, one that obligated men to avenge insults, underpinned this boast. Holbrook recalled how throughout his life he repeatedly confronted, sometimes with violence, males who allegedly insulted him. Although he conceded that such actions were "unchristianlike," Holbrook declared that a man must not tolerate attacks on his reputation or property. Neither should a nation. According to Holbrook, the War of 1812 was "a justifiable war" because "no country had ever been more grossly insulted" than the United States. If British attacks on America's sovereignty and its sailors' rights had remained unanswered, stressed Holbrook, then "our glorious Stars and Stripes would have decorated Westminster Abbey" and "the shackles firmly clenched and the boasted liberty of this great Republic thrown back upon our children with taunts and insults" (24, 30–31, 61, 58).

Like earlier seamen authors, Holbrook stressed that American mariners' defense of liberty and honor came at a high price, especially when they fought a formidable adversary. Holbrook especially illustrated this point when he recounted the fate of the United States frigate, the *Essex*. During its 1813–1814 Pacific cruise the *Essex* seized numerous British whalers before it was captured off the coast of Chile on March 28, 1814, by the HMS *Phoebe* and the *Cherub*.

Despite overwhelming odds and casualty rates of approximately 60 percent, the *Essex* fought ferociously for over two hours before surrendering. The ship quickly became a legend in American naval history. Broadsides emblazoned with the motto of the *Essex*, "Free Trade and sailor's rights," heralded the bravery and resolve of her crew and denounced the perfidy of her British captors. The *Essex*'s commander David Porter and other ship survivors received a hero's welcome when they returned to the United States as part of a prisoner exchange.[69]

The defeat and capture of the *Essex* made a particularly deep impression on Holbrook. He sailed on board the *Macedonian* with

[69] Charles E. Brodine, Jr., "The Pacific Cruise of the Frigate *Essex*" in *Against All Odds: U.S. Sailors in the War of 1812*, eds. Charles E. Brodine, Jr., Michael J. Crawford, and Christine F. Hughes (Washington, DC: Naval Historical Center, 2004), 1–26.

men who were part of the surviving crew of the *Essex*. Many of the
officers of the *Macedonian*, including its commander Captain John
Downes, had been junior officers of the *Essex*. No doubt Holbrook
heard graphic details from his shipmates about the battle which deci-
mated the *Essex*.

Holbrook used his autobiography to contribute to the rapidly growing legend surrounding this vessel. He reprinted extensive portions of
Captain Porter's official account of the *Essex*'s final battle and capture.
Of course this account was designed to vindicate Porter's decisions as
commanding officer and to portray his crew in the best possible light.
Holbrook also injected his own commentary and descriptions of the
battle, probably gleaned from his shipmates' eyewitness accounts. He
stressed the "fearless and patriotic spirit" which characterized "our
hardy sailors" in combat and how they richly deserved their reputation for bravery (336–37).

To dramatize this point Holbrook described the heroic deaths of
several men on board the *Essex*. One man ravaged by an eighteen
pound cannon shot died allegedly exclaiming: "I die in defence of
'Free trade and sailors' r-i-g-h-t-s'." Holbrook emphasized that the
sailor died "with the word *rights* quivering on his lips." Another
dying mariner, stated Holbrook, "died animating his shipmates to
fight bravly [*sic*] in defence of liberty." While a third, asserting he
would never "submit" to being a prisoner, jumped overboard to his
death.

It is impossible to know how factually accurate were Holbrook's
accounts of the dying words of sailors, especially those mortally
wounded. But to focus on this issue misses the crucial point: Holbrook
and countless of his countrymen believed that the men who died on
board the *Essex* did so because of their deeply felt commitment to
protecting American liberties and rights. The poignant death scenes
that Holbrook offered his readers, therefore, were not meant simply
to tug at their heartstrings. They were meant to bear witness to the
courage and determination of mariners who sacrificed their lives to
safeguard the United States and the rights of its free, proud men.

Antebellum seamen authors – whether they were veterans of the
War of 1812 or not, whether they were native-born or naturalized
Americans – challenged their readers to honor the sacrifices Jack Tar
made for the United States, especially during the War of 1812.They

fueled their countrymen's resentment of the British when they graphically described what American seamen suffered when impressed, imprisoned, and wounded. Yet such works also promoted American nationalism when they described how the country's seamen resisted British might and fought bravely against the formidable Royal Navy. Stories of American naval victories especially promoted Americans' belief that the War of 1812 upheld the honor and independence of both the nation and its fighting men.

This war, however, was not the only conflict that put antebellum American mariners in harm's way. So, too, did the revolutionary struggles for independence occurring in the Caribbean and South America during the late eighteenth and first half of the nineteenth centuries. Although these wars ultimately helped millions of human beings achieve a measure of dignity and freedom in their lives, U.S. mariners caught in these upheavals were understandably ambivalent about them. Their descriptions of the wars of independence in Haiti and South America offer a searing portrait of the turmoil roiling the southern hemisphere of the Americas during the formative years of the United States. Such accounts also highlight how seamen memoirists wove notions of manliness and nationalism into their narratives.

3

Exploring the Meaning of Revolution in the Americas

Sailor Narratives of the Haitian and South American Wars of Independence

American mariners who sailed the high seas in the late eighteenth and early nineteenth centuries quickly learned that they were living in a revolutionary age. This was especially true for those seamen who sailed to the Caribbean and to South America. Revolution began in the French Caribbean colony of Saint-Domingue in 1791 when enslaved blacks rebelled against their plantation masters as well as French rule. To highlight their independence from French colonialism black revolutionaries began to call their island nation "Haiti," a name long used by the indigenous people, the Tainos.[1]

By the first decade of the nineteenth century revolutionaries in Central and especially South America were campaigning against Spanish rule and demanding independence. Late in 1805 Francisco de Miranda, a quixotic Venezuelan revolutionary living in exile in London, traveled to New York City where he organized a naval expedition back to his homeland. He hoped to topple the colonialist government in Venezuela and instigate a war of independence throughout Latin America. Although Miranda's mission failed, he helped to educate and infuse with revolutionary fervor the next generation of independence leaders, Simón Bolívar and José de San Martín. These men

---

[1] Laurent DuBois, *Avengers of the New World: The Story of the Haitian Revolution* (Cambridge, MA: Harvard University Press, 2004). For the name change, see 299. See also Lester D. Langley, *The Americas in the Age of Revolution, 1750–1850* (New Haven, CT: Yale University Press, 1996), 87–144 and C. L. R. James, *The Black Jacobins: Toussaint L'Ouverture and the San Domingo Revolution* (1938; 2nd ed., rev., New York: Vintage Press, 1989).

realized Miranda's dreams by leading Latin America's wars of independence from 1808 to 1826.[2]

How did U.S. mariners who witnessed these developments interpret them? Chapter 3 explores this question by focusing on the autobiographies and memoirs of sailors who left especially rich accounts of their experiences in revolutionary Haiti and South America. Like their recollections of British impressment and the War of 1812, sailor authors constructed complicated narratives when they recalled their time in the southern hemisphere of the Americas. On one level their accounts became captivity narratives, especially when they described United States seamen caught in the vise of revolution in Haiti and South America. Yet this theme of captivity quickly gave way to other issues. Mariners' descriptions of the wars of independence south of the United States border helped to validate North Americans' faith in their own revolution and republican experiment.

Seamen narratives about revolutionary upheavals in the southern American hemisphere resonated with those about the War of 1812. Each of these accounts illustrated how mariners threaded themes of nationalism and manhood when recalling their seafaring years. This was apparent when sailor authors discussed their experiences in Haiti and South America. They stressed how they resisted both threatening Spanish colonials and revolutionaries, much as they had the British during the War of 1812 era. Such stories of course burnished North American sailors' reputation for courage and patriotism. More importantly, however, these accounts underscored how ideas about manliness and nationalism converged in the figure of Jack Tar. They also illustrated how concerns about race and slavery shaped mariners' responses to revolutionary struggles for independence. Analysis of sailors' recollections of the first, successful black

---

[2] Karen Racine, *Francisco de Miranda: A Transatlantic Life in the Age of Revolution* (Wilmington, DE: Scholarly Resources Inc., 2003), 141–72. John Charles Chasteen, *Americanos: Latin America's Struggle for Independence* (Oxford: Oxford University Press, 2008) and Langley, *The Americas in the Age of Revolution*, 147–213, offer overviews of the wars of independence in Latin America. See also John Lynch, *Simón Bolívar: A Life* (New Haven, CT: Yale University Press, 2006); Lynch, *The Spanish American Revolutions, 1808–1826* (New York: W.W. Norton, 1986); Leslie Bethell, ed., *The Cambridge History of Latin America*, vol. 3, *From Independence to c. 1870* (Cambridge: Cambridge University Press, 1984).

war of independence in the Americas, the Haitian Revolution, begins
to develop these arguments.

The Haitian Revolution appalled most of the white American mariners who witnessed it, including those who later published autobiographies and memoirs. Seamen authors graphically depicted the horrors
in Haiti. They especially stressed the ruthless, bloody efficiency with
which Haiti's black soldiers massacred white planter families. These
writers also emphasized how terrified they and their shipmates were
when caught in the maw of a particularly bloody revolution.

The theme of imperiled manhood was prominent in antebellum
white seamen's recollections of the Haitian Revolution. Paradoxically,
however, these accounts also nourished in their white readers a sense
of national identity and pride in the United States when they described
a revolution awash in gore and chaos in a nearby Caribbean island.

The autobiographical works of James Durand and Horace Lane
highlighted these themes. Durand offered a brief yet powerful account
of the carnage in Haiti. He recalled sailing several times as a merchant
sailor to Port-au-Prince in 1802.[3] His description of seeing the corpses
of one hundred and twenty whites, including those of infants, lying
exposed in a large hole conveyed the horror of what he witnessed (8–9).

But what Durand most stressed was the power that Haitian soldiers
wielded not only over their former masters but also American sailors.
He recalled, for example, how these soldiers boarded an American
ship about to leave for New York, took the French refugees hidden
below, and hung them shortly after reaching the shore. Unable to
intervene, the American captain, noted Durand, simply "sailed away"
(9). Durand also narrated how he and his shipmates watched helplessly when Haitians used their vessel's long boat to execute a terrible
task: rowing out to sea and drowning numerous refugees, including
women and children (10).

---

[3] Since many of the American sailors who sailed to Haiti during its war of independence did so on gun runners or commercial brigs, the kinds of sources found for
British and American naval ships, such as logbooks, muster and pay rolls, are generally not available. Unfortunately Durand did not state the name of the vessel that
he sailed on when he first went to Port-au-Prince in January 1802 (4). The events
he described occurred between then and before February 1803. During the latter
date he was in Baltimore, getting ready to sail on an unnamed brig bound to Turk's
Island in the West Indies (12–13).

Horace Lane offered an even more harrowing and detailed account of the bloodshed in revolutionary Haiti. In the summer of 1804, when he was fifteen years old, Lane shipped on board an American merchant vessel named the *Sampson* bound for Haiti. This vessel was one of the many Yankee gun runners and privateers to risk capture by the French in order to supply Haitian revolutionaries with provisions, including weaponry.[4]

Although welcomed by the newly emancipated Haitians with a gun salute and music, the *Sampson*'s crew saw plenty of evidence of recent massacres of the island's white inhabitants, including women and children. Lane grimly noted that there were "three hundred putrifying human bodies, lying in heaps across each other, in a church, not forty rods from where our boats landed." Days later Lane and his shipmates stumbled upon more corpses. As Lane's autobiography makes clear, the gruesome sight he saw seared his memory: "We came to a heap of bones, where there had been a massacre; the flesh on them was not wholly decayed, it was a horrid sight, and a sickening smell" (59–65).

Lane arrived in Haiti during a watershed in the black revolutionary struggle. Several years before in 1802, Napoleon Bonaparte had sent a French army to reconquer Haiti. Both sides massacred thousands of civilians. White masters played their part in the horrific carnage, torturing, raping, and murdering blacks and mulattoes. The latter retaliated in kind against the whites and soon the conflict degenerated into a race war. By 1804 yellow fever as well as the fighting abilities of Haiti's black armies combined to defeat Bonaparte's forces. The imprisonment of Toussaint Louverture in France catapulted to power Jean Jacques Dessalines, a black general. Dessalines took a hard line against white colonials and encouraged blacks to slaughter the whites, especially after rumors reached him that the latter were conspiring to foment a counterrevolution. To intimidate surviving

---

[4] No records of Lane's voyage on board the *Sampson* seem to have survived. But there is a consular certificate for the *Sampson* when it sailed from New York in late 1804 on another journey to the West Indies. See "Report and Manifest of the Cargo Laden at the Port of New York aboard the Ship Sampson," Bureau of Customs of New York, Oct.-Dec. 1804, RG 36, Box No. 0080, NA, Northeast Region, New York City.

whites, Dessalines ordered that piles of French corpses be left to rot in the open.[5]

By the time Lane and his shipmates arrived in Haiti, most of the French colonials had either fled or died. Yet some were in hiding. According to Lane, a promised reward by the French government, not compassion or benevolence, led his captain to try to smuggle out fugitive whites. The first attempt failed and threatened all of their lives. Two young French women were smuggled on board, dressed as young sailor boys and "smeared with filth and tar." Four children were also put in sacks and carried on board the *Sampson*. One, who was too young to keep quiet, died from an overdose of laudanum given to tranquilize him. Lane grimly noted that the child's weighted corpse had to be thrown overboard and that his remains were seen several days later in a shark's mouth. Unfortunately the French fugitives were caught by Haitian soldiers whom Lane described as "relentless blacks." These soldiers were so enraged that they threatened to kill everyone on board, including the crew. Although they finally accepted a bribe to "hush up" the incident, they killed the French women and children the next day (63–64).

Like Durand, Lane conveyed the horrors of Haiti's struggle for independence when he recounted the grisly events he witnessed on this Caribbean island. He also highlighted how precarious was the safety of American sailors who journeyed to Haiti during its bloodbath. He and his shipmates, stressed Lane, were caught in the maelstrom of an especially violent upheaval. They were buffeted by frightening revolutionary forces they barely understood and were powerless to affect.

Lane's autobiography also raised another issue that highlighted American seamen's powerlessness while in Haiti. He remembered that the captain of the *Sampson* summoned black Haitians to discipline the crew. This occurred when Lane and other sailors initiated a work stoppage to protest meager grog rations. A "bloody fight" ensued between the officers and sailors of the *Sampson*. It ended when the captain called for Haitian troops to quell the mutiny. They manacled nineteen of the crew and compelled them to do hard labor in Haiti for three months. Fortunately for Lane, he was not one of those imprisoned (61–62).

[5] Du Bois, *Avengers of the New World*, 251–301.

His brief recollection of these events belied the drama enacted on board the *Sampson*. Established racial hierarchies were turned upside down as armed black men shackled white men and carted them off to servitude. Lane was powerless to protect himself from such humiliating punishment. He escaped his shackled shipmates' fate only because the captain needed him and the rest of the crew to man the *Sampson*. When Lane deserted the *Sampson* Haitian soldiers soon recaptured him. Lane's captain ordered him flogged. The cat-o-nine tails, Lane recalled, "made my back feel as if fire was applied" (68).

Durand and especially Lane offered their readers powerful, racially charged images of endangered white manhood. Each of these writers stressed how they and other white mariners faced menacing black Haitian soldiers and were often powerless to stop the latter's massacring of French refugees. Of course Lane's recollection of Haitians shackling and abusing him evoked the image of slavery. Yet now the tables were turned – it was black men who ruled and maltreated white men.

Lane's ill usage violated not only white Americans' notions of racial hierarchy but also their sense of manhood. The two concepts were closely related in the early republic. The majority of Anglo-Americans racialized the idea of manliness, associating this quality with white males.[6] Being white, however, was a necessary but not a sufficient condition for manliness. Recall that a manly male had to show that he exercised agency over his life. He must be a "freeman," a male who was economically and politically independent from the domination of others.[7]

Manliness also demanded that white males control the blacks in their midst, especially slaves. This was essential to prevent slave revolts and the establishment of an inverted racial order in the United States, one in which black men subjugated whites. If this occurred

---

[6] Gregory L. Kaster, "Labour's True Man: Organized Workingmen and the Language of Manliness in the USA, 1827–1877," *Gender & History* 13, no. 1 (April 2001): 24–64, esp.26; David Roediger, *The Wages of Whiteness: Race and the Making of the American Working Class*, rev. ed. (1991; repr., London: Verso, 1999); Dana D. Nelson, *National Manhood: Capitalist Citizenship and Imagined Fraternity of White Men* (Durham, NC: Duke University Press, 1998). See also Gail Bederman, *Manliness and Civilization: A Cultural History of Gender and Race in the United States, 1880–1917* (Chicago: University of Chicago Press, 2005), 5–7.

[7] Kaster, "Labour's True Man," 38–45; Roediger, *Wages of Whiteness*, 55–56.

then white males would be allegedly stripped of their manly independence and honor. They would be degraded, shamed to the level of
slaves and therefore emasculated symbolically if not literally.

Not surprisingly, the "dread of enslavement" haunted slaveholders
in the antebellum South. As Bertram Wyatt-Brown and other scholars
have shown, slaveholders' idea of honor required that they display
their "manly autonomy" and power to rule over others, especially
slaves. Paradoxically, therefore, notions of white independence and
manliness in antebellum America, especially in the South, depended
on the continued domination of blacks.[8]

Haitians' violent overthrow of both slavery and white rule highlighted how fragile established racial hierarchies were; how quickly
cherished beliefs in white manliness and black emasculation could be
upended. Fears that the example of Haiti might precipitate slave insurrection and black dominance in the United States permeated its white
citizens' response to the Caribbean revolution. Numerous American
newspapers publicized the terror and slaughter perpetrated in Haiti,
especially after Dessalines came to power. Many of these accounts
were the eye witness testimony of Haitian whites who sought asylum
in American cities, especially New Orleans and Charleston. Their stories appalled white Americans, particularly Southerners, who feared
that the example of Haiti might precipitate slave insurrection and race
war in the United States.[9]

Several narrowly averted slave plots, including Denmark Vesey's
in 1822, exacerbated southern white fears that Haiti's violence would
spread to their shores. The fact that Vesey had been to the West Indies
when he was a young slave and that he wrote to the Haitian president
asking for help with his plot confirmed southern slaveholders' worst
fears about their land becoming another "Saint Domingue." In 1831

[8] Bertram Wyatt-Brown, *The Shaping of Southern Culture: Honor, Grace, and
War, 1760s-1880s* (Chapel Hill: University of North Carolina Press, 2001), 31–55,
63; Lorri Glover, *Southern Sons: Becoming Men in the New Nation* (Baltimore,
MD: Johns Hopkins University Press, 2007), 23, 34, 165, 169, 177–79; Orlando
Patterson, *Slavery and Social Death: A Comparative Study* (Cambridge,
MA: Harvard University Press, 1982), 77–101. See also Kenneth S. Greenberg,
Masters and Statesmen: The Political Culture of American Slavery (Baltimore,
MD: Johns Hopkins University Press, 1985), 20–22, 140–46.
[9] Alfred N. Hunt, *Haiti's Influence on Antebellum America: Slumbering Volcano in
the Caribbean* (Baton Rouge: Louisiana State University Press, 1988), 2, 107–46.

when the Nat Turner rebellion killed almost sixty whites in Virginia, many southern whites believed the main conspirators were inspired by Haitian rebels, even though there was no evidence to support this fear.[10]

The autobiographical works of white seamen authors capitalized on their countrymen's horror of the Haitian Revolution. Their recollections of being at the mercy of Haitian soldiers, many of them former slaves, stoked white readers' worst fears about black revolution and empowerment. These former sailors' accounts also implicitly challenged Americans' growing confidence in the United States, in their nation's ability to defend the honor of its flag and the safety of its citizens. This confidence gained momentum after the United States defeated the Barbary States and the British in the early nineteenth century. Protection of the bodies of American seamen and of "sailors' rights" galvanized Americans' support for these wars. But seamen's stories of their troubles in Haiti showed the United States unable to protect its mariners against a comparatively weak new country.

Durand and Lane recognized that their grim depictions of Haiti would strike a nerve in white Americans on both nationalist and racial grounds. They detailed their harrowing experiences in Haiti in hopes of gaining these readers' sympathy and money. Yet such writers also took a risk. Stories of sailors as victims, as men swept helplessly under the tow of revolutionary currents, undermined mariners' reputations as proud, manly males able to defend their liberty. The fact that white mariners symbolized as well as projected the emerging power of the United States made their powerlessness before black revolutionaries in a nearby Caribbean island all the more disturbing.

Durand and Lane ostensibly subverted popular images of Jack Tar. These men's recollections of the terror they witnessed or experienced in Haiti suggested that they had lost all control over their lives and were emasculated. Yet a closer look at their narratives reveals a more complicated story. Both Durand and Lane stressed that they managed to resist their Haitian adversaries by foiling the latter's efforts to massacre all island whites. According to Durand, he readily agreed when his captain "dared" him to go ashore and help rescue an elderly Frenchman, his wife, and daughter. Even though he risked his own

---

[10] Ibid., 119–21.

life by participating in this mission, Durand pointedly noted that he was determined "to get white people out of the reach of ... horrid murderous blacks." He proudly added that that his vessel succeeded in its rescue mission (12).

In a similar vein, Lane tempered descriptions of his terror in Haiti with an account of how he and his shipmates persisted in their efforts to smuggle out French refugees. When the *Sampson* left Port-au-Prince it had on board not only six hundred tons of coffee and other goods, claimed Lane, but also thirty-two white women and children (68).

Given the paucity of evidence regarding the merchant vessels on which Durand and Lane sailed, it is impossible to corroborate their stories of rescuing whites fleeing from Haiti. In the end, however, what is important is not so much the actual role Durand and Lane played in rescue operations but rather how they chose to remember, portray, these operations. Irrespective of whether or not they embellished their role in rescuing white refugees, Durand and Lane wanted their readers to think of them and their crew members as heroically risking their lives in order to defy Haitian black murderers and save endangered whites.

Such accounts paralleled narratives by Indian and Barbary captives as well as enslaved blacks in North America. Like these latter works, seamen narratives tried to strike a balance often difficult to achieve. On the one hand, they wanted to convey the sufferings they endured when confronted by an enemy with superior force. On the other hand, they took pains to convey their pride and determination in resisting an enemy through whatever means were available. For sailors it was especially crucial to stress the latter point since manliness required that men resist those who sought to strip them of their liberty and independence.

Durand and Lane sought to reassure their white readers not only about the manliness of their mariners but also about the wisdom of the American Revolution. Antebellum white Americans needed to be reassured about the latter development. They were well aware that it was their forebears who in 1776 initiated the process of waging wars of independence against European colonizers. The Haitian Revolution was a glaring reminder to antebellum whites in the United States of how quickly revolutionary violence could spread, of how difficult it was to stop the "contagion of liberty."[11]

---

[11] Bernard Bailyn used this phrase to discuss North Americans' fears of the radical legacy of their revolution, especially on southern slaves. See Bailyn, *The Ideological*

By the early nineteenth century many whites, fearful of the radical legacy of their colonial struggle against the British, began to reinterpret their revolution. They increasingly viewed the American Revolution in ways that de-radicalized it. Popular antebellum American culture portrayed the revolution as a unique political event, a "national coming of age," that contained rather than unleashed social upheaval.[12] Even the liberty tree, that symbol of Americans' radical defiance to tyranny, was increasingly erased from the dominant public memory or else reinterpreted as a "harmless metaphor, celebrating liberties already won." It was in France and Haiti rather than in the United States where the liberty tree remained a powerful symbol of people's continued struggle for freedom.[13]

The narratives of Durand and Lane promoted Americans' sanitized view of their revolution by detailing the bloodshed in Haiti. These texts helped to reassure the dominant white majority in the United States about their own war of independence and the republic it established. White Americans who read graphic accounts of the horrors in Haiti could congratulate themselves on having avoided a cataclysmic race war when their nation achieved independence. They could view the United States as a beacon for order and stability as well as liberty, one that offered refuge to former white colonials desperately fleeing revolutionary Haiti. As these comments suggest, mariner authors like Durand and Lane nourished in their white readers a sense of national identity and pride in the United States by offering a stark counter image of a revolutionary republic mired in violence.

But not all seaman authors shared such a grim view of Haiti. In 1839, the year that Lane's autobiography appeared in print, African American mariner Paul Cuffe Jr. published his memoir, praising Haiti's revolutionary republic. By the time Cuffe voyaged to the Caribbean in his father's brig the *Traveller*, Haiti had weathered its bloody beginnings and Jean Pierre Boyer, a racially mixed man, was president.[14] Cuffe therefore did not witness firsthand the gruesome

---

Origins of the American Revolution, enl. ed. (Cambridge, MA: Harvard University Press, 1992), 230–319, esp. 232–45.

[12] Michael Kammen, *A Season of Youth: The American Revolution and the Historical Imagination* (New York: Alfred A. Knopf, 1978), 186–220, esp. 219.

[13] Alfred F. Young, *Liberty Tree: Ordinary People and the American Revolution* (New York: New York University Press, 2006), 325–77.

[14] Cuffe said he traveled to Haiti on board the brig *Traveller* in the fall of 1812. See *Narrative of the Life and Adventures of Paul Cuffe, A Pequot Indian During*

violence that Durand and Lane saw. No doubt this fact contributed to his favorable impression of Haiti. But it is important to recognize that the issue of race shaped Cuffe's response to the Haitian Revolution just as it did white seamen's. Racial pride in the establishment of the first black republic in the Americas characterized Cuffe's portrayal of Haiti. His recollections of his journey to this island illuminated how antebellum African Americans contested the dominant notions of nationalism and manliness constructed by the white majority. To appreciate Cuffe's views one must first situate his memoir in a larger African American discourse about Haiti.

Most antebellum African Americans supported the Haitian Revolution. Public addresses, sermons, and newspaper editorials by black leaders praised Haiti as "a great nation," one that proved people of color had the intelligence, discipline, and power to govern themselves.[15] Many African Americans also lauded Haitian leaders, especially Touissant Louverture, as a symbol of black resistance and manhood. Leading black abolitionists, including Frederick Douglass, invoked this Haitian hero's memory to recruit African American men for the Union army during the Civil War. Douglass's admiration for Haiti continued when he served as the United States' first ambassador to Haiti in the postwar era.[16] In the antebellum years Douglass and other abolitionists, whites as well as blacks, used the example of Haiti to urge American slaveholders to end slavery and thereby avert a racial

Thirty Years Spent at Sea ... (Vernon, NY: Horace N. Bill, 1839), 5. But he was confused about the year since Jean-Pierre Boyer did not become president of Haiti until 1818 and served until 1843 ("Jean Pierre Boyer," *Encyclopedia Britannica*. 2007. Encyclopedia Britannica Online. 27 July 2007 http://www.search.eb.com/article-9016068). For discussion of the *Traveller*, see Sheldon H. Harris, *Paul Cuffe: Black America and the African Return* (New York: Simon and Schuster, 1972), 57,145–46,171–72.Cuffe Senior in a January 23, 1817, letter to James Forten said he was about to send the *Traveller* to Santo Domingo. His son may well have been on this voyage. See ibid., 247. Cuffe Jr. is listed as a seaman on board several merchant ships and whalers that sailed from New Bedford and surrounding areas during the period from the late 1820s to the mid-1850s. See the New Bedford Free Public Library's online "Crewmen Search Results" for "Cuffe" or "Cuffee," www.ci.new-bedford.ma.us/SERVICESLIBRARY/whalingproject/crewlistasp. Accessed 6/21/2007.

[15] Hunt, *Haiti's Influence on Antebellum America*, 157–61.
[16] Matthew J. Clavin, "American Toussaints: Symbol, Subversion, and the Black Atlantic Tradition in the American Civil War," *Slavery and Abolition* 28, no. 1 (April 2007): 89–90.

conflagration in the United States. A minority of African American activists, such as David Walker and Henry Highland Garnet, also urged slaves in the South to follow Haiti's example and violently overthrow their white masters.[17] Although most black leaders avoided such incendiary advice, recognizing how foolhardy it was to attack a heavily armed, majority white population, they were proud that now a black republic existed in the Americas. African Americans' admiration for Haiti led thousands of them to visit and even immigrate to the Caribbean island, attracted by the Haitians' warm welcome and President Boyer's promise of land and citizenship.[18]

Cuffe's narrative appeared when events in Haiti roiled the United States, heartening blacks but frightening whites. Like many African Americans, Cuffe expressed pride at seeing men of color in command of a republic in the Americas. He pointedly praised both Boyer and his presidential guard. The latter were "a fine looking set of fellows" who seemed "to understand military tactics to perfection" and to make "first rate soldiers." They were also "elegantly dressed in red frocks and trousers, faced with blue and green." Cuffe described President Boyer as "a personage of commanding appearance, who appeared to be a mulatto." He emphasized that Boyer was "most superbly dressed and equipped, and on horseback made an elegant appearance" (5).

This positive portrayal of Boyer and his guard served an important purpose in Cuffe's narrative. It challenged widely held racist stereotypes. At a time when black men were widely caricatured in the United States and elsewhere in the Western world as dirty, unkempt, and ignorant savages, Cuffe offered a startling counterimage: black men who were competent, knowledgeable, and well tailored.

His depiction of Haiti's president evoked images of the United States' first head of state. Like George Washington, Boyer was a "personage" of "commanding presence," a leader who inspired his fellow citizens with his dignity and elegance as well as his competence. To say this about a "mulatto" president who headed a revolutionary black republic that most whites in the United States feared and hated was a daring, even radical, public statement to make for any antebellum American, but especially an African American man.

[17] Hunt, *Haiti's Influence on Antebellum America*, 147–49, 153.
[18] Ibid., 169–71.

Cuffe's positive assessment of Haiti challenged white Americans' conceptions of both nationalism and manliness. Cuffe urged his white countrymen to reconsider how they interpreted the American Revolution and defined the national community of the United States. He implicitly urged whites to recognize the revolutionary nature of what began in 1776 when he proudly noted that Haiti was a country peopled by "free blacks, having a republican form of government" (5). Such language suggested that the American Revolution and the republic it established was not a unique event but one that reverberated throughout the world and helped to inspire other colonized peoples to fight for their independence, including Haitian slaves.

Cuffe also used his narrative to offer an alternative vision of what the United States could be. In exploring this issue, it is important to remember that his narrative appeared when the nation was expanding its political democracy.[19] Yet even as white working-class men participated more fully in the political process, the notion of citizenship remained racially exclusive. White Americans pointedly excluded people of color from citizenship. When African Americans tried to assert their rights as citizens, when they tried to vote, denounced slavery, challenged segregation, or marched in civic parades, such as annual Fourth of July celebrations, they faced violent white reprisals, including attacks by white mobs.[20]

Cuffe's depiction of black Haitians competently performing their duties of governance, his portrayal of President Boyer in ways that evoked Washington, implicitly rebuked white Americans' narrow vision of citizenship and national identity. Cuffe suggested that men of color could be responsible citizens of a republic. A newly established republic, an emerging democracy, need not fear when men of African descent demanded to be included as full citizens or even be elected president.

Such beliefs challenged how white Americans viewed manliness as well as nationalism. Cuffe affirmed the manly independence and

[19] For recent discussion of this process, see Sean Wilentz, *The Rise of American Democracy: Jefferson to Lincoln* (New York: W.W. Norton & Company, 2005).
[20] David Grimsted, *American Mobbing, 1826–1861: Toward Civil War* (New York: Oxford University Press, 1998), 30, 61–62,103–04, 135–47, 299nn 89–90; Paul A. Gilje, *Rioting in America* (Bloomington: Indiana University Press, 1996), 89–91; David Waldstreicher, *In the Midst of Perpetual Fetes: The Making of American Nationalism, 1776–1820* (Chapel Hill: University of North Carolina Press, 1996), 323–48.

dignity of black Haitians and by implication of black men in general when he praised Boyer and his soldiers. He urged his fellow Americans to forge a concept of manliness that included black as well as white males.

By contrast white seamen authors who journeyed to revolutionary Haiti portrayed the black males there in ways that questioned their manhood. Durand and Lane did this when they expressed skepticism about Haitians' capacity for self-rule. Ironically, Durand highlighted this point as much by what he omitted to discuss in his narrative as by what he actually said. Durand dwelled on the terror committed by blacks in Haiti but omitted discussing their struggles for liberty and an independent republic. He never mentioned the violence that white colonizers perpetrated against blacks nor how this earlier carnage fomented later bloody reprisals.

As for Horace Lane, he did concede early on in his autobiography that both Haitian whites and blacks committed "the most horrid acts of barbarous murder and massacre" against each other (55). But like Durand, Lane dwelled on the cruelties that blacks perpetrated against whites. He dramatized the alleged savagery of Haitian black rebels when he recounted how they massacred white women and children as well as men who had hidden in a church. The blacks, pointedly asserted Lane, were "too hardened with rage" to respect the "sacred rights" of a church; "they had no pity" (61).

It is tempting to argue that Durand and Lane's grim portrait of Haiti reflected not racial misgivings about black humanity, capability, or manliness but rather the fact that they visited this country when it was in the throes of revolutionary upheaval. As noted earlier, Cuffe visited Haiti when it had stabilized under Boyer and the worst of the violence was over. Yet even white mariners who traveled to Haiti after it had gained its independence were skeptical or contemptuous of the republic. This was the case with David Bunnell who recalled traveling to the Caribbean island shortly after it had gained independence.[21] He scoffed at the black army he saw in Haiti:

It was quite laughable to see the black army drawn out on parade; some entirely naked; others with one shoe on, and a few with a shirt. I saw several of the officers with great swords hung to their sides, with no other apparel

---

[21] Unfortunately, Bunnell did not state the exact year he was in Haiti.

on than a ragged pair of pantaloons and cocked hat. The president was also
very meanly clad. (16)

Even Bunnell's adding that Haitians lacked the "opportunity of pro-
curing clothing" since they had "not long been free from the bondage
of their tyrannical masters," could not erase the demeaning image
of blacks he created for his readers. By stressing their nakedness or
scanty, ragged clothing, Bunnell portrayed the Haitians as a mockery
or a caricature of disciplined, uniformed soldiers. He suggested that
it was folly to entrust such men with political and military power. In
fact, Bunnell presented Haitians as buffoons; they were not serious or
dignified; they were "laughable."

The stark contrast between Bunnell's and Cuffe's portraits of
Haiti highlights how contested and racially charged were notions
about manliness in the early republic. Like many other antebellum
African Americans, Cuffe proudly depicted Haitian revolutionaries
as "manly" men who had dignity, independence, and competency.
By contrast, Bunnell, Lane, and Durand depicted Haitian soldiers as
either laughable buffoons or sadistic savages.

Concerns about manliness and national identity swirled together
in complicated ways when seamen authors recounted their experiences in revolutionary South America as well as Haiti. As these writers described confronting colonialists, revolutionaries, and the British
Navy during Latin America's wars of independence, they underscored
Jack Tar's commitment to defending his nation and his own manly
independence.

Analysis of the narratives of Nathaniel Ames and Samuel Holbrook
develops these arguments. But several questions first warrant brief
discussion: What were the major events that precipitated the end of
Spain's colonial empire in South America? How did the U.S. government and its citizenry react to the revolutionary struggles for independence south of its border?

Many citizens of the United States initially supported Latin Americans'
rebellion against Spanish colonial rule, viewing them as part of the
global struggle for liberty begun by their own nation in 1776. Despite
this fact, the U.S. government was at first officially neutral in this
conflict. Congress's establishment in 1821 of a Pacific Station on the

west coast of South America reflected the United States' commitment to protecting its commerce and citizens against both sides in the wars of independence.[22]

These struggles became a pawn in the complicated chessboard of European politics. The Spanish received support from the Holy Alliance, the counter-revolutionary league formed by Russia, Austria, and Prussia during the Napoleonic Wars. Eager to check their continental rivals and protect their overseas trade, the British tacitly rejected their earlier policy of neutrality in Latin America's wars and began backing the independence movement. British banks provided crucial financial assistance to the revolutionaries and British mercenaries fought for Latin American independence.[23]

The United States also jettisoned its earlier stance of neutrality in Latin America. On May 4, 1822, it formally recognized the newly established republics of South America. Fearful of European efforts to recolonize this area, the U.S. government in December 1823 issued the Monroe Doctrine. It declared that the Americas were no longer open to further colonization by foreign powers. Enforcement of this decree by the formidable British navy gave this doctrine credibility. By 1824 the United States and Britain were openly helping the Latin American independence movement in numerous financial, military, and diplomatic ways.[24]

In early December 1824 the climactic patriot victory occurred at the Battle of Ayacucho in Peru. When the last royalist stronghold fell in Lima's main seaport Callao, in January 1826, Spain's defeat was complete. United States and British frigates played a role in this action by supporting the Peruvian Navy's blockade of Callao.[25]

[22] Edward Baxter Billingsley, *In Defense of Neutral Rights: The United States Navy and the Wars of Independence in Chile and Peru* (Chapel Hill: University of North Carolina Press, 1967), 76–120; Arthur Preston Whitaker, *The United States and the Independence of Latin America, 1800–1830* (New York: Russell & Russell, Inc., 1962), 275–316.

[23] Paul Johnson, *The Birth of the Modern: World Society, 1815–1830* (New York: Harper Collins, Publishers, 1991), 631–51.

[24] Whitaker, *The United States and the Independence of Latin America*, 370–563; John L. Johnson, *A Hemisphere Apart: The Foundations of United States Policy toward Latin America* (Baltimore, MD: Johns Hopkins University Press, 1990), 167–69, 181–86.

[25] Ibid.; David Bushnell, "The Independence of Spanish South America," in Bethell, ed., *Cambridge History of Latin America*, 3:145–46.

Many U.S. citizens entertained high hopes for Latin America after its liberation from Spanish colonialism. Some even expected that Latin Americans would emulate their nation's example and establish orderly republics after achieving independence. But by 1830 the civil strife and often anarchy that roiled the newly independent countries of Latin America made many in the United States pessimistic about the possibility of erecting stable, let alone democratic, governments south of the border. Anglo Americans' sense of racial superiority also made them skeptical about postcolonial societies with large numbers of racially mixed peoples being able to govern themselves effectively.[26]

Nathaniel Ames's *A Mariner's Sketches* (1830) reflected as well as promoted his countrymen's disillusionment with Latin America's struggles for independence. By the time Ames's ship, the forty-four-gun *United States*, commanded by Commodore Isaac Hull, arrived in Rio de Janeiro in early February, 1824, the Spanish colonial cause was largely lost.[27] Later that year Ames's ship helped to hasten Spain's capitulation by participating in the Peruvian blockade of Callao.

The growing diplomatic rapprochement between the United States and Britain and their naval cooperation in South America was fortunate for Hull. Aside from his flagship he had only the *Peacock*, an eighteen-gun sloop-of-war, to protect numerous American merchant vessels sailing near Peru's long coastline.[28] By contrast, the British had a formidable squadron: the *Cambridge* (84 guns), two frigates, and several sloops-of-war, under the command of Captain Thomas James Maling.[29]

---

[26] Johnson, *A Hemisphere Apart*, 56–57, 78, 175–81.

[27] The muster and pay rolls of the *United States* show a William Ames as a crew member (no. 405). His dates of service match Nathaniel Ames's stated times of service (237). The muster rolls for 1823–1844 are in the "Miscellaneous Records of U.S. Navy, Naval Records & Library," roll 129, T829, RG 45, NA, Washington, D.C. For the pay rolls for 1823–1840 see roll 131, ibid. Ames's name and dates of service appear on p. 18.

[28] Linda M. Maloney, *The Captain from Connecticut: The Life and Naval Times of Isaac Hull* (Boston: Northeastern University Press, 1986), 364–412, and Maloney, "The U.S. Navy's Pacific Squadron, 1824–1827" in Robert William Love, Jr., ed., *Changing Interpretations and New Sources in Naval History: Papers from the Third United States Naval Academy History Symposium* (New York: Garland Publishing, Inc., 1980), 180–91, discuss the role of the *United States* in Callao. See also Billingsley, *In Defense of Neutral Rights*, 194–201.

[29] Maloney, *Captain from Connecticut*, 384.

Hull's relationship with Maling became so cordial that the British captain came on board the *United States* to celebrate Fourth of July festivities. British as well as American flags flew together that day as the officers of both ships banqueted and toasted each other's countries. "Old hatchets were buried," Hull's biographer Linda Maloney has noted, as both the commodore and his British counterpart worked closely together to enforce the blockade and protect the shared interests of their nations.[30]

Ames's memoir did not emphasize the cooperation between British and American naval forces. Instead, Ames depicted the British Royal Navy in disparaging ways. By contrast he portrayed the U.S. Navy as an impressive force ready to avenge any insults to the American flag. Of course, such an account misrepresented the relative strengths and weaknesses of the two navies. But this did not matter to Ames. He used his narrative to bolster the martial reputation of the U.S. Navy and to deflate that of the British.

This was especially evident when he compared the British frigate the *Tartar* to the *United States*. Although the *Tartar* belonged to "the largest class of *English* frigates," emphasized Ames, he was "astonished" to see that it was only "two thirds the length of the *United States*" (196). After surveying the respective guns of each vessel, Ames proudly proclaimed that his ship was superior in every way. In fact the *United States* had such an obvious advantage that: "many of our men wondered, not that we had taken any English frigate during the last war, but that any British officers should be found who had the temerity to engage such disproportionate force, or the hardihood to fight as long as they did" (196).

Ames's boast reflected his pride in the American navy as well as his resentment of the British one. He also disparaged the Brazilian navy and the man who had headed this force since 1822, Admiral Thomas Cochrane. This British aristocrat and naval officer came to South America after his involvement in a London stock scandal and other controversies ruined his career in the Royal Navy. Cochrane quickly established himself as the redoubtable commander of rebel naval forces in several South American countries.[31]

[30] Ibid.
[31] David Cordingly, *Cochrane: The Real Master and Commander* (New York: Bloomsbury, 2007) is the most recent scholarly biography. See 296–314 for discussion of Cochrane's three year command of the Brazilian navy.

Under his authority the Brazilian navy impressed sailors from different nations, including the United States. This policy rankled Ames and he applauded his ship's efforts to free impressed American sailors from their captivity. "We made his Lordship give up one American," he dryly recalled, but then angrily added that this rescued sailor was "probably only one of many" (192).

But Ames reserved his greatest venom for General José Ramon Rodil, the commander of the Spanish garrison in Callao. By 1824 Rodil was in an increasingly desperate situation. He sought to break through the blockade by firing on American, British, and Peruvian ships. His gun boats also seized American merchant vessels and at one point Rodil imprisoned and abused the American captain and crew of one such vessel. This action so angered Hull that he prepared to attack the Spanish. News of the patriot victory at Ayacucho, however, caused Rodil to release the Americans and so a full-scale confrontation between Spanish and United States forces were averted.[32]

Ames bristled with resentment when he recalled how Rodil fired upon his ship. He dismissed the possibility that Spanish firepower was intended for the nearby Peruvian navy. Instead Ames stressed how "the shot fell so thick and so fast around us that I have no doubt they were intended for us, for the Protector frigate, the nearest of the Peruvians, was broad off on our brow, and not within three hundred yards" (207).

But what most angered Ames about Rodil was not that he attacked American vessels but that he was allegedly disrespectful towards Hull's Pacific squadron. Rodil, claimed Ames, offered the *United States* "repeated insults," by firing on the ship's landing boats and demanding "a flag of truce" before communicating with Hull. When the *United States* tried to avoid escalating the confrontation, recalled Ames, Rodil allegedly mistook "our quietness for fear." This Spanish officer had "the impudence" to threaten to fire upon the American vessel if it came "within gunshot" (211–12).

Ames's language is revealing here. He depicted Rodil not as an embattled commander defending an increasingly untenable position but rather as an "impudent" man, one who "insulted" the *United States* and the nation it represented. Ames's sense of wounded nationalism

[32] Maloney, *The Captain from Connecticut*, 387–89.

is palpable here. Significantly he asserted: "it is impossible to give any idea by description of the indignation and wrath that filled the minds of our men at these [Rodil's] continual insults" (212).

Ames stressed that he and his shipmates made Rodil pay dearly for his impudence. The *United States*, he recalled, not only "rigorously enforced" the blockade of Callao but also protected a convoy of American merchant vessels, sending a menacing Spanish privateer "certain 'winged messengers,' called twenty four pound shot... with our compliments" (205).

Ames made clear that that he and his mates gave a good account of themselves when they fought colonial forces. They accomplished their mission even though they were in the crosshairs of Spanish guns. His major disappointment was that the Spaniards did not engage the crew of the *United States* in a climactic battle. Such a confrontation, he asserted, would have led to the colonialists' quick defeat, thereby "putting every thing to rights in a ship-shape manner and proving our courage and patriotism" (212).

Ames's use of the last phrase was especially telling. It underscored how entwined the themes of nationalism and manhood were in sailor narratives. Like so many other seamen authors, Ames emphasized how eager he and his shipmates were to vindicate their country's honor and display their manly courage through combat. It is no wonder that he repeatedly portrayed the crew of the *United States* as spoiling for a fight.

The nationalism that Ames displayed in his memoir could make him belligerent towards non-Anglo-Saxon peoples, especially Latin Americans and the Spanish. Significantly Ames peppered his narrative with remarks like the following: "South American governments require a sound thrashing about once a year, each, to make them understand... the civil law and the law of nations" (192); "I have often thought that the only way to get along with a Spaniard, a Portuguese, or Italian... was to knock him down first" (196).

Nathaniel Ames expressed various emotions in his narrative – strident nationalism, anger against those who insulted or threatened his nation and ship, hostility towards foreign peoples, and pride in American sailors. All of these emotions were on display when Ames recalled Bolívar's visit to his ship. In a gesture redolent of symbolic significance, the liberator of South America came on board the *United*

States on February 22, 1825, to celebrate the birthday of George
Washington. Hull, an admirer of Bolívar, accorded him full military
honors. Even the ship's logbook, usually a terse, dry document, conveyed some of the excitement that Bolívar's visit evoked when it noted
that the general received a twenty-one-gun salute.[33]

But Ames recalled this historic occasion in a sarcastic, derisive way.
"His Liberatorship" was merely "a soldier of fortune" with "little or
no principle." Ames added that Bolívar looked like King Charles I,
the Stuart monarch whose advocacy of absolutism led to his behead-
ing and precipitated the English civil war of the 1640s. He was even
more scathing in describing the officers who "swarm[ed]" around
Bolívar. The large whiskers they sported made them look ridiculous
rather than manly: "each one resemble[ed] a rat with his nose through
a bunch of oakum, or an old baboon peeping through a prickly bear
bush" (217–20).

Ames also portrayed Bolívar and his officers as effeminate, naïve,
and childish.[34] The leader of the Latin American independence movement allegedly had a "whining, shrill, and querulous" voice, much
"like that of a sick and peevish child." He also gushed in "admiration and astonishment" when the ship fired its guns for "his entertainment" and declared in "perfect ecstasy" that the ship "must be
invincible." Ames suggested the effeminacy of Bolívar's officers when
he described their uniforms as "dresses," covered with "gold lace
and embroidery." He also stressed that one cavalry officer had such a
"diminutive body and slender legs" that he seemed to be "an append-
age" to his whiskers (219–20).

Ames offered a counter image of the crew of the *United States*,
depicting them as "all young and remarkably stout, fine looking men."
Significantly he noted that Bolívar was very impressed with the crew.
Indeed, this commander allegedly seemed "to have eyes for nothing
else" and repeatedly walked to the mainmast to have a closer look

[33] Logbook of the *United States*, February 22, 1825, "Records of the Bureau of Naval
Personnel, Log of U.S. Naval Ships, 1801–1915," RG 24, NA, Washington, DC. See
also Maloney, *The Captain from Connecticut*, 391–92.
[34] Amy S. Greenberg, *Manifest Manhood and the Antebellum Empire*
(Cambridge: Cambridge University Press, 2005), esp. 96–106, 108–12, discusses
how Americans' denigration of Latin American men, including claims that they
were effeminate, was used to justify Manifest Destiny expansionism in Central
America.

at the men. By contrast, asserted Ames, the crew took little notice of Bolívar, and "wish[ed] him at the devil" for delaying their dinner (220).

Ames belittled South American revolutionary leaders and the cause they represented through such comments. He encouraged his countrymen to view dismissively what Latin Americans had accomplished when they fought successfully to become independent of Spanish colonial rule. He also contributed to a larger public discourse in the antebellum United States one that affirmed its citizens' belief in their own national identity as well as in the manliness of their sailors. Ames's contemptuous portrait of Bolívar implicitly reminded U.S. citizens of how lucky they were to live in a nation allegedly founded by brave, selfless men who had the foresight to establish an orderly, stable republic.

A Mariner's Sketches appeared when American popular culture was lionizing the founding father of the nation. Hagiographic biographies and iconography portrayed George Washington as a dignified, imposing man who embodied the qualities needed to make the United States a success: courage, honesty, determination, and selflessness. Washington was heroic not only because he led the military campaign against the British but also because as first president he moderated the fledgling republic's commitment to liberty and yoked it to civic responsibility and social restraint. For antebellum Americans Washington struck the right balance between order and freedom and thereby helped to establish a viable republic in North America.[35]

Of course, Ames's depiction of Bolívar offered a stark contrast to George Washington. Bolívar was not a genuine liberator, asserted Ames, but a despot like the hated Charles II. To add insult to injury, Ames suggested a homoerotic dimension behind Bolívar's admiration of the *United States* crew. Portraying the mariners of this ship as the embodiment of a youthful, hardy manhood only sharpened Ames's image of the alleged effeminacy of Bolívar and his officers.

It is tempting to dismiss Ames as an idiosyncratic xenophobe who seemed to hate anyone who was not an Anglo American. Yet

---

[35] Early-nineteenth-century biographies of Washington, such as Parson Weem's bestseller, contributed to the idealization of the first president. See Scott E. Caspar, *Constructing American Lives: Biography and Culture in Nineteenth-Century America* (Chapel Hill: University of North Carolina Press, 1999), 68–72.

in the end his narrative articulated in a particularly pronounced way what other seamen authors expressed: an ardent, at times bellicose, nationalism; a persistent animosity against the British navy; and perhaps most importantly of all, pride in the U.S. Navy and its mariners.

Samuel Holbrook reprised these themes in his 1857 autobiography. Since he was in South America almost four years before Ames, his work offers a different perspective on the wars of independence, especially in Peru. Holbrook's text deepens our understanding of how issues of manliness and nationalism shaped antebellum sailor narratives, especially when they discussed revolutionary struggles in the southern hemisphere. Discussion of Holbrook's naval service while in South America lays the groundwork for analyzing his narrative.

Late in 1820 Samuel Holbrook was ship's carpenter on board the USS *Macedonian* when it voyaged to South America under the command of Captain John Downes.[36] Holbrook arrived in Peru when the wars of independence were raging and the United States was still officially neutral in this conflict. Recently independent Chile and colonial Peru warred with each other. Thomas Cochrane led the Chilean navy and imposed a blockade around Callao in order to deprive the nearby capital city of Lima of needed supplies. With a small fleet of ships Cochrane could impose only a "paper blockade" on Peru's long coastline and most neutral countries, including the United States, refused to recognize its legality. Nevertheless Cochrane's forces periodically seized North American merchantmen and this action angered the United States.[37]

The *Macedonian* sailed into the middle of these conflicts. Downes was under orders to provide safe passage to U.S. vessels through the

[36] The "Invalid Navy Pensioners List Complete to November 17, 1848," Records of the Veterans Administration; and "Pension Application Files. Miscellaneous Service. Old War Series," File No. 762 (both sources in RG 15, NA, Washington, DC), confirm Holbrook's service as carpenter on board the *Macedonian*. David Bunnell was also on board the *Macedonian* and told a similar, briefer account of the events Holbrook described. See Bunnell's *Travels and Adventures*, 146–49. For confirmation of Bunnell's service on board the *Macedonian* see "Pension Application Files...," File No. 216, ibid. See also the Muster Roll of USS *Macedonian*, 1813–1821, Roll 55, "Miscellaneous Records of the U.S. Navy Naval Records & Library," T829, RG 45, NA, Washington, DC Bunnell is no. 218 (p. 201) and Holbrook, listed as ship's carpenter, is no. 396 (p. 207).

[37] Cordingly, *Cochrane*, 268–95.

blockade and to protect them from seizure by Spanish privateers and pirates. Early in November 1820 he decided to defy the Chilean blockade and enter Callao.[38]

Holbrook's rousing account of the *Macedonian*'s near showdown with the Chilean fleet underscored how seamen writers used their narratives to depict Jack Tar as the embodiment of a proud, defiant American nationalism as well as a manly warrior ethic. It captured the tension yet also the determination on board the *Macedonian* as the crew prepared to enter Callao *"blockade or no blockade"* (257). Ready for a showdown with Cochrane's fleet, the *Macedonian* prepared for battle: "We beat to quarters, had all bulk heads down, deck sanded, guns double shotted, and matches lit." Holbrook stressed that "the whole blockading fleet were now ... coming towards us" (258). But Cochrane chose not to stop the *Macedonian*, probably because he had no wish to further antagonize a neutral United States nor deflect his limited resources from attacking the Spanish.

In his official report to the U.S. Navy Downes minimized his near confrontation with the Chilean navy, merely noting that Cochrane was "polite" when informed that the *Macedonian* was entering Callao.[39] Holbrook's account of this incident could not have been more different. Even after almost forty years later Holbrook's anger against Cochrane and pride in the *Macedonian*'s resolve are palpable. His autobiography conveyed the bravery and determination of the *Macedonian*'s crew as it faced the Chilean navy. It also stressed how many of Callao's residents crowded the shore to see one American man-of-war take on the Chilean navy. Not surprisingly, Holbrook boasted that in battle the *Macedonian*'s crew would have given a good account of themselves. All on board his ship would have fought as long as "there remained a man to load a gun." Of course Holbrook declared that they would have been victorious: "I am sure that we could have blown them out of water in a very few minutes" (258–59).

Holbrook wove together the themes of nationalism and manhood when he recalled how the *Macedonian* defied the Chilean blockade of Callao. He also did this when he discussed an incident that became legendary in Latin American and British naval history. On November 5,

[38] Billingsley, *In Defense of Neutral Rights*, 76–100.
[39] Ibid., 102–03.

1820, Cochrane made a daring attack on the formidable Spanish fleet anchored in Callao. He and his men captured or "cut out" from the Spanish fleet its flagship, the forty-four-gun *Esmeralda*. While the crews of the nearby *Macedonian* and the British ship the *Hyperion* watched, the Chilean navy scored one of its greatest naval victories. The loss of the *Esmeralda* as well as the deaths of many of the seamen on board enraged the Spanish and their Peruvian allies. They correctly recognized that Cochrane's victory gutted Spanish naval power in the area and made Peruvian independence only a matter of time.[40]

Unfortunately the *Macedonian* bore the brunt of the Spaniards' anger. Since it was anchored nearby during the attack, the colonialists mistakenly believed that it had supported Cochrane's forces. Seeking revenge, the Spanish hammered the *Macedonian* with a barrage of gunfire from their fort. Battered by the bombardment, this American ship managed to sail out of the harbor and beyond the range of Spanish guns. But it remained in the crosshairs of Peru's colonial rulers. When the *Macedonian* commander sent a boat ashore for provisions, the Spaniards killed or badly wounded most of the over dozen men on it. Wounded American sailors remained in danger, even when they were hospitalized in Callao. Mobs tried to murder them and also attacked any foreigners in Callao, especially Americans. Only when the Spanish viceroy in Lima was convinced that the *Macedonian* had not been involved in the destruction of the *Esmeralda* was its crew safe from harm.[41]

Spanish hostilities against the *Macedonian* occurred at a time of growing tensions between the United States and its mariners on the one hand and Peruvian loyalists and their Spanish rulers on the other. Chilean independence had been greatly helped by North American arms shipments despite the United States' declaration of neutrality. Many Chilean privateers had been initially American vessels, bought in the United States. Former American naval officers and mariners

[40] Thomas Cochrane, *Narrative of Services in the Liberation of Chili, Peru, and Brazil, From Spanish Domination* (London: James Ridgway, 1859), 1:83–86; and the logbook of the *Macedonian*, November 6, 1820 entry, "Records of the Bureau of Naval Personnel, Logs of Ships and Stations, 1801–1946," RG 24, NA, Washington, DC. See also Cordingly, *Cochrane*, 288–91.

[41] Different sources corroborate Spanish attacks on the *Macedonian*. See Cochrane, *Narrative of Services*, 1:91–92; *Macedonian* logbook, November 8, 9, and 12, 1820 entries, ibid. See also Billingsley, *In Defense of Neutral Rights*, 111–113.

became major officers in the Chilean navy. Countless American sailors volunteered to serve in the Chilean navy. Many did so in hopes of gaining prize money from captured Spanish vessels.[42]

Holbrook did not mention his countrymen's service in the Chilean navy or their attacks against Peru. Nor did he mention that support for the Latin American cause of independence led many of the officers of the *Macedonian* to quietly whisper encouragement to Cochrane and his men as they got ready to board the *Esmeralda*.[43] Understandably, Holbrook focused on the fact that the Spaniards tried to destroy his ship and kill him and his shipmates. Like other seamen authors, he used his narrative to convey his anguish at facing threatening forces beyond his control. He had troubling memories of the Spanish bombardment of the *Macedonian*: "The[ir] shot flew round us like hail, cutting away our cross-jack yard, and much of our rigging. Many of the red hot shot struck very near us" (263). The murder of his crew mates on the provision boat also haunted Holbrook. He recalled seeing their "blood and brains scattered round upon the inside [of the boat] as though a bullock had been killed in her" (264). Holbrook also reminded his readers of how Spanish mobs in Callao tried to murder wounded American sailors and how they killed "every foreigner they could find" in the city, including one unfortunate American sailor in a grog shop who had his throat slit (263–66).

Through such grim recollections Holbrook vented his rage against the Spanish. He painted these men as cowardly murderers, not manly warriors who followed a martial code of honor. By contrast, Holbrook repeatedly stressed the grit and resolve of his shipmates as they were bloodied by the Spanish and menaced by Cochrane's navy.

He also made it a point of noting how the *Macedonian*'s crew managed to give the Spanish and Cochrane's forces their comeuppance. Holbrook relished recounting the *Macedonian*'s liberation of an American merchant vessel that was captured by the Chilean navy when it tried to run the blockade around Callao. A handpicked group of *Macedonian* men silently boarded the captured vessel and cut her out from the Chilean line of ships without the loss of one life. Holbrook could not help boasting of a mission well done: "this well

---

[42] William L. Newmann, "United States Aid to the Chilean Wars of Independence," *The Hispanic American Historical Review* 27, no. 2 (May 1947): 204–19.

[43] Cochrane recalled this event in his *Narrative of Services*, I: 90.

♥

planned and successful scheme, and the brilliancy of the achievement is equal, if not superior to the cutting out of the Esmeralda" (284).

Such comments highlighted Holbrook's pride in the military prowess and courage of the *Macedonian*'s crew. This pride was also evident when Holbrook recalled how Captain Downes obtained the release of approximately seventy American and British prisoners of war from Peruvian jail. These men were mariners captured from Chilean war vessels. Many of them had been imprisoned in terrible conditions for almost two years. According to Holbrook, "they were much emaciated,...heavily chained, and scarcely able to crawl" (271). Although the Spanish and Peruvians initially balked at releasing these men, Holbrook recalled that his captain "demanded their release as American citizens." This occurred despite the fact that half of the men were British. Perhaps to underscore the shortcomings of the British government in protecting its sailors as well as the magnanimity of the Americans, Holbrook stressed that "no distinction was made between English and American, all were claimed as Americans, and received the same protection" (271).

Holbrook offered a dramatic and perhaps inflated account of what the *Macedonian* accomplished. The ship's log downplayed the release of prisoners of war from Spanish prison. A September 13, 1820, entry, for example, merely listed the names of over twenty men released from prison "by permission of the Vice Roy [sic]."[44] Holbrook, therefore, may not have been entirely accurate in depicting the actual events in which the *Macedonian* challenged the Spaniards or Cochrane's navy. But it is how Holbrook remembered or chose to present these events in his narrative that matters here. Like other seamen authors, he did not merely recall but reinterpreted events that occurred many years earlier in order to affirm Americans' pride in their country, their navy, and the sailors who manned it.

Throughout their narratives about South America's wars of independence and the Haitian Revolution, seamen authors asserted that Jack Tar personified the best of American nationalism and manhood. He therefore deserved the respect and esteem of his countrymen. Many of these writers also argued that American mariners deserved

---

[44] *Macedonian* logbook, September 13, 1820 entry, "Records of the Bureau of Naval Personnel," RG 24, NA, Washington, DC.

protection, not so much from foreign enemies (Jack Tar was supposedly eager to fight these) but from their own officers.

A Mariner's Sketches offers a good entry point for understanding what seamen authors meant. Ames recounted an incident he found disturbing, one that occurred as he sailed on board an unnamed U.S. frigate in the Pacific. A sailor from a nearby American brig requested protection from his abusive captain. This commander had allegedly caused the death of one of his crew by whipping him with "savage barbarity."

Ames's anger was evident as he recalled this story. "So much for 'sailor's rights,'" he groused, "we allow nobody to kick and cuff, flog and shoot our seamen, but our own negro-driving skippers of merchantmen" (103). Other sailor memoirists would have added that such abuse occurred on board American naval as well as merchant ships. Behind such comments was a growing movement to reform how American seamen were disciplined at sea, a movement which sailor authors shaped in crucial ways.

4

Defending One's Rights as a Man and an American Citizen

Sailor Narratives as Exposés of Flogging

The most riveting part of *Two Years Before the Mast* occurs when Dana describes how his shipmates writhed in agony and begged for mercy when they were flogged for little or no reason. Dana portrayed the captain of the *Pilgrim* as a sadistic tyrant, a man who "danced about deck, calling out as he swung the rope, – 'If you want to know what I flog you for, I'll tell you. It's because I like to do it! – because I like to do it! – It suits me! That's what I do it for!'" Dana recalled that he felt so "disgusted, sick, and horror-struck" at his captain's actions that he "turned away" and refused to watch punishment (155).

Dana may have looked away during the infliction of floggings on board the *Pilgrim* but his vivid recollection of these punishments forced readers to face the pain, horror, and sadism of this form of discipline. Although earlier seamen authors such as Nathaniel Ames had condemned the practice of flogging, Dana offered the most famous discussion of this issue. The success of his 1840 memoir encouraged later sailor writers to detail how they and their shipmates regularly suffered a range of punishments, including confinement in irons, beating with fists, rattans, and other weapons. But like Dana, these men singled out flogging as a particularly objectionable form of discipline.

Seamen authors stressed that this punishment threatened a mariner's manhood and rights as an American citizen. These writers also asserted that flogging sailors jeopardized the interests of the United States by hindering the recruitment of qualified American mariners and promoting mutiny on board the nation's naval and merchant vessels. In developing these arguments seamen authors articulated grievances against flogging that resonated with larger American concerns about pain, discipline, enslavement, and emasculation. These ex-mariners also illuminated how issues of class, race, and ethnicity complicated Americans' discussions about these concerns. Situating seamen narratives in an antebellum discourse about how to discipline the body offers a useful context for exploring why their authors targeted flogging as a particularly egregious form of punishment for seafaring men.

Starting approximately in the early 1820s but especially during the 1830s and 1840s a growing chorus of evangelical reformers, former naval officers, and Congressional leaders campaigned to end the whipping of sailors on board American merchant and naval vessels.[1] Opponents of flogging had their work cut out for them since it was a traditional form of discipline on the high seas. Officers inflicted this punishment for a wide variety of offenses, including disobedience of orders, drunkenness, stealing, and neglect of duty. The loss of many log books and the fact that some punishments, especially if they were casually administered, were not recorded, makes it impossible to determine with certainty how often officers inflicted the lash on their men. Extant records, however, suggest that the use of this punishment varied from ship to ship. Some officers frequently used flogging to keep their men in line, especially during a long sea voyage, while others rarely did.

Officers who did use the lash were increasingly under pressure to end this punishment as the campaign against flogging on the high seas gained momentum during the 1830s and 1840s. Congress initially responded to the public clamor by requiring quarterly reports of naval punishment starting in 1840. Finally on September 28, 1850,

---

[1] Myra C. Glenn, *Campaigns Against Corporal Punishment: Prisoners, Sailors, Women, and Children in Antebellum America* (Albany: State University of New York Press, 1984) and Glenn, "The Naval Reform Campaign Against Flogging: A Case Study in Changing Attitudes Toward Corporal Punishment, 1830–1850," *American Quarterly* 35 (Fall 1983): 407–25; Harold D. Langley, *Social Reform in the United States Navy, 1798–1862* (Urbana: University of Illinois Press, 1967), 131–206.

Congress prohibited the use of flogging on both naval and commercial vessels.[2]

The campaign against maritime flogging was part of a broad antebellum movement against sanguinary punishments in the United States. Restricting, if not abolishing altogether, the infliction of corporal punishment in schools, prisons, asylums, as well as on seafaring vessels increasingly gained public support in the United States, especially among middle-class Americans in the urban Northeast, the epicenter of antebellum reform.[3]

Opposition to such punishment in turn reflected a fundamental belief gaining ascendancy in the Western, especially Anglo-American world, namely, that it was barbaric to inflict pain and suffering on others. Such a belief propelled various transatlantic developments, including campaigns against cruelty to animals, war, dueling, and the growing use of anesthetics. Groups that had long been targeted for abuse, such as the insane, criminals, and slaves, were now objects of sympathy. Abolitionists' barrage of factual narratives and sentimental fiction as well as their powerful visual images of slaves suffering mobilized a widespread movement against the "peculiar institution." Opponents of capital punishment argued that it was immoral for the state to destroy criminals' bodies, no matter how heinous their

---

[2] The best discussion of flogging and other punishments on board American naval ships prior to 1815 is Christopher McKee, *A Gentlemanly and Honorable Profession: The Creation of the U.S. Naval Officer Corps, 1794–1815* (Annapolis, MD: Naval Institute Press, 1991), 233–54; 261–67. For analysis of these issues during the 1815–1860 period, see the sources cited in endnote 1 and Matthew Raffety, "Discipline But Not Punish: Legality and Labor Control at Sea, 1790–1861," in *Pirates, Jack Tar, and Memory: New Directions in American Maritime History*, eds., Paul A Gilje and William Pencak (Mystic, CT: Mystic Seaport, 2007), 183–205; Raffety, "The Republic Afloat: Violence, Labor, Manhood, and the Law at Sea, 1789–1861" (PhD diss., Columbia University, 2005), 99–186. See also James E. Valle, *Rocks & Shoals: Order and Discipline in the Old Navy 1800–1861* (Annapolis, MD: Naval Institute Press, 1980). On legislation regarding naval flogging see Leo F.S. Horan, "Flogging in the U.S. Navy: Familiar Facts Regarding Its Origin and Abolition," *United States Naval Institute Proceedings* (September 1950): 965–75. For quantitative data on flogging in antebellum American vessels, see McKee, *A Gentlemanly and Honorable Profession*, 479–83; Glenn, *Campaigns Against Corporal Punishment*, 155–64; Briton Cooper Busch, *"Whaling Will Never Do for Me" : The American Whaleman in the Nineteenth Century* (Lexington: University Press of Kentucky, 1994), 26–27.

[3] Glenn, *Campaigns Against Corporal Punishment*.

offenses. Similarly, reformers demanded humane treatment for those incarcerated in prisons and asylums.[4]

The belief that every human being had an innate right to control his/her own body, to exercise self ownership over it, fueled these various reform movements. Closely related to this belief was another, namely, that it was necessary to protect the body from abuse and degradation because it was a creation of God and therefore invested with inalienable rights. The body, argued a growing number of reformers, possessed an innate integrity, rights, and independence that must be respected by others.[5]

The campaign against the flogging of sailors was ultimately part of a much wider movement against practices that violated the integrity and dignity of the human body. The narratives of former mariners, like those of paroled convicts and runaway slaves, made a crucial contribution to the campaigns against sanguinary and degrading punishments. Such works were part of a relatively new genre of literature, what the historian Thomas Laquer has called "humanitarian narratives."[6] Their graphic descriptions of cruelty were grist for the reformers' mill. They offered firsthand accounts of how numerous punishments, particularly the lash, felt on the human body. In the case of seamen narratives, these works fleshed out the dry statistics on punishment recorded in ships' logs and naval reports to Congress.[7]

[4] The following works offer an overview of these developments: Lynn Hunt, *Inventing Human Rights: A History* (New York: W.W. Norton & Company, 2007), 70–112; Elizabeth B. Clark, "'The Sacred Rights of the Weak': Pain, Sympathy, and the Culture of Individual Rights in Antebellum America," *Journal of American History* 82, no.2 (September 1995): 463–93; Karen Sanchez-Eppler, *Touching Liberty: Abolition, Feminism, and the Politics of the Body* (Berkeley: University of California Press, 1993); G.J. Barker-Benfield, *The Culture of Sensibility: Sex and Society in Eighteenth-Century Britain* (Chicago: University of Chicago Press, 1992); Thomas W. Laqueur, "Bodies, Details, and the Humanitarian Narrative" in *The New Cultural History*, ed. Lynn Hunt (Berkeley: University of California Press, 1989), 176–204. Michel Foucault, *Discipline and Punish: The Birth of the Prison*, trans. Alan Sheridan (New York: Pantheon Books, 1977), argues that newer forms of discipline could be more oppressive and invasive than earlier ones. Yet this does not alter the fact that most reformers were seeking more humane ways to govern human beings and genuinely sympathized with their sufferings and pain.

[5] See esp. Hunt, *Inventing Human Rights*, 29–30, 82–83; Clark, "Sacred Rights of the Weak" and Sanchez-Eppler, *Touching Liberty*.

[6] Laqueur, "Bodies, Details, and the Humanitarian Narrative."

[7] See endnote 2 for discussion of antebellum records on punishment.

Narratives by former seamen, convicts, slaves, and other groups who suffered harsh discipline challenged the American public to view the recipients of abuse not simply as nameless, abstract victims but as individuals with as much claim to their personhood and rights as anyone else. They also highlighted a crucial point: the power to punish was the power to control, subjugate, those who were being disciplined.[8]

To highlight this point seamen authors detailed the ritualistic, performative aspects of inflicting flogging on the high seas.[9] They described how armed officers in full dress uniform assembled on the quarterdeck while the crew assembled on the spar deck, after hearing the boatswain's cry "all hands ahoy to witness punishment." The prisoner, often dressed in his best clothes in hopes of softening the captain's disposition, appeared on deck with a guard of marines and the master-at-arms. His hands and feet were then tied to the grating and the boatswain commenced whipping, often with the cat-o-nine tails.[10]

In the end, maritime flogging was a carefully constructed spectacle, a drama, designed to highlight and reinforce the hierarchy of power on board a vessel. The way in which this punishment was inflicted was almost as important as the act itself. The ritual or spectacle of flogging on the high seas dramatized the authority of the officers, especially the captain, and the subordination of the crew. Flogging both figuratively and literally inscribed the power of the captain on the bodies of the victims. But it also imprinted this power on the minds of the spectators, on those forced to witness the gory performance repeatedly during a voyage.[11]

Antebellum sailors used their narratives to illuminate the power relationships that fostered flogging on the high seas as well as to convey the anguish of the men who experienced or witnessed this punishment. What made their discussion of these issues so compelling was how they viewed them through the prism of concerns about manliness

---

[8] My analysis builds on the work of other scholars. See the texts cited in endnote 4 and Janet Moore Lindman and Michele Lise Tarter, eds., *A Centre of Wonders: The Body in Early America* (Ithaca, NY: Cornell University Press, 2001),esp. 2–6.

[9] On the theatrics of flogging with the cat-o-nine tails, see Greg Dening, *Mr. Bligh's Bad Language: Passion, Power and Theatre on the Bounty* (Cambridge: Cambridge University Press, 1992), 144–45.

[10] Leech, *A Voice from the Main Deck*, 24–25, and Hazen, *Five Years Before the Mast*, 220–21. See also Langley, *Social Reform in the United States Navy*, 139–41.

[11] Dening, *Mr. Bligh's Bad Language*, 116, 144–45, and Raffety, "The Republic Afloat," 8, 142–44, 194.

and nationalism. Analysis of seamen authors' recollections of maritime flogging develops these arguments and deepens our understanding of their autobiographical works.

James Durand's account of the whippings he saw or suffered while on board the *Constitution* during the years 1805 to 1807 undoubtedly jarred his fellow Americans.[12] Most of them viewed the *Constitution* or "Old Ironsides" as the premier ship in the U.S. Navy. Its exploits, especially during the War of 1812, were already legendary by the time Durand's memoir first appeared in 1817.[13]

This former mariner sought to puncture his countrymen's heroic view of the *Constitution* by portraying many of its officers as cruel, even sadistic disciplinarians. The first lieutenant, Durand asserted, had a "fiendish disposition." This officer ordered Durand to be flogged when he erred in finding his station shortly after his arrival on board. Thinking that the boatswain did not lash Durand hard enough, the lieutenant took over the job. Bitterly Durand remembered that "the Lieutenant flog[ged] me until he was weary" (24).

Durand's recollection of flogging was at the cusp of seamen authors' accounts of punishment on the high seas. Later sailor autobiographies and memoirs, especially those published after Dana's book, offered graphic, detailed discussions of what mariners suffered at the hands of allegedly tyrannical officers. These works targeted whipping as a particularly painful and humiliating punishment for Jack Tar, one that threatened his manliness.

Sailors' recollections of maritime discipline risked titillating the public, of encouraging a sadistic taste for cruelty. Much like the penny press's sensationalistic coverage of brutal crimes, exposés of punishment whetted the public's appetite for the "pornography of pain."[14]

---

[12] Unfortunately there is no extant logbook for the USS *Constitution* for the 1805–1807 period. But the "Muster and Pay Rolls of the U.S. Frigate *Constitution*" lists James Duran as being on board. See muster roll, no. 737, p. 89 and pay roll, no. 887, p. 125, "Miscellaneous Records of the U.S. Navy, Naval Records & Library," Roll # 93, RG 45, NA, Washington, DC.

[13] Tyrone G. Martin, *A Most Fortunate Ship: A Narrative History of Old Ironsides*, rev.ed. (Annapolis, MD: Naval Institute Press, 2003), 1–207.

[14] Karen Halttunen, *Murder Most Foul: The Killer and the American Gothic Imagination* (Cambridge, MA: Harvard University Press, 1998), 60–90; Halttunen, "Humanitarianism and the Pornography of Pain in Anglo-American Culture," *The American Historical Review* 100, no. 2 (April 1995): 303–34.

Yet this was a risk that recipients of harsh punishment had to take if they were to delineate the cruelties that occurred in institutions generally off limits to the public. Seamen memoirists and autobiographers understood this. Like slaves abused in a remote plantation or inmates incarcerated in a penitentiary or asylum, sailors suffered punishments that most Americans never saw. Vivid, even lurid, depictions of harsh discipline on the high seas, therefore, were necessary to expose a world isolated from the public's prying eyes.[15]

Such descriptions were also necessary to undermine Americans' pride in their maritime officer corps. The recent sea victories in the War of 1812 had burnished the reputations of American officers, especially those in the U.S. Navy. Former sailors sought to deflate these reputations by exposing the cruelty that allegedly lay behind the benevolent face officers showed to the public.

They often portrayed officers in much the same way that popular antebellum crime narratives demonized murderers. Both kinds of narratives encouraged the public to view the perpetrator of violence as fiendish, a man in name only who was beyond the pale of civilized society.[16] Seamen authors' depiction of officers who flew into rages and relished inflicting the lash also seemed much like the monstrous Simon Legree in *Uncle Tom's Cabin*. Ironically, however, author Harriet Beecher Stowe made Legree a former sailor.[17] By contrast, ex-mariners who authored recollections of their seafaring years suggested that it was seemingly gentlemen officers, not sailors, who were the true monsters on the high seas.

As they fleshed out their arguments, seamen memoirists and autobiographers challenged the confident nationalism that antebellum Americans began constructing after the War of 1812 ended. They

---

[15] Michael Meranze, *Laboratories of Virtue: Punishment, Revolution, and Authority in Philadelphia, 1760–1835* (Chapel Hill: University of North Carolina Press, 1996), esp. 204–13, and Karen Halttunen, "Gothic Mystery and the Birth of the Asylum: The Cultural Construction of Deviance in Early Nineteenth-Century America" in *Moral Problems in American Life: New Perspectives on Cultural History*, eds. Karen Halttunen & Lewis Perry (Ithaca, NY: Cornell University Press, 1998), 41–57, have shaped my analysis of how exposés described punishments increasingly hidden from public view.

[16] Halttunen, *Murder Most Foul*, 4–6, 35, 46–49, 56–59.

[17] Harriet Beecher Stowe, *Uncle Tom's Cabin or Life among the Lowly*, ed. Ann Douglas, Penguin Classics (1852; repr., New York: Viking Penguin Inc., 1986), 477, 527–29.

exposed the dark underside of the much praised naval and commercial fleet of the United States. Abuse and tyranny, they repeatedly declared, all too often marred the lives of the men who made possible the nation's successes in sea battle and overseas commerce.

William Murrell's 1840 memoir, an account of his naval service on board the *Columbia* during its 1838–1840 voyages around the world, offered an especially rich illustration of how sailor writers developed the above issues.[18] Although it purported to be a description of the *Columbia*'s global journeys, Murrell's book became an exposé of harsh, even cruel maritime discipline. The author pointedly rebuked those who naively believed that officers were decent men. "Landsmen," he fumed, "would not credit the various scenes of cruelty and tyrannic oppression" which he witnessed and suffered at the hands of "gentlemen of the epaulette" (45).

Murrell vilified the *Columbia*'s commanding officer, Commodore George C. Read, as a "sea monster" filled with "pride, hatred, and revenge" (177). He was "a wretch, deaf to all feelings of humanity" (36); a man who "trample[d] underfoot all the laws and rights of civilized humanity" (175–76). Read allegedly ordered numerous men, including Murrell, to be flogged for trivial offenses.[19] One incident in particular enraged Murrell. Read supposedly had thirteen gravely ill men whipped for being too slow in reefing the sail. These men could "scarcely *crawl* round the decks," exclaimed Murrell, and still they were flogged (176).

Murrell's scorching portrait of Read was diametrically opposed to the one offered by the chaplain of the *Columbia*, the Reverend W. Fitch Taylor. In his memoir Taylor portrayed Read as an outstanding commander, one who displayed the bravery and professionalism of the United States' naval forces. Taylor was so impressed with Read that he dedicated his book to him.[20]

---

[18] Murrell's name appears on the muster roll of the USS *Columbia*. He is number 363, discharged on June 27, 1840. See "Muster Rolls from the USS *Columbia*, October 31, 1837 to October 25, 1847," vol. 506, box 41, RG 217, NA, Washington, DC.

[19] Murrell discussed numerous incidents of flogging throughout his book. On his flogging, see 137–38.

[20] Fitch W. Taylor, *A Voyage Round the World, and Visits to Various Foreign Countries, in the United States Frigate Columbia ...*, 2 vols. (New Haven, CT: H. Mansfield & New York: D. Appleton & Co., 1846).

The logbook of the *Columbia* offered another perspective on Read. Although this document had no record of the cruel incident Murrell described or of his being flogged, it did show that sailors were regularly whipped for significant breaches of naval discipline. These included theft, fighting, drunkenness, sleeping on duty, and attempted desertion.[21] At the very least, Read was a commander who readily used the lash to discipline his men.

To sift through the different documents available on the *Columbia*'s 1838–1840 voyages is to recognize that Murrell may have elided the complex reality surrounding the administration of punishment on board his vessel. His graphic if skewed recollection of Read sought to jolt readers into recognizing that seemingly humane officers could become sadistic tyrants once they were at sea.

Jacob Hazen also offered a gripping exposé of the cruelty of maritime officers in his 1854 memoir. He had joined the USS *Independence* early in 1839 while it was in Rio de Janeiro. He did so hoping to return to the United States after a brief impressment in the Brazilian Navy and service on board American whalers. Frequently transferred to different American frigates before his discharge from the U.S. Navy in January 1842,[22] Hazen saw plenty of his shipmates flogged. He also experienced the lash himself.

His narrative conveyed how angry he was with those who had a positive view of America's maritime officers. Significantly, Hazen

[21] Logbook of the *Columbia*, January 13, 1838 to June 28, 1840, is in "Records of Bureau of Naval Personnel, ... Logs of U.S. Naval Ships, 1801–1915," vol.1, RG 24, NA, Washington, DC. Murrell could very well have been flogged and his punishment not recorded, especially if it was administered summarily with a colt. Unlike the cat-o-nine tails, the colt was often casually inflicted by subordinate officers. See Horan, "Flogging in the U.S. Navy," 971–72; Langley, *Social Reform in the United States Navy*, 141. Significantly, Murrell recalled that the second lieutenant ordered the boatswain to whip him on the spot when he accidentally spilled some ink on a ladder (137–38).

[22] According to Hazen, *Five Years Before the Mast*, 161,164, he joined the *Independence* about three months before April 1839. There is corroboration for the major ships on which Hazen says he served. The "Muster Roll of the USS *Columbus*," vol. 480, No. 1279, Box 37, RG 217, NA, Washington, DC, shows him coming on board on December 1, 1840 and being discharged on January 11, 1842. The logbook of the *Fairfield* shows that a number of men from the *Columbus*, including Hazen, were received on board on May 27, 1841. For logbook see "Records of the Bureau of Naval Personnel ... Logs of US Naval Ships, 1801–1915," vol. 14, RG 24, NA, Washington, DC.

made it a point of noting how he tried to disabuse a "lady missionary" who visited the USS *Columbus* that the ship's officers were "very
polite and agreeable" men. Confined in irons and awaiting punishment, Hazen was obviously exasperated with this woman's gullibility.
He recalled that he shocked her when he stressed how many officers cursed and flogged their men for trivial offenses. Appearances,
pointedly added Hazen, were deceiving. Echoing Murrell, Hazen
asserted: "if you were to encounter Satan himself, you would most
likely meet him with a smile on his face and an epaulet on his shoulder" (214–17).

Hazen dramatized his scathing indictment of naval officers by
providing a particularly graphic discussion of what floggings did to
mariners. His words conveyed not only how painful and gory these
punishments were but also how they unmanned sailors, those who
witnessed as well as experienced the lash. This was evident when
Hazen recalled his reaction to seeing a sailor whipped on board the
Columbus for attempted desertion:

When they [the cat-o-nine tails] were elevated over the shoulder of poor
Summers, I could scarcely repress a tear in commiseration of the torment
he was about to suffer.... The blow descended, and the skin flew, while the
excoriated marks of the cords that stretched from shoulder to shoulder, were
immediately suffused with gore... (221)

What made this incident so poignant for Hazen was that he was next
due to be flogged. His alleged offense was that he had failed to obey
an order and do his duty. Repeatedly the captain silenced Hazen as he
tried to explain that he was a member of the *Preble*'s crew who had
been sent by some "unaccountable means" on a work detail with the
men of the *Columbus* and mistaken as a member of this ship.

In his memoir Hazen conveyed the agony of what he endured as he
was stripped naked and whipped with a cat-o-nine tails that had been
"soaked in salt water":

I turned my face away, and for a minute became unconscious of what was
passing around me. I heard only a confused murmur, and a rushing sound,
while a heavy blow descended on my back, suspending my breath, and pen-
etrating every fibre of my body with a pain more excruciating than if molten
metal had been poured upon me, seething and scorching my flesh to the very
marrow. Could I at that instant have recovered my breath, I would perhaps
have yelled out for mercy, but I was unable to do so. (223)

Fortunately Hazen's punishment abruptly ended when the first lieutenant of the *Preble* came on board, corroborated his story, and pro-
cured his release. But later on board the *Fairfield*, a vessel noted for
harsh discipline, Hazen suffered the full dozen lashes with a colt for
not removing a spot of paint from his hammock.[23] He recalled that he
"almost fainted with pain" from this punishment (294–95).

Images of sailors almost crying or fainting, of being so overcome
that they could not even scream for mercy, illustrated how a flogging
stripped mariners of their manly qualities and made them behave in
ways gendered feminine in antebellum America. Depictions of sailors
agonizing under the lash also suggested that Jack Tar was subject to
a particularly degrading, emasculating punishment since it was one
regularly inflicted on slaves.

Many seamen authors made explicit the comparison between slaves
and American mariners. They repeatedly hammered away at a central
point: to whip Jack Tar was to debase him to the level of a slave and
thereby strip him of his manly independence and pride. Not surprisingly, this argument became prominent in sailor narratives published
during the 1840s and 1850s, decades when the antislavery movement
gained momentum and the trope of the whipped slave became a standard image in abolitionist iconography.

Dana arguably offered the most vivid illustration of how the lash
allegedly enslaved and therefore emasculated white American sailors
when he recalled a heated exchange between the *Pilgrim*'s captain and
a sailor about to be flogged. When the latter objected to his punishment
by declaring: "I'm no negro slave," the captain responded: "Then I'll
make you one." The commander whipped this sailor and another who
interceded on his behalf. Throughout the ordeal the captain screamed
to his crew: "I'll make you toe the mark, every soul of you, or I'll
flog you all, fore and aft,... You've got a driver over you! Yes, a *slave
driver* – a *negro-driver*! I'll see who'll tell me he isn't a negro slave!"
(152–53, 156).

Dana stressed that each man reacted in different ways to his punishment. John was a "foreigner and high-tempered" whose chief reaction

[23] There is no record of Hazen's punishment in the *Fairfield* logbook but this is
not surprising since he was whipped with a colt and not the cat-o-nine tails. For
punishment on board the *Fairfield* in the late 1830s and early 1840s, see also
endnote 26.

to his flogging was anger and desire for revenge. But it was the other whipped man who especially troubled Dana. His name was Sam and Dana stressed that he was a white American from a slave state who had often "amused" his shipmates with "queer negro stories." But such tales ended after his whipping. This punishment, stressed Dana, "seemed to completely break him [Sam] down. He had a feeling of the degradation that had been inflicted upon him, which the other man was incapable of ... he seldom smiled; [and] seemed to lose all life and elasticity ..." (184–85).

Dana's recollection of this incident highlights several important issues surrounding the antebellum discourse over flogging, issues which were fleshed out in later seamen narratives. First, Dana dramatized how whipping Jack Tar emasculated or "broke" him. It is for this reason that Dana looked away during punishment. He was appalled not only by the gore and pain of the lash and his captain's sadism but also by the humiliation that shipmates endured when subjected to a punishment associated with slavery.

Charles Nordhoff made a similar point in his 1855 memoir *Man-of-War Life*. Forced to witness the "barbarous" lashing of twenty of his shipmates on board the USS *Columbia* for smuggling liquor on board, Nordhoff recalled the horror and "dark humiliation" he felt at seeing "the manhood" of his fellow sailors "scourged out" of them (122). The fact that he received twelve lashes for attempting to desert undoubtedly contributed to Nordhoff's revulsion against the "barbarous tyranny" of flogging.[24] Like Dana, Nordhoff stressed that he turned his face away "from the sickening scene" when his shipmates were flogged (122).

Dana's description of how differently the foreign and the Anglo-American sailor reacted to punishment highlights another crucial issue: the nativist and racial dimensions of the antebellum discourse over flogging. What made this punishment particularly offensive was that it was inflicted on white American men. Although he felt revolted at seeing any sailor, "a man – a human being ... flogged like a beast"

---

[24] John B. Hattendorf, ed., *Man-of-War Life*, xvii, notes Nordhoff's flogging on December 13, 1846. For original source see John D. Hayes, "Record of Punishments, USS *Columbus*, 15 May 1845–26 February 1848," Nimitz Library, Annapolis, MD. Significantly, Nordhoff did not mention his punishment in his memoir. Perhaps it was too painful or humiliating to discuss.

(153), Dana also suggested that it was particularly upsetting to see Anglo-American sailors whipped.

John Ross Browne echoed Dana's views in his 1846 memoir. An Irish-born Kentuckian, Browne was quite open in his contempt for people of color, including the dark skinned Portuguese sailors with whom he served on a seventeen-month whaling cruise in the early 1840s.[25] Yet Browne had nothing but respect and affection for those sailors whom he saw as white Americans. These "genuine son[s] of Neptune" had "blunt, manly qualities," including a "noble generosity" (166).

That many of these men suffered the lash and other harsh discipline while at sea enraged Browne. He asserted that they were as oppressed as slaves, perhaps even more so. Indulging in hyperbole, Browne claimed that there was "no class of men in the world who are so oppressed, so degraded" as the seamen who served on board American whaling vessels. They were allegedly "beyond the sphere of human rights" and during their voyages were "slaves" to "arrogant and despotic" officers (504–06).

Ben-Ezra Stiles Ely shared Browne's view that Jack Tar was as oppressed as a slave. While denouncing the "inhuman" practice of flogging on the high seas in his 1849 memoir, Ely bitterly contended that mariners were subject to "as horrible slavery at sea, as any of the children of Africa in any part of the world." Not content with this statement, Ely asserted that "in nine cases out of ten" American sailors endured worst treatment than any "slave on shore suffered" (41).

It is easy to dismiss such comments as histrionics. But they underscored the sense of grievance and anger seamen authors felt about maritime discipline. Ultimately these writers rebuked their society when they asserted that the practice of flogging degraded Jack Tar to the level of a slave. Why, insistently asked sailor memoirists and autobiographers, did the United States allow free white men who protected the nation's sovereignty and commerce to be subjected to a punishment associated with enslavement and emasculation?

Ely raised this issue in a particularly blunt manner when he chided "gentle reader[s]" who cried "horrible, horrible!" as they read about

---

[25] On Browne's life, see John Seelye's introduction to *Etchings of a Whaling Cruise*, 1–27; *Dictionary of American Biography*, s.v. "Browne, John Ross."

the agony of whipped seamen. These people, complained Ely, needed to recognize their complicity in mariners' sufferings. Flogging on the high seas was "sanctioned by our maritime laws, and these laws have been enacted...by our legislators...elected by the humane people of the United States" (41).

Seamen authors like Ely participated in a larger public discourse when they entwined discussions of flogging with the issue of slavery. During the 1830s and 1840s various genres of literature asserted that white American sailors subject to the lash were no better than slaves. Former petty officers Solomon Sanborn and William McNally, for example, stressed this point in their respective exposés.[26] Although neither man was whipped himself, their narratives offered a litany of abuses, especially floggings, on the high seas. Both authors emphasized that the whip was a slavish and therefore particularly degrading punishment to use on American mariners. Sanborn declared that flogging violated "the Rights of Man" for which America's founders had fought (5). The harsh discipline that he saw on American men-of-war, he claimed, "far exceed[ed] any thing I have every witnessed where slavery exists in its most odious form" (28).

McNally was even shriller when he excoriated Americans for railing against slavery while permitting the lash to debase men who served their country:

Never let American citizens in the northern states rail at slavery, or the punishment inflicted on slaves, or say that it is wrong, so long as their own sons, their own flesh and blood, their own seamen, their own free citizens, and the men to whom they look for protection in case of war, are daily subject to the same treatment as the slaves ... (128)

Perhaps Herman Melville offered the most eloquent indictment of naval flogging in his novel *White Jacket*. Appearing less than a year

---

[26] William McNally, *Evils and Abuses in the Naval and Merchant Service*...(Boston: Cassady and March, 1839). Most of Solomon H. Sanborn, *An Exposition of Official Tyranny in the United States Navy* (New York: n.p. 1841) is an exposé of the abuses he saw when he served as master-at-arms on board the *Fairfield* during the approximate period 1837 to early 1841. Mc Nally, 87–88, also discussed punishments on board this vessel. The muster roll of the USS *Fairfield*, 1828–1829, p. 15, lists McNally as a "boy"; the roll for 1837–1839, p. 89, lists Sanborn as a corporal. See "Miscellaneous Records of US Navy, Naval Records & Library," T829, Roll #43, RG 45, NA, Washington, DC.

before Congress prohibited this punishment, Melville's work was
a fictionalized account of the author's service on board the *United
States* in 1843–1844.[27] Like other critics of the lash, Melville underscored the connection between slavery and whipping: "You see a
human being, stripped like a slave, scourged worse than a hound"
(139). Melville stressed the shame, the humiliation, which a sailor felt
at suffering such punishment: "But what torments must that seaman
undergo, who, while his back bleeds at the gangway, bleeds agonized
drops of shame from his soul!" Significantly, Melville then asked his
readers: "Is it lawful for you, my countrymen, to scourge a man that
is an American? – to scourge him round the world in your frigates?"
(143–44).

That question resounded throughout Melville's text. In the "name
of immortal manhood" he demanded the immediate prohibition of
flogging in the navy. Such a practice, he resolutely declared, must
end immediately because it was "opposed to the essential dignity of
man...oppressive,...utterly repugnant to the spirit of our democratic
institutions; [and] involves a lingering trait of the worst times of a
barbarous feudal aristocracy..." (148).

Congressional opponents of flogging on the high seas shared
Melville's views. Significantly these opponents were also leaders in
the antislavery movement. New Hampshire Senator John Parker Hale,
for example, was the first senator elected on an antislavery ticket. His
indefatigable opposition to slavery was matched only by his opposition to flogging in the U.S. Navy. In fact Hale led the successful
Congressional campaign to prohibit this punishment. He repeatedly
denounced both slavery and flogging as "relics of barbarism." Despite
his opposition to slavery, Hale was not above playing the race card
in his quest to end flogging on board American seafaring vessels.
Ignoring the growing numbers of African American and foreign-born
men on American vessels, he claimed sailors were "not the descendants of the curly headed African" but rather "our brethren...the
fair-haired rosey-cheeked [*sic*] sons of New England and the West."
He therefore wondered how Congress could allow mariners' continued subjection to the "degradation and cruelty" of the lash.[28]

---

[27] Andrew Delbanco, *Melville: His World and Work* (New York: Alfred A. Knopf,
2005), 59–61.
[28] Glenn, *Campaigns Against Corporal Punishment*, 39–40, 112–13, and Langley,
Social Reform in the United States Navy, 169–70. For quotes by Hale, see Langley,

The seamen memoirists and autobiographers who condemned flogging on the high seas did so in the context of these widespread attacks on the "slavish," degrading lash. Although their works rarely approached the eloquence of Melville's novel they did illuminate how fears about enslaving and emasculating American men, especially white European American men, fueled growing objections against flogging on the high seas.

As the movement to prohibit maritime flogging came to a head in the 1840s seamen authors played another trump card in condemning this punishment. They asserted that whipping denied Jack Tar his rights as an American citizen and violated the democratic ideals of the United States. Significantly it was a naturalized American citizen, the English born Samuel Leech, who especially developed this argument.

His 1843 autobiography threaded together concerns about democratic rights, national identity, and manliness and put them at the center of the discussion regarding maritime flogging. Like other seamen authors, Leech condemned American naval officers for their use of the lash. But his indictment was particularly compelling because he began his narrative by counter posing the British and U.S. navies, to the latter's advantage.

Even after more than thirty years Leech had bitter memories of the officers on board his British man-of-war, the *Macedonian*. The midshipmen were "little minions of power" who "ordered and drove" him and other boys "round like a dog" (16). One first lieutenant, ironically named Hope, was "harsh, severe, and fond of seeing the men flogged" (31). But Leech reserved his greatest anger for the men who commanded the *Macedonian*. Lord Fitzroy, he claimed, was a sadist who "gloat[ed]" like a "vulture" as he watched men being flogged (33). His successors were just as bad if not worse. During one captain's tenure flogging was "an almost every-day scene," while Captain Carden was a "heartless, unfeeling lover of whip discipline." Like Shylock, he demanded to have "the whole pound of flesh" from men who pleaded for mercy while they were flogged (40, 51–52).

Leech graphically described how flogging violated mariners' bodies. While describing one *Macedonian* sailor who received four

176; Glenn, 118. For original sources, see the *Congressional Globe*, 30th Cong., 2nd sess., 18:489 and 20: 508 (February 9, 1849 and February 12, 1849).

dozen lashes for drunkenness, Leech recounted the havoc that the cat-o-nine tails caused on this man's body: "His flesh creeps – it reddens as if blushing at the indignity; the sufferer groans; lash follows lash,...the lacerated back looks inhuman; it resembles roasted meat burnt nearly black before a scorching fire ..." (25).

Yet Leech was not content to simply focus on the pain and gore flogging inflicted. He also explored how this punishment degraded sailors by stripping them of their sense of manliness. Flogging, he emphatically declared, "robbed" a seaman of "all self – respect" and made him "a pitied, self-despised, groaning, bleeding wretch" (25). The humiliation inflicted by the lash seared a sailor's character long after the physical scars healed: "the whip...wounded the spirit; it struck the *man*; it begat a sense of degradation he must carry with him to his grave" (66).

The harsh discipline meted out on board British men-of-war, believed Leech, was symptomatic of officers' refusal to recognize the manly worth of their sailors: "[T]he difficulty with naval officers is that they do not treat with a sailor as with a *man* ... they are apt to look at them [their crews] as pieces of living mechanism, born to serve, to obey their orders, and administer to their wishes without complaint." Leech pointedly added that this was "a bad morality and a bad philosophy," especially since there was "often more real manhood in the forecastle than in the ward-room..." (77–78).

Leech highlighted how the issue of manhood permeated former sailors' recollections of flogging on the high seas. He stressed how this punishment stripped or denied mariners of their manliness. He also questioned the manhood of officers who resorted to such a form of discipline. No doubt Leech recognized that his indictment of the British officer corps would play well in the Anglophobic United States.

So too would his initial praise for the U.S. Navy and its officers. Recall that Leech praised both the crew and commander of the *United States*, the ship that defeated and captured the *Macedonian*, as magnanimous victors. He also lauded the American navy for defending "sailors' rights" and renouncing impressment (95, 97). When he recalled his service in 1813 on board the U.S. brig the *Syren*, Leech made it a point of contrasting the "lenient and favorable" treatment he received there with the harsh discipline of the *Macedonian*. In fact he painted an almost idyllic picture of life in the U.S. Navy when he asserted that the captain and officers of the *Syren* were so "kind" that "our crew were as comfortable and as happy as men ever are in a man of war" (118).[29]

This initially rosy view made Leech's later indictment of the American navy all the more powerful. Bitterly he recounted how his illusions about this institution were smashed when he shipped on board the American brig the *Boxer* as an eighteen-year-old ordinary seaman in 1816.[30] There he quickly discovered that American officers could be as cruel as their British counterparts. Leech recalled how the *Boxer*'s captain "flew into a passion" after his steersman committed an error in piloting the brig on the Mississippi and peremptorily decreed that he receive one hundred lashes with a rope's end. Even several days after punishment the pilot's back looked "as if it had been roasted" and he was unable "to stand upright" (163).

It is not a coincidence that Leech's description of this flogging echoed his earlier accounts of the punishment on board the *Macedonian*. Leech wanted his American readers to recognize that their navy could be as cruel and despotic as the British one; that some of their officers behaved much like the "naval demi-gods" and "demi-fiends" that disgraced the British Navy (25, 158–59).

He also wanted his American readers to recognize how their nation betrayed its professed commitment to democracy and individual rights when it emulated the autocratic British Navy. According to Leech it was particularly appalling that the United States, a nation that prided itself on being a republic and safeguarding the rights of its citizens, flogged its mariners. American men, he argued, should be secured "the rights of a citizen, as well on the *planks* as on the *soil* of his country" (161).

Despite his assertion that "a MAN" should never endure "the indignity and brutality" of the lash (165), Leech made it clear that what he found particularly objectionable was the use of the whip on free white men in the service of their nation. Significantly he stated: "Flogging may be needful to awe a slave writhing under a sense of unmerited

---

[29] Michael J. Crawford in his edition of *A Voice from the Main Deck*, xii–xiii, discusses Leech's service in the U.S. Navy.

[30] Leech deserted the *Boxer* on December 20, 1816. See Muster Rolls of U.S. brig *Boxer*, 1815–40, pp. 15, 20, 27, 30, and Payrolls of U.S. brig *Boxer*, 1813–35, pp.24, 46, RG 45, NA, Washington, DC.

wrong, but never should a lash fall on a freeman's back, especially if he holds the safety and honor of his country in his keeping" (32).

Leech's last comments underscore how issues of race and slavery shaped seamen authors' campaign against maritime flogging. These issues continued to resonate in sailor narratives published after Congress prohibited flogging on board naval and commercial vessels. Samuel Holbrook illustrated this point in his autobiography. By the time he published his work in 1857, maritime flogging had been prohibited for almost seven years. Yet Holbrook knew that many southern Congressional leaders and naval officers sought its reinstatement, especially to discipline the growing numbers of foreign seamen in the American Navy.[31]

Holbrook sought to bolster arguments against the lash by reprinting an undated speech of Robert F. Stockton, the former naval commander who became one of the most outspoken critics of naval flogging, especially after he became Senator from New Jersey.[32] Like Stockton, Holbrook stressed that "genuine Tar[s]" who were "American citizens" should never be subject to the "brutalizing lash" (346).

Echoing earlier critics of the lash, Holbrook highlighted the association of whipping with slavery. Significantly, he first discussed the horrors of slavery before turning to the issue of flogging on the high seas. While recalling an 1821 trip to Brazil, Holbrook described the abused slaves he saw on a plantation. Their bodies were emaciated, beaten, and naked. Their faces were a "perfect blank." Indeed the slaves Holbrook saw seemed so stripped of their humanity that he glumly stated: "They looked like anything but human creatures, and I think that if I had ever any doubts about the negro belonging to our race, I am sure that such doubts would now be confirmed" (314). Fears that a whipped sailor could become as dehumanized as those slaves he saw in Brazil haunted Holbrook. It infused with urgency his campaign to scuttle efforts to reinstate the "brutalizing lash."

Ex-mariners used their autobiographical works to dramatize their heartfelt hatred of flogging and to galvanize the public's opposition

---

[31] On efforts to reinstate naval flogging, see Glenn, *Campaigns Against Corporal Punishment*, 130–31, Langley, *Social Reform in the United States Navy*, 199–201.

[32] On Stockton's campaign against naval flogging, see Glenn, ibid., 119, 137–38; Langley, ibid., 183–85, 199.

against it. These writers coupled their denunciations of the lash with recollections of how they and other tars resisted this punishment. Documenting such resistance was imperative for the same reason that documenting opposition to impressment, incarceration, and military attacks were. Defense of one's manhood required resistance to oppression.

This theme reverberated throughout the public discourse over maritime flogging in antebellum America. During the congressional debates over this punishment, Senator John Parker Hale warned that the use of the lash provoked resistance because "sailors are men, and have the feelings of men."[33] Similarly, William McNally declared that proud American mariners would resist being disciplined as slaves: "Seamen know that they are born free, and freemen will never submit to the lash of slavery."[34]

Antebellum federal court records noted how sailors mobilized to protest and halt the practice of whipping on seafaring vessels. As the historian Matthew Raffety has shown, New York courts during the antebellum period repeatedly dealt with cases involving mariners who refused to be punished, especially through whipping. Many of these men risked death or long prison sentences rather than endure the lash.[35] It was not discipline per se to which these men objected, persuasively argues Raffety, it was discipline that "centered on disrespect," that symbolized "personalized attacks on honor and manhood."[36]

The autobiographical narratives of former seamen offered vivid, often poignant illustrations of how they and their shipmates opposed officers who sought to whip them. Moses Smith's 1846 memoir provided a particularly good discussion of this point. He asserted that many "proud, spirited" American sailors would "rather die" than receive a flogging (23). To illustrate his point Smith recalled how one sailor tried to kill himself rather than "be tied up so, like a slave" and whipped. The man gnawed off the ropes that bound him and jumped ship. Fortunately he was rescued from drowning and in the end was not flogged (42).

---

[33] Glenn, *Campaigns Against Corporal Punishment*, 118. For original source, see *Congressional Globe*, 30th Cong., 2nd sess., 20:508 (February 12, 1849).

[34] Mc Nally, *Evils and Abuses in the Naval and Merchant Service, Exposed*, 130.

[35] Raffety, "Republic Afloat," 139–86.

[36] Ibid, 169, 171.

their readers that this punishment fomented violent confrontations between commanders and their crews and even led to mutiny. Such an argument turned the tables on those who defended the practice of whipping sailors by claiming that it was needed to discipline unruly men and preserve order while at sea.[39] It was the use of the lash, cogently countered seamen authors, which caused mariners to become insubordinate, even mutinous.

Seamen authors struck a powerful nationalist chord when they noted how maritime flogging imperiled the order and security of the nation's seafaring vessels. They also appealed to Americans' sense of nationalism when they recalled how native-born sailors deserted or refused to reenlist in order to escape the lash. Such arguments fueled their countrymen's concerns about the failure of the maritime services to attract a sufficient number of American recruits and their increasing reliance on foreign sailors.[40] They offered needed ammunition to the congressional leaders and naval officers who campaigned against the use of flogging on the high seas by invoking these concerns.[41]

Seamen memoirists and autobiographers staunchly defended the countless mariners who protested the lash by deserting or refusing to reenlist. Significantly these writers invoked a sailor's right as a free man and an American citizen to resist cruel, degrading punishment. John Ross Browne did this when he defended one mariner who deserted a cruel captain and was then recaptured and imprisoned in irons for months. What right, angrily asked Browne, did anyone have to punish this deserter when he was justifiably asserting his "rights

[39] For discussions of antebellum defenders of maritime flogging, see Glenn, *Campaigns Against Corporal Punishment*, 115–17, 130–31; Langley, *Social Reform in the United States Navy*, 181–82.
[40] Langley, ibid., 89–92, 98–100.
[41] See, for example, naval surgeon John P. Lockwood [Anonymous], *An Essay on Flogging in the Navy; Containing Strictures Upon Existing Naval Laws and Suggesting Substitutes for the Discipline of the Lash* (New York: Pudney & Russell, Printers, 1849), esp. 27. This essay originally appeared as "Flogging in the Navy," *United States Magazine and Democratic Review* 25 (1849): 97–115; 225–42; 318–37; 417–32. Stockton made a similar point in the *Cong. Globe*, 32nd Cong., 1st sess, 24 : Part 1 :219–20 (January 7,1852). See also Sanborn, *Exposition of Official Tyranny in the United States Navy*, 4. McNally, *Evils and Abuses in the Naval and Merchant Service, Exposed*, 134, stressed that the practice of flogging also hindered recruitment on board whalers.

as a man and an American citizen" by seeking to escape his "slavish position" (488).

Seamen authors made it clear that they spoke from painful personal experience when they defended mariners who deserted. Holbrook made no apologies for planning to desert a ship where the lash was frequently used. Just hearing the "dreadful" shrieks of flogged men and witnessing their humiliation, he declared, caused feelings that "work[ed] like an avalanche upon me." Only his promotion to a warrant officer, which put him "out of the reach of the lash," prevented Holbrook's desertion (98, 101).

Most seamen authors were not as fortunate as Holbrook. They either suffered the lash or faced the threat of it during their seafaring years. Some of these writers admitted that they deserted vessels characterized by harsh treatment. Horace Lane regularly deserted vessels where he suffered floggings and other harsh treatment. Early in his seafaring career, for example, Lane deserted a merchant vessel because the captain repeatedly cursed and taunted him for wanting to go to school. This officer also gave Lane "many severe floggings, for trifling, frivolous reasons." When the next merchant vessel he shipped on proved to be as abusive, Lane again deserted (33–34). Similarly, Leech deserted the *Boxer*. After six years of witnessing the "ill usage" of his crew mates and "trembling for my own back," Leech recalled that he "became completely sickened" with "man-of-war life" and resolved "to get free of it at once and forever" (43–44, 177).

Other seamen authors got free of the lash by refusing to reenlist. Hazen, for example, stressed that it was primarily his hatred of flogging that caused him to decide against continuing in the U.S. Navy. This was apparent when he recalled why he was so jubilant when his naval service ended: "the reign of terror and cat-o-nine tails was over, and I was about to stalk once more into the world an unfettered American citizen" (393). Nordhoff echoed these views when he recounted why he refused to extend his naval service. "I had had a surfeit of bondage," he stated, and only sought "to fling off the long-borne yoke" (255).

Such stories of course burnished mariners' reputation as proud, free American men who bristled at efforts to oppress them, especially through the lash. At times seamen authors misrepresented their past behavior in order to highlight their opposition to this punishment.

Durand may have done this when he recalled how after enduring twelve lashes for a minor offense he deserted the *Constitution* shortly after its arrival in Boston in the fall of 1807. The fact that Durand was punished months after his term of service had expired also aggrieved him. Durand's memoir conveyed his sense of pride in leaving the *Constitution*, even though he lost over $350 in pay: "I considered myself my own man...and quitted the ship" (37–38).

Institutional records offer a very different spin on Durand's desertion. In May of 1826 Congress denied Durand's request to receive the pay he had been owed for his services on board the *Constitution*, noting that he forfeited the money when he deserted. In his petition, however, Durand claimed he had not meant to abandon his ship. The night before the *Constitution* sailed to New York, he was allegedly "engaged in a frolic" in Boston, had "overslept," and missed his vessel's departure.[42]

One will never know the actual reason as to why Durand left the *Constitution* – perhaps it was to protest what he regarded as abusive punishment or perhaps he was too drunk to return to the ship in a timely manner. But for our purposes what is important is how Durand crafted his memoir. His book broached a theme that later seamen narratives fleshed out: Jack Tar was a manly man who resolutely defended his independence and rights by refusing to tolerate a punishment he found cruel, unjust, and emasculating.

The assertion that the use of the lash thwarted the recruitment and retention of native-born American sailors became an effective rhetorical ploy in seamen narratives by the mid 1850s. This was particularly evident in the autobiography by Roland Gould, a work which detailed its author's service on board the USS *Ohio* during its 1839–1841 cruise of the Mediterranean.[43] Gould emphatically asked:

[42] "On a Claim to Pay as a Seaman, Withheld for Alleged Desertion," *American State Papers. Documents, Legislative and Executive, of the Congress of the United States, From the First Session of the Eighteenth to the Second Session of the Nineteenth Congress, Inclusive: Commencing May 13, 1824, and Ending January 5, 1827* (Washington, DC: Gales & Seaton, 1860), vol. II: Naval Affairs, 19th Cong., 1st sess., no. 316, p. 722.

[43] Gould's name appears on both the muster and pay rolls of the *Ohio*. See "Muster Rolls & Pay & Receipt Rolls," USS *Ohio*, no. 376, vol. 1210, box 101, RG 217, NA, Washington, DC. He plagiarized much of his account of the events on board the *Ohio* from F. P. Torrey's *Journal of the Cruise of the United States Ship Ohio...* (Boston: Samuel N. Dickinson, 1841), 49. Torrey's name does not appear on either

What American, who feels the noble impulse of freedom throbbing in his bosom, would ever consent to rivet the chains of slavery upon himself? The clanking of the chains which have been riveted on the few native seamen, who are found in naval service, has served to deter others from selling their birthright for a mess of pottage (191).[44]

Gould's aggrieved tone perhaps reflected his anger over his own treatment on board the *Ohio*: he experienced nine lashes in February 1841 for having a dirty hammock.[45]

Like earlier seamen authors, Gould used his memoir to expose the alleged cruelty of his commander. Captain Joseph Smith, claimed this embittered former mariner, was "a cruel, unmerciful, and heartless tyrant, ... a commander destitute of every manly and ennobling sentiment" (114–15).[46] To document this contention Gould cited the frequent and often illegal floggings that marred the *Ohio*'s voyage, including the practice of whipping sailors more than the stipulated twelve lashes for relatively minor offenses.[47]

Not surprisingly, Gould recalled in his narrative how determined he was to leave the *Ohio* once it arrived in Boston in July 1841, especially since his service had expired months earlier. When officers threatened to confine Gould in double irons, this former mariner proudly recounted how he stood his ground: "I told the master-at-arms, that my term of service had expired, and that I was a citizen, and that if he laid his hands on me he would do it at the peril of his life" (199). Fortunately for both men the captain intervened and set Gould free.[48]

---

the muster or pay rolls of the *Ohio*, suggesting that he used an alias. Linda M. Maloney, *The Captain from Connecticut: The Life and Naval Times of Isaac Hull* (Boston: Northeastern University Press, 1986), 446, speculates that Torrey was the pseudonym of John Peirce Jr., a teacher of mathematics who tutored the *Ohio*'s midshipmen during the voyage.

44 These words also appear in Torrey, *Journal of the Cruise of the United States Ship Ohio*, 111.

45 See the *Ohio* logbook for February 17, 1841. "Records of the Bureau of Naval Personnel...Logs of US Naval Ships, 1801–1915," vol. 3, Log, USS *Ohio*, RG 24, NA, Washington, DC.

46 These words are taken verbatim from Torrey's *Journal*, 49.

47 Gould, *Life of Gould*, 77–78, 83, 106–10. The logbook of the *Ohio* for the period October 11, 1838, to August 3, 1841, corroborates that there was much flogging on board for numerous offenses. During the first week in March 1841, for example, thirty-nine men were flogged. See "Records of Bureau of Naval Personnel...Logs of U.S. Naval Ships, 1801–1915," vol. 3, RG 24, NA, Washington, DC.

48 The logbook, ibid, did not record this incident but it did note on July 18, 1841, that the captain allowed seventy men to go on shore since their terms of service had expired.

Gould's autobiography reprised many of the themes that fueled earlier seamen authors' denunciation of flogging on the high seas. According to these writers, this punishment threatened Jack Tar and the nation on several levels. First, the use of the lash violated the United States' democratic values by allowing maritime officers to act like tyrants. Second, this punishment jeopardized the welfare of the country's naval and commercial fleet by causing American mariners to mutiny, desert, or refuse to re-enlist.

Although seamen authors compellingly argued the above points, what they most stressed was that flogging on the high seas violated Jack Tar's rights as a man and an American citizen. Their graphic images of white male citizens in the service of their country being stripped, tied, and flogged was a powerful and disturbing trope in antebellum America, one that evoked fears of these men's enslavement and emasculation.

Of course the notion of manhood was hardly monolithic in the early republic. Ultimately antebellum Americans refracted discussion of this issue through the lens of class, ethnic, and racial concerns. This was evident when Anglo-American seamen tackled the topic of maritime punishment in their narratives. A minority of these writers revealed how fear of some sailors tempered their defense of Jack Tar's manly rights, particularly his right not to be flogged.

Richard Henry Dana was undoubtedly the most famous example of these authors. Despite his obvious hatred of the lash, Dana asserted towards the end of his memoir that captains must retain the power to whip in order to discipline motley crews drawn from all over the world. What especially alarmed Dana were the growing numbers of men of color, including darker skinned southern Europeans, manning American vessels. There were, he stressed, more "Spaniards, Portuguese, Italians ... together with Lascars, Negroes." But even white Anglo Saxons worried Dana if they were marginal, rootless, and unruly. The "off-casts of British men-of-war," as well as native-born white Americans who went to sea because they "could not be permitted to live on land," he asserted, were "the worst of all." Such sailors could be "pirates or mutineers" and therefore needed strict discipline, including the whip (470–71).

Dana's comments illustrate how class, racial, and ethnic fears intersected to limit his opposition to flogging on the high seas. In the end

Dana's dread of disorder trumped his hostility to this punishment. He upheld a captain's right to flog because he worried that without this power unruly mariners, especially if they were black, dark skinned foreigners, or lower-class Anglo Americans, would take over a ship.

Racial and nativist fears led John Ross Browne to qualify his solidarity with mariners who rebelled against harsh punishment while at sea. During his discussion of sailors' protests against floggings this memoirist boldly declared that mutiny is "a species of crime...inherent in every manly heart" and is sometimes needed to resist "brutal tyranny" (503). But Browne imposed obvious racial limits on rebelling against harsh discipline. He made clear that only "American freemen,"[49] a term coded in the antebellum period to mean white European American men,[50] should resist the oppression of the lash and other forms of tyranny.

Browne even objected to southern European sailors exercising the same rights to rebel as did Anglo Americans. As noted earlier, he regarded his Portuguese shipmates with disdain. He described them as "mere brutes" and claimed that they spent most of their free time "reveling in filth, beating harsh discord on old violas, jabbering in their native language, smoking, cursing, and blackguarding" (41–43). Browne vehemently opposed a work stoppage initiated by these men to protest their captain's harsh discipline and failure to grant them shore leave. He recalled that he became "really wolfish" against the Portuguese and that his "blood boiled with indignation and contempt" when they pressured him to join their protest (311).

Given the virulence of racial and ethnic prejudice in the antebellum United States, Browne's opposition to his shipmates' rebellion is not surprising. Neither is Dana's defense of the lash as a necessary way to discipline unruly men, especially American blacks and swarthy foreigners. The prospect of dark-skinned men rising up to resist treatment that they deemed unmanly and abusive alarmed most Anglo Americans, whether this occurred in Haiti or on board U.S. seafaring vessels.

[49] When Browne used this phrase, it was evident from the context that he meant Anglo-American men like himself. See *Etchings of a Whaling Cruise*, 378, 496.

[50] Gregory L. Kaster, "Labour's True Man: Organized Workingmen and the Language of Manliness in the USA, 1827–1877," *Gender & History* 13, no. 1 (April 2001): 24–64, esp. 26; David Roediger, *The Wages of Whiteness:Race and the Making of the American Working Class*, rev. ed. (London: Verso, 1999), 55–60.

Like so many of their white countrymen, Dana and Browne ultimately had a constricted view of manhood. They were primarily concerned with protecting the manly independence and freedom of men
like themselves. Their grim scenarios about dark skinned seamen taking over U.S. vessels resonated with white citizens increasingly concerned about the diverse crews manning the nation's seafaring fleet.

But it is important to recognize that Browne and Dana were atypical seamen authors. Recall that Dana was the scion of a distinguished,
well-to-do New England family. This Harvard-educated youth sailed
only once as a seaman before settling down to a prosperous life in
Boston. Browne was also a "gentleman sailor." After his seventeen-
month whaling voyage ended, he became a reporter for the *Louisville
Public Advertiser*, a newspaper his father owned. By the time Browne
published his memoir in 1846 he had established himself as a successful journalist and had worked for various government agencies.[51]

These men's privileged backgrounds and relatively short stints as
mariners ultimately limited their identification with the men of the forecastle and made it more likely that their fears of disorder at sea would
outweigh their commitment to defending Jack Tar against the lash.[52] But
this was not the case with most seamen authors. Several factors made
these writers express a greater sense of camaraderie with mariners than
Dana or Browne did. They generally came from the same hardscrabble backgrounds that the majority of seamen did. Unlike "gentlemen
sailors," these men were often mariners for a significant part of their
lives.[53] Finally, many also experienced the lash themselves.

These experiences nurtured in most sailor authors a sense of solidarity with mariners who were flogged. Significantly, the majority of
retired white seamen who published antebellum accounts of their seafaring years demanded an end to this punishment. They stressed that
Jack Tar, irrespective of his color or ethnicity, should never be subject
to such a cruel, humiliating, and unmanly form of discipline.

---

[51] See endnote 25 for information on Browne's life.
[52] Dana scholars have stressed the class divisions that separated this "gentleman sailor"
   from the typical men in the forecastle. See, for example, Bryan Charles Sinche,
   "'The Test of Salt Water': Literature of the Sea and Social Class in Antebellum
   America" (PhD diss., University of North Carolina at Chapel Hill, 2006), 70–100;
   Hugh McKeever Egan, "Gentlemen-Sailors: The First-Person Sea Narratives of
   Dana, Cooper, and Melville" (PhD diss., The University of Iowa, 1983), 59–135.
[53] Chapter 1 discusses these writers' lives.

Perhaps Holbrook best articulated most seamen authors' firm opposition to the lash when he addressed the issue of how to punish foreign-born seamen on American vessels. Strict discipline, he asserted, was especially necessary when dealing with a "heterogeneous mass" of foreign men, everyone "from the Chinaman to the Laplander." Yet Holbrook emphasized that flogging should not be part of this discipline: "abolish the whip. It...should never be upon the back of a man" (347).

Behind such comments was a fundamental belief that all mariners possessed inviolable rights as men which must be respected. Unlike Dana, Holbrook was not willing to compromise this belief when it was foreign-born or nonwhite sailors being disciplined. In the end he upheld the principle that flogging was wrong, irrespective of whether it was used on a sailor who was an Anglo-American citizen of the United States or one who was a "Chinaman" or "Laplander."

Holbrook challenged the dominant white majority in antebellum America to forge a more inclusive notion of manliness when he excoriated maritime flogging. So, too, did Jacob Hazen. His memoir pointedly injected the issues of class and race into the discussion over punishment on the high seas. But unlike "gentlemen sailors," Hazen did this to bolster his arguments against the lash. Punishment, he provocatively argued, reflected profound class differences. Privileged officers allegedly cared little for sailors, men who were "the washerwoman's son, or the orphan child of poverty." Hazen added that officers rarely "dwell on such lowly objects" as mariners, "except by way of discipline, which always carries with it a strong presumption in favor of the cat-o'-nine tails" (231).

No doubt Hazen's impoverished early life and experiences with flogging heightened his animosity against the officer corps. But they also helped him to recognize how maritime discipline both reflected and reinforced positions of power based on class differences in antebellum America. Hazen also articulated how a hierarchy of power based on race and ethnicity as well as class shaped the dynamics of punishment on board seafaring ships.

His memoir offered a gripping account of how he and other Anglo-American sailors joined African American and Portuguese shipmates to protest abusive treatment on the high seas. Hazen described how during one voyage on board a whaler named the *Hudson* the crew went on strike to protest the flogging by the first mate of a fellow sailor William Peterson who was a "negro." Their strike came at a particularly opportune time since the captain needed the crew to unload over one hundred barrels of oil.

Significantly the leader of the mutiny was an African American seaman, Samuel Maloney. Hazen identified "old black Sam" as his friend. He also stressed that the work stoppage ended only when the captain promised to end floggings and publicly rebuked the first mate. Yet Hazen noted that he deserted ship when it arrived in Rio de Janeiro since he feared punishment for his role in the strike (106, 110–19).[54]

Hazen's story illustrates a point noted by scholars of maritime history: a seafaring life could blunt the most virulent forms of racism found on land and foster a sense of camaraderie among antebellum mariners, one that at times outweighed racial and ethnic divisions in the forecastle.[55] But perhaps what is more important for this study is how Hazen's account offered a view of manhood that was racially and ethnically inclusive. Like Holbrook, Hazen urged his white readers to defend the manly independence and rights of all mariners, irrespective of their color, country of origin, or family background.

Seamen authors marshaled powerful arguments against the practice of flogging on the high seas, ones that challenged their countrymen's ideas about nationalism and manhood. They stressed that this punishment was an egregious violation of Jack Tar's rights as an American citizen and also threatened his manhood. Given its associations with slavery, flogging symbolized how a mariner was stripped of the most basic control over his body, how in a sense he was enslaved, emasculated. That it was American officers and not foreign enemies who did this to Jack Tar made flogging all the more objectionable and humiliating.

Seaman memoirists and autobiographers who discussed why flogging occurred in the naval and merchant services often raised an

---

[54] The crew list for the *Hudson's* 1837–1839 voyages appears in Captain Henry Green's journal, Mystic Seaport Museum. It identifies Peterson and Maloney respectively as "Black" and "Negro." Hazen appears as "Jacob Hays" and is listed as a "Raw Hand" who "ran away in Rio." See July 23, 1838, entry.

[55] Raffety, "Republic Afloat," 254; W. Jeffrey Bolster, *Black Jacks: African American Seamen in the Age of Sail* (Cambridge, MA: Harvard University Press, 1997), 131–57; Busch, *Whaling Will Never Do Me*, 32–50.

issue that bedeviled antebellum reformers, namely, mariners' abusive drinking. Sailor narratives stressed that drinking was a leading cause of flogging and other punishment. Many of these works argued that drinking and the carousing that often accompanied it threatened Jack Tar's "manly" independence. In developing these arguments, seamen authors expressed conflicted views about religion and evangelical efforts to reform sailors.

5

Straddling Conflicting Notions of Masculinity

*Sailor Narratives as Stories of Roistering
and Religious Conversion*

In the spring of 1840, the brother of well-known abolitionist and temperance advocate William Lloyd Garrison was at the brink of suicide. James Holley Garrison's alcoholism had destroyed his health and his sixteen-year career as a sailor. By December 1839 he became so incapacitated by drink that his brother pleaded with Secretary of the Navy James Kirk Paulding to release James from naval service. No doubt this must have been a particularly difficult task for William since Paulding was a public defender of slavery.

Shortly after his dismissal from the navy, James began writing penitential reminiscences about his misspent life that he significantly entitled his "confessions." He recalled his numerous drunken bouts on shore leave and how they led to gambling, whoring, theft, and imprisonment. He also recollected suffering repeated whippings and confinement in irons in the navy because of drunkenness. Finally, James detailed the horrors of delirium tremens and admitted several attempts to commit suicide. Toward the end of his life, when he was cared for by different relatives, especially William, James confessed his anguish and yearned for death: "I feel that my constitution is broken, and my frame debilitated,...I do not wish to live under such existing circumstances....(Merrill, 112)." Forty-one-year-old James Holley Garrison finally died in his brother's home on October 14, 1842.[1]

---

[1] Walter McIntosh Merrill, ed., *Behold Me once More: The Confessions of James Holley Garrison* (Boston: Houghton Mifflin Co., 1954). For quote, see 112.

James's confessions make for painful reading as they detail his growing sense of degradation and shame at being a drunkard. Yet another contemporary of Garrison's, William Otter, was anything but contrite as he recounted his drunken, raucous behavior in his 1835 autobiography. Otter's various occupations – he was at different times in his life a conscripted sailor in the British Navy, a New York plasterer, tavern keeper, slave catcher, and local Maryland politician – underscored his restlessness. But irrespective of what occupation he followed, Otter remained a die hard drinker, brawler, bully, and prankster. His autobiography regaled his readers with graphic descriptions of what he called his "sprees," drunken debauchery and fighting in taverns, dance halls, whorehouses, and the public streets. Otter also recounted a litany of sadistic pranks he played on others, especially African Americans and Irish immigrants, as well as his cruelty to animals. Openly contemptuous of both religion and domesticity, Otter seemed to value only one bond, the one he forged with the "jolly fellows" who shared his rowdy, often violent masculine pastimes.[2]

Fortunately, most antebellum American men were neither debauched, sadistic bullies like Otter nor broken down alcoholics like Garrison. Yet the writings of these two men warrant attention because they illuminate an important aspect of antebellum American society: the persistence of a traditional "rough" masculinity, especially among working-class men. Abusive drinking, brawling, whoring, gambling, and participation in blood sports remained for many men a way to prove one's manhood and establish camaraderie with other men. Urban, working-class youths, the B'hoys, as well as firemen, sailors, and waterfront workers, were legendary for embracing a culture of "rough" masculinity.[3] The allure of traditional masculine

[2] Richard B. Stott, ed., *William Otter: History of My Own Times* ... (Ithaca, NY: Cornell University Press, 1995). See also Mechal Sobel, *Teach Me Dreams: The Search for Self in the Revolutionary Era* (Princeton, NJ: Princeton University Press, 2000), 97–103.

[3] Amy S. Greenberg, *Cause for Alarm: The Volunteer Fire Department in the Nineteenth Century City* (Princeton, NJ: Princeton University Press, 1998); Michael Kaplan, "New York City Tavern Violence and the Creation of a Working-Class Male Identity," *Journal of the Early Republic* 15 (Winter 1995): 591–617; Elliot J. Gorn, *The Manly Art: Bare-Knuckle Prize Fighting in America* (Ithaca, NY: Cornell University Press, 1986); Richard B. Stott, *Workers in the Metropolis: Class, Ethnicity, and Youth in Antebellum New York City* (Ithaca, NY: Cornell University

pastimes was evident both among those who reveled in them such as Otter as well as men like Garrison who repeatedly failed to rehabilitate himself.

Yet by the mid-1820s middle-class, evangelical reformers had begun mobilizing against "rough" masculinity and offered an alternative model of manhood. They contended that true manliness demanded piety, sobriety, and self-discipline. The temperance crusade was in the front lines of reformers' efforts to attack traditional notions of masculinity. As the historians Bruce Dorsey and Elaine Frantz Parsons have stressed, this crusade was ultimately "a battle over the nature of manhood in antebellum America." Temperance reformers sought to break the traditional association of manliness with drinking. They argued that liquor enslaved, emasculated men by depriving them of autonomy over their bodies. Liquor "unmanned" a man while abstinence liberated him.[4]

Temperance advocates also argued that alcohol jeopardized the nation's future. Repeatedly they stressed how drinking threatened to plunge the United States into worldly and moral ruin by causing a number of ills – impiety, poverty, crime, disease, and domestic discord. What made this prospect especially appalling for evangelicals was their belief that the United States had been chosen by God to usher in the millennial age, one culminating in the glorious Second Coming of Christ. Alcohol, therefore, was evil because it threatened to destroy the nation entrusted with initiating the regeneration of the world.[5]

Press, 1990), 247–76. For discussion of sailors' embrace of the "rough" masculinity of working-class youth, see Paul A. Gilje, *Liberty on the Waterfront: American Maritime Culture in the Age of Revolution* (Philadelphia: University of Pennsylvania Press, 2004), 10–11, 35–37. By the late nineteenth century, sailors were a symbol of an "oppositional" masculinity that challenged Victorian values. See Valerie Burton, "'Whoring, Drinking Sailors': Reflections of Masculinity from the Labour History of Nineteenth Century British Shipping," in Margaret Walsh, ed., *Working Out Gender: Perspectives from Labour History* (Aldershot, UK: Ashgate, 1999), 84–101.

[4] Elaine Frantz Parsons, *Manhood Lost: Fallen Drunkards and Redeeming Women in the Nineteenth Century United States* (Baltimore, MD: Johns Hopkins University Press, 2003), 53–74; Bruce Dorsey, *Reforming Men and Women: Gender in the Antebellum City* (Ithaca, NY: Cornell University Press, 2002), 113–31. For quote, see 124.

[5] Robert H. Abzug, *Cosmos Crumbling: American Reform and the Religious Imagination* (New York: Oxford University Press, 1994), 79–104, especially develops this theme.

Temperance crusaders conjoined themes of nationalism and manhood. They sought to protect the United States and its allegedly millennial mission by promoting an evangelical model of manhood, rooted in piety, sobriety, and self-restraint. Sailors played an important role in this endeavor. Evangelicals increasingly targeted seamen for reformation while the waterfront culture with its traditional pleasures and rowdiness retained its allure.[6] Seamen's bodies, how to discipline and reform them, became a major concern. For many reformers debauchery was as much a threat to a sailor's manhood and the nation's progress as the practices of impressment and flogging.

As these comments suggest, American sailors were once again at the center of an important public discourse in antebellum America, one dealing with evangelical efforts to prohibit drinking and other traditional male pastimes regularly found in seaports. How did sailors experience and regard the waterfront culture? How did they respond to reformers' efforts to destroy that culture? To what extent did antebellum mariners embrace the evangelical model of masculinity espoused by reformers? Historians have begun exploring these questions by utilizing a wide range of sources, including sailors' songs, broadsides, diaries, and letters.[7]

Chapter 5 will contribute to this literature by focusing on the published autobiographies and memoirs of antebellum mariners. Such writings offer vivid descriptions of how these authors and many of their comrades experienced the raucous waterfront culture and the evangelical crusade against it. They also suggest the obstacles mariners faced in forging successful lives for themselves after their seafaring years ended.

[6] Dan Hicks, "True Born Columbians: The Promises and Perils of National Identity for American Seafarers of the Early Republican Period" (PhD diss., The Pennsylvania State University, 2007), 114–24; Gilje, *Liberty on the Waterfront*, 195–227; Gilje, "On the Waterfront: Maritime Workers in New York City in the Early Republic, 1800–1850," *New York History* 77 (October 1996): 395–426; Steven H. Park, "'Three Sheets to the Wind': Marine Temperance in Antebellum Nineteenth-Century America," *International Journal of Maritime History* 13, no. 1 (June 2001): 137–49.

[7] Besides the works cited above, see Margaret S. Creighton, *Rites & Passages: The Experience of American Whaling, 1830–1870* (Cambridge: Cambridge University Press, 1995); Briton Cooper Busch, *"Whaling Will Never Do for Me": The American Whalemen in the Nineteenth Century* (Lexington: University of Kentucky Press, 1994), 104–34.

Yet the narratives of sailor authors did not merely describe seamen's experiences. They also interpreted those experiences and the values underpinning them. In many respects sailor authors were cultural mediators. They mediated between career seamen and the middle-class Americans who bought and read most books, including theirs. Even when they supported prescribed evangelical values, sailor authors often interpreted them in ways that challenged middle-class reformers. Their narratives were often conflicted texts, straddling competing notions of masculinity. Seamen authors professed allegiance to reformers' model of masculinity, one characterized by sobriety, discipline, and restraint. Yet these writers often challenged, even subverted, this model when they depicted the attractions of the traditional, roistering masculinity prominent on the waterfront. To explore these tensions, one must first examine the evangelical crusade to reform Jack Tar.

As James Holley Garrison lay dying in his brother's home and William Otter continued his roistering, the temperance movement gained momentum. Supporters of this movement spread their message through various means. Temperance parades and meetings run much like revivals attracted thousands. After 1815 temperance works flooded the literary market. They included plays such as "The Drunkard" and the prolific T. S. Arthur's numerous short stories and novels, including the 1854 bestseller *Ten Nights in a Bar-Room*. Dramatic performances by recovering alcoholics like John Gough as well as sermons and lectures by noted revivalist preachers such as the Reverend Lyman Beecher also enjoyed widespread popularity. The Washingtonians, an organization of recovering alcoholic men mostly from the working class, popularized the temperance message in the 1840s through their graphic testimonials of the horrors of abusive drinking. As these developments suggest, the temperance movement became a form of mass entertainment as well as a moral crusade by the mid-1840s.[8]

---

[8] Graham Donald Warder, "Selling Sobriety: How Temperance Reshaped Culture in Antebellum America" (PhD diss., University of Massachusetts at Amherst, 2000); William R. Sutton, *Journeymen for Jesus: Evangelical Artisans Confront Capitalism in Jacksonian Baltimore* (University Park: Pennsylvania State University Press,1998), 267–76; Teresa Anne Murphy, *Ten Hours' Labour: Religion, Reform, and Gender in Early New England* (Ithaca: Cornell University Press, 1992), 101–30. Earlier works on antebellum temperance remain essential reading. See particularly Ian R. Tyrrell, *Sobering Up: From Temperance to Prohibition in Antebellum America, 1800–1860* (Westport, CT: Greenwood Press, 1979). See also the works cited in endnote 4.

Temperance advocates singled out sailors, long renowned for their drinking, as targets for reform. In fact the trope of the intoxicated, debauched sailor became a staple of antebellum temperance literature. Didactic tales purportedly written by former sailors who were recovering alcoholics cautioned young men against succumbing to the lure of alcohol and other vices. The titles of such works underscored their temperance message: *My Drunken Life, The Disenthralled*, and *The Reformed*.[9] Paradoxically, these stories reinforced a seaman's reputation for drunkenness even as they promised his reformation by conversion to the temperance cause.

Like most stereotypes, that of the drunken sailor offered a distorted, simplistic image of a complex reality. Of course most mariners were not alcoholics, nor did many suffer James Garrison's tragic denouement. Yet the logs of numerous vessels document that alcohol abuse was a serious problem for many antebellum seafaring men. Naval ship logs, for example, show that sailors were punished because they were caught smuggling liquor on board, stealing the grog ration, drinking while on duty, or returning from shore leave "three sheets to the wind."[10]

Such records were grist for the reformers' mill and promoted a movement to abolish the grog ration in the navy. Many of the same people who led the opposition to naval flogging also led the movement to abolish the grog ration. Senators John Parker Hale and Robert Stockton, for example, pointed out that alcohol related offenses were a major cause of punishment on the high seas. For this reason, they intertwined their campaigns against the lash and grog. Reformers argued that abolition of the grog ration would end much of the insubordination and incompetence that caused flogging on the high seas. Their efforts finally led to Congressional abolition of the grog ration on July 14, 1862.[11]

---

[9] Jacob Carter, *My Drunken Life, in Fifteen Chapters, ...* (Boston: The Author, 1847); Joseph Gatchell, *The Disenthralled: Being Reminiscences in the Life of the Author ...* 3rd ed. (Troy, NY: N. Tuttle, 1845); John Elliott, *The Reformed: An Old Sailor's Legacy* (Boston: Usher & Strickland, 1841).

[10] Myra C. Glenn, *Campaigns Against Corporal Punishment: Prisoners, Sailors, Women, and Children in Antebellum America* (Albany: State University of New York Press, 1984), 155–64.

[11] Harold D. Langley, *Social Reform in the United States Navy, 1798–1862* (Urbana: University of Illinois Press, 1967), 207–69, esp. 249–55, 265–66.

The movement against grog was ultimately part of a much broader agenda to armor Jack Tar against vice. Reformers established a network of institutions designed to replace the raucous boarding houses, brothels, dance halls, and taverns that traditionally graced the waterfront. These included mariner churches where dynamic preachers like the ex-sailor the Reverend Edward Taylor evangelized seamen. Numerous Bethel societies as well as seamen's saving banks and "dry" boarding houses known as Sailor Homes underscored the ambitious agenda of the reformers. The American Seamen's Friend Society, formed in 1826, and its flagship journal *The Sailor's Magazine and Naval Journal* served as clearing houses for many reform endeavors.[12]

Sailors responded in different ways to reformers' efforts. Although a minority converted to the evangelical agenda,[13] countless others continued to indulge in the traditional pleasures of the waterfront and to enjoy their daily grog ration while at sea. Significantly antebellum court records referred to sailors as unusually "aggressive" and "disorderly" men, characterized by drunken, raucous behavior.[14] Efforts to end or decrease the grog ration sometimes resulted in sailors rioting as they did in 1839 in the New York harbor.[15] For many mariners, grog was a needed stimulant on cold, wet nights as well as one of their few sources of pleasure while at sea.

Many sailors also resisted what they regarded as reformers' meddling in their traditional shore leave practices. By the mid-nineteenth century, missionaries in the Pacific and elsewhere were often at loggerheads with sailors over the latter's quest for liquor and native women. The fact that missionaries began to enlist the cooperation of indigenous people to outlaw various forms of carousing in the Pacific

---

[12] Roald Kverndal, *Seamen's Missions: Their Origin and Early Growth* (Pasadena, CA: William Carey Library, 1986), 407–538; Gilje, *Liberty on the Waterfront*, 195–227; Gilje, "On the Waterfront."

[13] Gilje, *Liberty on the Waterfront*, 221, notes that during the 1840s about thirty-five hundred to four thousand sailors stayed in the New York Sailor Home (there were over fifty thousand sailors shipping out from this seaport during this decade) and that about half that number of sailors signed a temperance pledge. Creighton, *Rites & Passages*, 156–60, and Busch, "*Whaling Will Never Do for Me*," 120–21, cite examples of individual sailors expressing disgust for their shipmates' drunken debauchery and noting their commitment to evangelical values.

[14] Dorsey, *Reforming Men and Women*, 108.

[15] Matthew Taylor Raffety, "The Republic Afloat: Violence, Labor, Manhood, and the Law at Sea, 1789–1861" (PhD diss., Columbia University, 2005), 76.

islands made them particularly unpopular with many sailors. No doubt one mariner's grousing in his diary expressed the frustration of many of his comrades when he complained that the missionaries had gotten "glory pumped into the natives good and at both ends."[16]

When retired antebellum sailors published their memoirs and autobiographies they did so in the context of the growing tensions between reformers and mariners. These men expressed a range of views about sailors' drinking and carousing and campaigns against such pastimes. As they grappled with these issues, seamen authors highlighted how conflicted their notions of manliness were.

Commitment to evangelical values was the litmus test for sailor authors seeking admission or reintegration into mainstream America. For this reason, most of these writers paid at least lip service to the reform agenda. But retired seamen who had experienced religious conversion and were church members did much more than this. They staunchly promoted evangelical ideas. Like mainstream reformers, these men sought to transform the United States into a nation characterized by Christian piety and probity. They also advocated allegiance to Protestant Christian values, especially temperance, as the linchpin of manliness.

Samuel Leech offers an especially revealing case study of an evangelical sailor author. Religious values permeated his 1843 text and enabled him to weave together several popular kinds of life stories – a boy's coming-of-age, an intemperate youth's conversion to Christianity and sobriety, and an impoverished immigrant's upward mobility in the United States – into a compelling narrative.

Leech's account of his religious conversion illustrated how the above themes intersected. He began this part of his autobiography by recalling how difficult life was for him after his seafaring life ended and he tried to establish himself in his adopted country. When he sought a fresh start in Hartford, Connecticut, Leech met only rejection. He roamed the streets of that city "lonely and sad." The only people who initially helped Leech were religious ones. A "kindhearted Presbyterian" fed

---

[16] For quote see Busch, "*Whaling Will Never Do for Me*," 106. On the tensions between evangelical reformers, including overseas missionaries and sailors, see ibid., 105–34; Gilje, *Liberty on the Waterfront*, 220–24; Gilje, "On the Waterfront," 413–14; Creighton, *Rites & Passages*, 139–61.

and lodged him on his first night in wintry Hartford. When he tramped to Coventry, a church deacon took him home and fed him (178–79).

As Leech bounced from one job to the next, what gave him stability and fellowship was attending revival meetings. As he poignantly remembered: "a sweet calm came over me; peace and joy filled my soul." Like many others in the throes of conversion, however, Leech admitted that his road to salvation was a rocky one. He gave into temptation and caroused with "many light-minded, trifling young men." Contritely he noted: "my peace and calm were lost...and the wretchedness of a back-slider in heart filled my soul." His apostasy caused him to despair. Leech declared that he felt as if he was in a "dreary wilderness" and "heedlessly stumbled into its gloomy shadows." Edward Taylor's preaching finally led Leech to Christianity. Infused with a sense of God's grace and love, Leech turned his life around after he joined the Methodist Episcopal Church. It was only then, he stressed, that he achieved the fellowship, stability, and prosperity that he had sought (184–86/193).

Toward the end of his autobiography Leech offered a paean to his adopted nation as well as to his evangelical beliefs. Although he returned briefly to England to visit relatives, he stressed that he had no desire to leave the United States since he was well satisfied with his life: "Happiness presided at my domestic board, prosperity accompanied my temporal enterprises, and religion reigned as the ruling genius over the whole" (194).

Of course Leech's life story hit all the right notes with his American readers. British tyranny, poverty, and youthful dissipation were exchanged for American freedom, prosperity, and evangelical probity. Immigration to the United States as well as conversion to evangelical Protestantism enabled yet another destitute immigrant youth to come into his own manhood; to achieve in his adopted country the manly independence and respectability he vainly sought in his native homeland. Such a heartening life story confirmed the master plot evident in numerous antebellum accounts about upward mobility. Religious piety dovetailed with worldly success and all was well

Eager to establish his credentials as an evangelical reformer, Leech used his text to publicize how mariners' abusive drinking threatened both their manhood and the welfare of the nation they represented. Leech first did this when he recounted the drunkenness that occurred on board the HMS *Macedonian*. He stressed how fighting, cursing, and insubordination replaced order when liquor appeared on board this British ship (36–37).

But what especially perturbed Leech was how both the officers and sailors on board the *Macedonian* profaned Christmas by indulging in a debauch:

> The men were permitted to have their "full swing." Drunkenness ruled the ship. Nearly every man, with most of the officers, were in a state of beastly intoxication at night. Here, some were fighting, but were so insensibly drunk, they hardly knew whether they struck the guns or their opponents ... (37)

Leech's language made clear what he found especially reprehensible: mariners unmanned themselves when they got drunk. They degraded themselves to the level of beasts and became capable of all sorts of terrible behavior. Leech offered a vivid example of such behavior when he recalled two drunken sailors on board the USS *Boxer* quarrelling violently until one shot the other to death. Leech pointedly asserted that "RUM," the "great instigator of crimes," was to blame for this tragedy. Drunkenness had allegedly caused these sailors to lose any sense of manly restraint or self discipline (166).

According to Leech, drunkenness and other alcohol-related offenses also jeopardized Jack Tar's manliness by causing him to suffer the degrading, emasculating shipboard punishment of flogging. He recalled, for example, how sailors were whipped on board the *Macedonian* when they returned drunk from shore leave (69). One shipmate of Leech's received four dozen lashes for being drunk on duty. The next night when he was inebriated again and addressed the captain as "Billy, my boy," the man was put in irons and later suffered five dozen lashes (32–33).

Leech also stressed that men's drunkenness endangered their ship. While recalling the debauchery on board the *Macedonian* during the Christmas holiday, he declared: "Had we been at sea, a sudden gale of wind must have proved our destruction; had we been exposed to a sudden attack from an enemy's vessel, we should have fallen an easy prey to the victor..." (37). Leech's story of an intoxicated sailor committing murder on board the *Boxer* reminded Americans that abusive drinking could imperil the order of their ships and therefore the welfare of the United States.

Evangelical sailor author Samuel Holbrook also entwined concerns about manhood and nationalism in his autobiography when he excoriated mariners' drinking. He peppered his narrative with accounts of how drunkenness degraded proud, independent, competent American mariners into brawling, besotted brutes who endangered their ship and nation.[17]

Holbrook especially illustrated the terrible effects of liquor when he recounted the sad tale of one of his shipmates, a man named William. Addiction to alcohol, claimed Holbrook, destroyed not only William's ability as a mariner but also his manliness: "He [William] would sob and cry like a child" as he "bitterly lament[ed]" his "thirst for rum." William's repeated insubordination when drunk led to frequent and humiliating punishments that further emasculated him: "He had been whipped at the gangway, kicked and knocked about like a dog ..." Significantly, Holbrook ended his account of William's tragic life by describing this drunken mariner in much the same way that he portrayed abused Brazilian slaves. Recall that Holbrook had depicted the latter group as seemingly devoid of humanity, their faces "a perfect blank" (314). Holbrook suggested that William was also enslaved and unmanned when he sadly concluded: "Whiskey had usurped [William's] intellectual empire, and what *might* have been a brilliant mind, was doomed to be a blank" (248).

Holbrook conveyed both his relief and pride at having escaped a similar fate. He pointedly noted that his rigorous commitment to evangelical values, especially temperance, enabled him to "*command* respect" from other seafaring men, including officers (213–14). Somewhat smugly Holbrook remembered that he "escaped the general ruin" and "drunkard's grave" of other youths because he took the temperance pledge (58–60).

For Holbrook this pledge was a way to achieve manly independence and success. It helped him to practice self discipline in the midst of temptation (58–60). Not surprisingly, Holbrook praised the establishment of an evangelical network of institutions designed to instill this same restraint in other sailors. Organizations such as Bethel societies and temperance boarding houses, he stressed, would end the vices that degraded sailors as well as protect them from the landlords,

[17] Holbrook, *Threescore Years*, 56, 82, 87, 93, 209, 213–14, 248.

tavern and brothel keepers who fleeced lonely, vulnerable men on shore leave (348–49).

Perhaps because he published his autobiography when the reform network Holbrook approvingly referred to was just emerging, Leech was even more adamant in his call to evangelize sailors. Significantly Leech stressed that only conversion to the reform agenda, especially temperance, could save sailors from "immorality." He exhorted his readers to financially support "sailors' missionaries, bethels, and the like." They must not rest, he added, until the sailor was "elevated to his proper position, which is that of a CHRISTIAN MAN!" (173).

Of course Leech and Holbrook cemented their status as respectable, middle-class men when they equated manliness with strict adherence to Protestant Christian values. By proselytizing this message they sought to participate in the national civic culture being shaped by antebellum evangelicals. Their status as former mariners gave their comments about how best to reform Jack Tar particular legitimacy.

But a closer look at Leech's narrative suggests how even an evangelical seaman author undercut the model of manliness promulgated by reformers. This text was ultimately paradoxical. Leech subverted his professed temperance message when he recalled his shipmates "laughing," "hallooing" and "singing libidinous and bacchanalian songs" on board the *Macedonian*. Even the "chaos" and "confusion" that Leech claimed to hate seemed to have its allure. On Christmas the *Macedonian* became a ship where "confusion *reigned in glorious triumph*" (37; emphasis added).

Elsewhere in his narrative Leech noted how pleasurable drinking was. He declared that "almost every sailor" viewed being drunk as "the *acme* of sensual bliss" (36). Leech conceded that at times he participated in his shipmates' drunken revels while on shore leave. He seemed especially wistful when he recounted one such spree while in New York City: "Drinking, swearing, gambling, going to the theatre, and other kindred vices, took up all our time as long as our money lasted...We felt as if New York belonged to us and that we were really the happiest, jolliest fellows in the world" (155).

Such stories challenged readers to recognize that mariners who roistered engaged in a crucial form of male bonding. Much like the culture of the B'hoys or of firemen, that of sailors depended on initiating young males into a fraternity of proud, tough men. An important part of this process was when older mariners taught "green hands" how to chew tobacco, curse, drink, brawl, and whore. All of these activities represented a masculine rite of passage, a way for a youth to transform himself into a man.[18]

Sailor writers emphasized that it was unwise for a "green hand" to resist this process of initiation. Refusal to participate in the bawdy pleasures of the waterfront suggested that a male was not man enough to be accepted into the fraternity of sailors. For this reason David Bunnell recalled that he soon learned to drink with his shipmates: "if I did not drink, I was called 'no sailor'." He therefore decided to become a "jovial companion," to "drink, laugh, sing, and tell stories," as other tars did (92).

Sailor authors who came from genteel backgrounds stressed that participation in drunken revelries helped them to gain acceptance in the forecastle. Dana and Nordhoff highlighted this theme in their memoirs. Dana declared that a man had an obligation to drink with his shipmates and treat them, even if it meant "getting cornered." Refusal to drink not only alienated a man from his crewmates but also endangered him at sea since Jack Tar "will not be a shipmate to you on board" if you are not "shipmate to him on shore" (169). As for the grog ration, Dana admitted that he drank it along with the rest of the crew of the *Pilgrim* since it provided needed warmth and comfort on cold, wet nights (393).

A note of defiance characterized Dana's recollections of his drinking with his fellow tars. As noted earlier, one of the reasons why Dana shipped out to sea was to escape the stifling restraints of his family. Rebellion against those restraints fueled his desire to join the fraternity of mariners, a group renowned for their "rough" masculinity. Significantly in his memoir Dana recalled that he joined his shipmates' revels in order to end their "suspicion" of him because of his privileged "birth and education." He resolved *not* "to put on the gentleman" or act "ashamed" of his fellow sailors when they caroused in seaports. Instead he "dressed like the rest, in white duck trowsers,

---

[18] Creighton also stresses this point throughout *Rites & Passages* and "American Mariners and the Rites of Manhood, 1830–1870" in Colin Howell and Richard Twomey, eds., *Jack Tar in History: Essays in the History of Maritime Life and Labor* (Frederickston, NB: Acadiensis, 1991), 143–63.

blue jacket and straw hat," and drank and caroused with the best of them (168–69).

Although Nordhoff professed to be disgusted with the "scenes of drunkenness and riotous debauchery" that he witnessed repeatedly on shore leaves, he conceded that participation in such revelry was a way for a youth to establish his credentials as a manly sailor. According to him, "green hands" quickly learned that the "easiest and quickest way to become a thorough sailor was to drink rum and chew tobacco"(31–32).[19] Nordhoff admitted that he drank his grog ration while at sea (92, 34). One wonders if at times he also participated in his shipmates' carousing while in port.

Nordhoff stressed that alcohol was so important to seafaring men that they resorted to violence when it was denied them. He recalled that when his shipmates on leave boarded a steamboat and found the bar closed to them, they were indignant. Viewing the closure as "an infringement on the ever-to-be respected doctrine of Free Trade and sailors' rights," the seamen commandeered the bar and helped themselves to liquor without paying for it (33–34).

Such incidents illustrate what Paul Gilje and other historians have recently noted: one of the multiple meanings of liberty for antebellum sailors was the freedom to do as one pleased while on shore leave, including getting very drunk.[20] By the time Nordhoff published his narrative in 1855 he rejected the association of sailors' rights or liberty with debauchery. His work was ultimately one of cultural interpretation. Nordhoff sought to explain, if not justify, the behavior and values of mariners to middle-class American readers. When he recalled how his shipmates invoked the notion of "sailors' rights" to justify their requisitioning of the steamboat bar, Nordhoff challenged his readers to recognize these men as more than roisterers in search of liquor. Rightly or wrongly these sailors believed they were defending their traditional rights. They espoused increasingly contested notions of manhood, liberty, and sailors' rights that deserved to be understood, if not approved.

Seamen authors asserted that mariners ultimately sought to reclaim the manly freedom denied them on long sea voyages when they

[19] All references are to Nordhoff's *Man-of-War Life*.
[20] Gilje, *Liberty on the Waterfront*, 3–31; Raffety, "The Republic Afloat," 10.

roistered during shore leave. Significantly, John Ross Browne declared that: "A sailor let loose from a ship is no better than a wild man. He is free; he feels what it is to be free. For a little while, at least, he is no dog to be cursed and ordered about by a ruffianly master" (275).

But perhaps it was Richard Henry Dana who best conveyed the sense of liberation and renewed manhood so many seamen experienced while on leave when he stated:

I shall never forget the delightful sensation of being in the open air, with the birds singing around me, and escaped from the confinement, labor, and strict rule of a vessel – of being once more in my life, though only for a day, my own master. A sailor's liberty is but for a day; yet while it lasts it is perfect. He is under no one's eye, and can do whatever, and go wherever, he pleases. This day, for the first time, I may truly say, in my whole life, I felt the meaning of a term which I had often heard – the sweets of liberty. (168)

Dana added that he and his shipmates used their liberty to drink. They "steered for the first grog shop" in "sailor-like" fashion (169).

Sailor memoirists and autobiographers readily conceded that Jack Tar often acted irresponsibly while on shore leave. Significantly, many of these writers compared a mariner on shore leave to an animal newly released from captivity and too busy savoring its newfound freedom to exercise any restraint. Bunnell, for example, stated that a sailor in port was "like a wild bird liberated from its cage; their money flies like chaff" as they drink and carouse.[21]

Seamen authors undoubtedly recognized that they reinforced stereotypes about mariners when they recalled their drinking sprees during shore leave. Yet these writers also defended Jack Tar and implicitly rebuked landsmen who would judge sailors too harshly. The language that they used, especially their repeated assertion that seamen on shore leave were like birds freed from a cage, is especially suggestive. Mariners who caroused, they declared, sought a needed respite from a harsh seafaring life that often repressed, demeaned them. By exercising liberty in ways that challenged the authority of both maritime officers and reformers, roistering sailors allegedly asserted their rights as free men.

---

[21] Bunnell, *Travels and Adventures*, 39; see also Leech, *Thirty Years from Home*, 68; Delano, *Wanderings and Adventures*, 30.

The narratives of many retired mariners revealed their ambivalence about the evangelical model of manhood. Even those who agreed with reformers that the bawdy life of the waterfront had to end still wistfully remembered their proverbial misspent youth and the camaraderie among shipmates as they drank, whored, and brawled together. Their alluring descriptions of the traditional "rough" masculine pastimes found on the waterfront often subverted their professed opposition to such activities.

Conflicted notions of manliness were perhaps most evident in the memoirs and autobiographies of retired sailors who were lifelong alcoholics and trying to reform. Not surprisingly, these narratives offered the most graphic accounts of how drinking ravaged mariners' lives and those of their families. Such stories showcased the need to embrace an evangelical definition of manhood, one characterized by sobriety and restraint.

Paradoxically, however, many of these works also seemed drawn to a traditional "rough" masculinity. They provided detailed and enticing descriptions of waterfront pleasures, especially drinking and whoring. Such descriptions titillated readers, offering them a seductive alternative to middle-class society with its incessant calls for restraint. If only vicariously, readers could experience the proscribed pleasures of waterfront culture. But at the same time they could be reassured that transgression of evangelical values brought ultimate ruin. Narratives by alcoholic former sailors, therefore, were both repentant accounts of dissipation and voyeuristic looks at a bawdy culture.

The autobiographical writings of three such men, Ned Myers, Horace Lane, and Reuben Delano, illustrate these points. All three detailed the downward trajectory of their lives, and by implication the loss of manhood, because of abusive drinking.[22] In his autobiography, Myers recounted a litany of woes that alcohol caused him. These included: mishaps on board seafaring vessels, especially one accident that broke his collar bone and necessitated his hospitalization; estrangement from his family; and the loss of the woman he loved because his prospective mother-in-law thought him "too wild." Although Myers stated that he "cared for no one," his narrative

---

[22] For discussion of how antebellum Americans associated failure to succeed with loss of manhood see Scott A. Sandage, *Born Losers: A History of Failure in America* (Cambridge, MA: Harvard University Press, 2005), 44–69.

suggested a sadder truth: that no one cared for him. Significantly Myers described himself as drifting or floating through life, images that illustrate his instability, powerlessness, and fatalism. In the mid-1830s, shortly after his discharge from the Navy Yard hospital in Brooklyn for alcohol-related illness, Myers almost killed himself.[23] His recollection of this time in his life underscored how alcohol destroyed not only his body but also his self-respect and sense of kinship with his fellow human beings:

I had undoubtedly brought on myself a fit of the "horrors," by my recent excesses. As I went along the streets, I thought every one was sneering at me; and, though burning with thirst, I felt ashamed to enter any house to ask even for water.... I shaped my course for [the Navy Yard], feeling more like lying down to die, than anything else. ... I sat down under a high picket-fence, and the devil put it into my head, that it would be well to terminate sufferings that seemed too hard to be borne, by hanging myself on that very fence. (245)

Only the fear of what his former shipmates might think of him stopped Myers from committing suicide (246).

When Delano and Lane recounted how alcoholism devastated their lives they stressed their failure to fulfill the expectations of men. Delano, a Nantucket native who served twelve years on board whalers and whose alcoholism caused his institutionalization in the State Lunatic Hospital in Worcester, Massachusetts, illustrated this point in his 1846 memoir. He published his work when he was only thirty-seven years old and still an inmate of the asylum.[24] Delano began his memoir by recalling his pride at the age of fourteen when he began his sailing career: "I felt that I was a man then" (17).Yet manly pride quickly gave way to feelings of shame and disgust, he sadly recalled. Repeated bouts of drunkenness and carousing soon made him a "burden to society" and an "outcast." It caused his family, especially his mother, "misery" and made Delano "unfit for the society of the good

[23] Cooper, ed., *Ned Myers*, 182, 138, 143, 152, 238, 242–46. See also William S. Dudley's introduction and notes of *Ned Myers*, esp. x–xv, xvii–xviii.

[24] Delano's seaman protection certificate, number 2170, shows that he shipped out from New Bedford at the age of fifteen on July 6, 1824. See "Seamen's Protection Certificates," Abstracts of Registers, 1815–1834, New Bedford. Records of the United States Customs Service, RG 36, NA, Washington, DC. Privacy laws prevent access to inmate records at the Massachusetts State Hospital in Worcester. Since Delano was born in 1809, he would have been thirty-seven and not thirty-five as he stated in *Wanderings and Adventures*, 99.

and the virtuous" (70). Delirium tremens destroyed Delano's health, including his mind: "I had the horrors to such a degree that I could scarcely see, and my mind was in a perfect state of torment" (88). It was this tragic denouement that led to Delano's institutionalization in an insane asylum.

Horace Lane also used his autobiography to convey the anguish he and those unfortunate enough to love him experienced because of his alcoholism. He recalled, for example, feeling mortified when he recognized that drinking made him unfit to be a sailor. He also detailed how alcohol ruined his health. At one point, Lane noted, he wandered the streets of a French port hatless and shoeless under the grueling sun. He became ill and allegedly "discharged something like a half-pint of blood each day" (170).

Life in the United States was no better for Lane. He offered bitter recollections of suffering delirium tremens and destitution as he wandered the streets of New York in a disheveled state (181). He also offered a graphic account of how his poverty and desperation drove him to thievery and led to his imprisonment, including in Auburn and later Sing Sing Prisons (190–97).

But it was his mistreatment of Samoorah, a Malaysian woman whom he loved and with whom he had a child, that caused Lane the most anguish. As he recalled his callous treatment of Samoorah, Lane conveyed the shame and regret he felt for acting in ways that did not become a man. He recalled how Samoorah often waited for him outside the taverns where he drank and caroused with a "rough group." He also sheepishly noted his inability to care for their baby, who died soon after birth. His failure to care for his family, Lane ruefully admitted, "lashed my guilty conscience many a time since then." But what caused Lane the most remorse, however, was when he shipped out on board a vessel bound for the Isle of France sometime in 1820, in a desperate effort to resume his seafaring career and "dry out." Recalling his farewell to Samoorah, Lane stated: "It was a solemn day for me. I don't think I ever felt so sorrowful before or since" (161–63).

Lane, Delano, and Myers offered case studies of how alcohol destroyed sailors' manly independence and self respect. Yet each of their narratives also offered readers a happy ending, one that suggested how these authors recovered their manhood. All three writers claimed they had overcome their alcoholism. They also advocated complete abstinence and urged their readers, especially the young, not to repeat the mistakes they made. Lane, for example, hoped that his work would serve as a "warning" to "careless youth" to avoid the vices, the "quicksands" that caused him "so much trouble and distress" and to appreciate the need for "an internal, heart-felt reformation" (v). Proudly Lane stated that he had been sober and "enjoying a regular course of civilized society" for over six years (209). Similarly, Myers claimed that he was now "a perfectly sober man for the last five years" and that because of this he now enjoyed "the happiest period" in his life (269–70, 278). Delano was equally upbeat even though he resided in an insane asylum. He professed to have freed himself from his cravings for liquor and recovered his sanity (100).

Such accounts dovetailed with popular temperance stories flooding the antebellum literary market. Remorse for misspent lives, cautionary tales to the young about the perils of alcohol, and joy in finally achieving sobriety and respectability – these were the salient and increasingly shopworn characteristics of temperance stories. Lane, Delano, and Myers infused these temperance themes with poignant meaning when they detailed their tragic lives.

By appropriating and reinvigorating temperance themes, all three writers reached out to an evangelical audience. They demonstrated their commitment to participating in their nation's civic culture as reformed men. But the lives of these former mariners after their narratives were published belied their optimistic conclusions. Recall that Lane and Myers spent their last years destitute and in ill health due to alcohol-related diseases. Delano also seems to have had a troubled life after his discharge from the asylum. Like other marginal men, he did not leave behind many records. There are, for example, no probate records for him. Yet the federal census of 1870 shows him living in Taunton, Massachusetts, earning his living as a watchman. According to his death certificate, Delano died of "mania" in 1878 when he was in his late sixties.[25] Such a cause of death suggests that alcoholism as well as mental illness dogged Delano in his final years.

---

[25] According to the 1870 United States Federal Census for Taunton, Massachusetts (Bristol County), p. 2, Delano was a watchman living with his wife Sarah and other family members in Taunton. Delano died on August 22, 1878. His death certificate listed his occupation as "sailor." See "Records of Death," 1878, vol. 301, p. 142, no. 2146, Massachusetts Archives, Public Records Division, Boston, MA.

The sad outcome of these men's lives underscored the power alcohol had over them. Their narratives' vivid depiction of the evils of drinking echoed countless temperance works. But like the Washingtonians and other advocates of abstinence, these ex-mariners also subverted their professed message of temperance by recalling the joys of indulging in drunken sprees and other pastimes associated with a traditional masculinity.

Delano did this when he remembered his revels in a fancy saloon and whorehouse in Antwerp. The "Grand Salon" had "a splendid hall, with a marble floor, glass sides, decorated with elegant paintings, and illuminated with nine costly and splendid chandeliers." There were not only musicians but also a "magnificent bar-room" and "females of different nations." When Delano entered, "the drinking, dancing, singing, and talking were all in full blast." Although he said this scene was a "perfect representation of the Devil's head-quarters," he clearly enjoyed himself at the time. Later he went to a French public house where sailors could enjoy "a lass and a glass." Delano quickly found not only the bar but also "a young French damsel." As he dryly noted: "I soon made myself at home" (91–92).

Horace Lane offered similarly enticing descriptions of drunken carousing in waterfront brothels and taverns. He recalled, for example, the delights offered by "French Johnny," a New York City brothel. For a shilling Lane entered a world that he admits captivated him. There were "glittering chandeliers," excellent musicians, plenty of liquor, and fourteen young pretty women, "tipped off in fine style" with "winning smiles" and sexually available bodies (103–04).

Lane also conveyed the pleasurable sensations of drinking liquor, of getting drunk. Liquor, he stated, had "a riveting grasp on the sailor"; it made "his heart leap for joy" and enabled him to endure the hardships and loneliness of seafaring life. The most pleasurable part of drinking, he added, was when one hovered on the verge of inebriation. This was "the most exquisite period of the pleasure," when one became talkative and carefree. Sailors on the verge of drunkenness allegedly exchanged melancholy and solitude for "gayety and warmth" (37).

Such accounts evoke earlier roguish, picaresque tales. At times the narratives by Lane and Delano echoed the unrepentant memoir by William Otter, who like Lane frequented "French Johnny" when he was a sailor. Lane's and Delano's texts also suggest a subversive genre of antebellum literature. Like George Lippard, George Thompson, and some professed advocates of reform, including John Gough, these former mariners wrote narratives that portrayed vice in such alluring ways that they attracted as much as repelled the reader.[26]

It is tempting to argue that Lane and Delano merely gave lip service to values they knew most of their middle-class readers embraced. Both men were destitute; one was a recidivist criminal and ex-convict and the other was the inmate of an insane asylum. Each man hoped that publication of their narratives would turn their lives around, earning them badly needed money and an opportunity at a respectable, middle-class life.

Yet these facts do not mean that Lane and Delano merely invoked the notion of reformed manhood as a rhetorical ploy or marketing device. These men's anguished descriptions of the devastation that alcoholism caused them and their families suggested a genuine commitment to becoming the kind of men evangelicals urged. The fact that they failed to achieve long-lasting reformation made their advocacy of abstinence poignant rather than insincere.

Lane, Delano, and other seamen authors risked appearing as emasculated males when they recounted their enthrallment to liquor. In a society in which manhood meant mastery over one's body, to be a slave to liquor was to lose one's manhood. Delano particularly articulated this point when he recounted how his alcohol addiction caused him to lose the sense of manliness that he felt when he became a mariner. Images of being enslaved, even swallowed up, by alcohol recurred throughout his narrative: "I was a slave to the intoxicating bowl"; "I had become...engulfed in the abyss of intemperance"; "when the tyrant rum holds us in his slavish embrace we struggle in vain for freedom and deliverance" (66, 70, 84).

The fact that sailors personified a robust manliness in antebellum America made stories of their destruction through alcohol especially disturbing. So too did the fact that Jack Tar symbolized the nation in the early republic. The desire to safeguard the United States by protecting

[26] David Reynolds, *Beneath the American Renaissance: The Subversive Imagination in the Age of Emerson and Melville* (Cambridge, MA: Harvard University Press, 1988), 54–91, discusses the subversive nature of reform literature.

seamen's rights and bodies was a major concern for many Americans. It fueled the campaign against flogging on the high seas. It was also one of the major reasons why the United States fought the Barbary Wars and the War of 1812. In fact what galvanized public support for these wars were fears that the nation's sovereignty and honor were imperiled when its sailors were enslaved by Barbary State corsairs or impressed by the British. Seamen authors' vivid descriptions of how drunkenness blighted their lives exacerbated Americans' growing concern that alcohol threatened Jack Tar and the country he represented as much as any foreign enemy or abusive American officer did.

But these ex-mariners pointedly counter posed their stories of alcoholism with accounts of how conversion to temperance led to liberation from addiction and reclamation of manhood. Delano, for example, declared that the temperance movement empowered him to break "the bondage of the evil habit that chained me" (100). Lane declared that temperance enabled him to become once again "master of my own ship and cargo" (218). Similarly, Myers proudly recounted the transformation he experienced after a three-month stay in a hospital deprived him of liquor and forced him to become sober: "I left that place, into which I had entered a miserable heart-broken cripple, a happy man.... I was lightened of the heaviest of all my burthens, and felt I could go through the world rejoicing, though, literally, moving on crutches" (270).

Freedom, joy, empowerment – these were recurrent images when seamen authors recalled their struggles to become sober by embracing abstinence. Like the Washingtonians and other recovering alcoholics, these former mariners proudly remembered when they allegedly became free of their addiction as a time of renewed manly independence and self respect.

Through their testimonials about reformed manhood seamen authors challenged their countrymen to accept them into the mainstream of U.S. society. These writers also sought to convince their fellow Americans that they could contribute to a national discourse about how to reform mariners. Perhaps some of these men even hoped to become a poster child for the temperance movement by offering a tragic case study of how alcoholism debased him.

Not surprisingly, seamen authors often folded their stories about personal redemption and reclaimed manhood into a larger national narrative about the need to regenerate America through religious conversion. Like countless other antebellum Americans, these writers portrayed Christian piety as the linchpin of reform. Myers, for example, stressed that it was reading the Bible as well as other religious literature in the hospital that gave him strength in his repeated efforts to achieve sobriety (265). Similarly, Lane declared that "the thundering voice of conviction...made such a tremendous noise about the hatchway of my soul" that it steered him from "the coast of eternal despair" and gave him the strength to become temperate (204).

Other seamen authors who were abusive drinkers also credited their reformation to religious conversion. Nicholas Peter Isaacs offered a particularly powerful account of his conversion in his 1845 work *Twenty Years Before the Mast*. He recollected that this event occurred when he was tempted by a strong urge to resume drinking after eight years of sobriety. God's grace allegedly rescued him as he felt himself being enveloped in "a horror of darkness." His autobiography conveyed the joy and strength that he felt during this experience:

a glorious light broke into my soul, and my mind rejoiced with joy unspeakable, and full of glory. Indeed it seemed to me that the light of God's presence filled my room. A radiant circle glowed round my bed for a moment, and when it disappeared a sweetly calm assurance filled my overflowing soul... the love of Christ welcomed me and mine to join him...

That night of "glorious experience" resonated throughout Isaacs's narrative thirty years later. It anchored him and gave him the will to resist despair and the "fierce temptations" of the sailor's life. Significantly he also claimed that it freed him once and for all from the "slavery of drunkenness" (170–71).

Such testimonials echoed countless evangelical works that trumpeted religious conversion as the sine qua non of reformation. Yet seamen authors were not content to merely reiterate the evangelical message. They also sought to reshape it in order to better address the needs of Jack Tar. In doing this sailor memoirists and autobiographers often revealed misgivings about the process of evangelization and reform roiling antebellum American culture.

Not all sailor authors, however, expressed reservations about these developments. Recall that Leech and Holbrook, both staunch Methodists, unequivocally supported evangelical reform efforts. But ultimately these men were the exception not the rule among seamen memoirists and autobiographers. Many of these writers expressed skepticism, even disdain, for reformers and missionaries. They accused evangelical activists of using oppressive and patronizing means in their efforts to "elevate" Jack Tar into a "Christian MAN." In the end such methods, groused many sailor authors, alienated mariners and inadvertently thwarted their conversion to reformed manhood.

Nathaniel Ames was one of the first seamen memoirists to level these criticisms. In two memoirs – published, respectively, in 1830 and 1832 – Ames declared that reformers and missionaries too often substituted a narrow dogmatic sectarianism for compassion and morality. He also chided temperance advocates for berating hard drinking seamen instead of rewarding mariners who voluntarily gave up their grog ration with money and public praise. But Ames reserved his sharpest barbs for the evangelicals who published and disseminated countless missionary tracts. Such publications, he fumed, were riddled with sectarian dogma and did more harm than good, especially when people were pressured to read them. Bitterly Ames declared: "Nothing has so powerful a tendency to make religion contemptible as the attempts of … hot-headed and wrong-headed zealots to thrust it down the throats of uneducated people in the disgusting form of religious tracts."[27]

What this former mariner found especially offensive about the Protestant evangelical establishment was that it allegedly denied Jack Tar his due as a man. Reformers, angrily claimed Ames, patronized, infantilized seamen. He believed this was glaringly obvious in the *Sailors Magazine*. Ames singled out this periodical for scorching criticism in *Nautical Reminiscences*, calling it "an exceedingly silly periodical," written in a style "too puerile, too silly for children of five years old." Sailors, asserted Ames, were not "easily gulled" by "the fabricators of this pious magazine." They rightly recognized that this journal insulted them. Ames emphatically noted that reformers would never be effective until they dealt with seamen as "rational and accountable beings" or in other words, as men (47).

Dana also criticized reformers in his memoir. He particularly targeted temperance reformers for begrudging Jack Tar his grog ration

---

[27] Ames, *Nautical Reminiscences*, 40–48 (42 for quote); Ames, *Mariner's Sketches*, 44–45, 58–59,198–99,241–43.

while allowing a captain to drink "as much as he chooses." Most sailors, he asserted, resented being deprived of their traditional right to enjoy rum, especially when no suitable non-alcoholic drink, such as hot coffee or chocolate, was available. They allegedly viewed the temperance movement as yet another infringement on their rights and liberties. In fact, stressed Dana, seamen generally regarded efforts to enforce temperance on board seafaring vessels as "a new instrument of tyranny" (392–93).

Sailor authors who led hardscrabble lives after their years at sea ended were even more bitter towards reformers than a successful attorney and writer like Dana. Jacob Hazen, for example, bristled at how naïve, condescending, and even callous such people were towards mariners. He was openly contemptuous of the female missionaries who distributed religious tracts on board the *Columbus* when he was in irons awaiting punishment. In his memoir he portrayed such women as naïve and ignorant of the hardships and abuses sailors like he faced. When one young "lady" missionary tried to give him religious literature Hazen snarled that he had "been damned long ago." When she persevered he told her to give the tracts to the officers whose curses would shock her. The young woman then abruptly left Hazen but not before telling him "you terrify me." Her reaction of course merely confirmed what Hazen thought when he first saw the missionaries come on board: they were incapable of providing genuine compassion and solace to him and would prove to be "a Job's comforter at best" (214–17).

Hazen's story underscored the belief of many seamen authors that evangelical activists demeaned rather than helped Jack Tar. In their narratives some former mariners articulated their sense of being betrayed by reformers who raised hopes for Christian fellowship and badly needed financial help but in the end failed to deliver on either.

This theme was prominent in Lane's autobiography. This author excoriated "benevolent men in authority" for failing to provide any assistance to newly discharged convicts like him. He bitterly remembered how his desperate efforts to find charity if not work were repeatedly rebuffed after his release from Sing Sing. Lane's anger was palpable when he chided reformers: "When your example agrees with your profession of benevolence, and not till then, need you expect to reclaim the vile wretch over whom you have influence, and over whom you sit in authority" (203–4).

Lane's condemnation of reformers perhaps reflected his fears that the evangelical agenda was yet another snare, oppressing and humiliating rather than liberating him. Since he was a recidivist thief and alcoholic, reformers' reproaches against backsliders and their campaigns to ostracize such men must also have given him pause. Like a seafaring career, evangelical reform might have promised more than it delivered, at least for seamen authors like Lane.

Mainline churches also bitterly disappointed many seamen authors. Whereas Leech and Holbrook remembered finding solace in these institutions, other former sailors groused that churches were welcoming in name only but not in fact. In his 1854 memoir merchant seaman Cyrene Clarke[28] resentfully noted how most churches kept mariners at arm's length despite their professed concern for them. Congregations regarded sailors as being in "the lowest class of society" and blanched at the prospect of having them sit with virtuous and refined churchgoers in "their finely cushioned pews." Instead sailors were "shove[d] into the nigger's pew" (74).

Clarke's comments occurred at a time when changing attitudes towards masculinity undermined sailors' standing in American society. By the mid-nineteenth century this society had become less tolerant of a rowdy, roistering masculinity that it had earlier endured, if not condoned. The public, for example, demanded the disbanding of urban volunteer fire companies because of their persistent drinking and brawling.[29] The evangelical movement became more insistent in promulgating its model of manliness. Men who violated reformers' injunctions were increasingly denounced and marginalized in genteel American society.[30]

---

[28] Clarke's *Glances at Life* discussed his voyages on two whaling voyages on board the *Bengal* and the *Parana*. Unfortunately, there seems to be no extant crew list or logbook for the *Parana* for the 1853 voyage Clarke discussed but the crew list of the *Bengal* notes Clarke on the whaling voyage leaving from New London on September 23, 1850, for the Pacific Ocean. See "List of Persons Composing the Crew of the Ship Bengal...," NA, Northeast Region, Boston, MA (NARA).

[29] Greenberg, *Cause for Alarm*, 41–79.

[30] Reformers focused on ending drinking, prostitution, and other traditional male pleasures especially did this. See Dorsey, *Reforming Men and Women*, esp. 113–31, and Burton, "Whoring, Drinking Sailors."

Seamen authors were well aware of the fact that the model of manliness prescribed by "respectable" Americans could hurt Jack Tar. Their narratives, especially those published after the mid-1840s, articulated both anger and anguish over how many of their fellow citizens ostracized mariners. Clarke of course expressed these sentiments when he bitterly noted how white American mariners were forced to sit in church pews reserved for the lowliest, most marginal members of American society.

Other sailor authors had painful memories of how they were shunned by "respectable" landsmen. Ben-Ezra Stiles Ely ruefully recalled how even his own relatives initially avoided him after his whaling voyage. His filthy and ragged condition appalled them: "I stood surrounded, with all eyes turned on me, as if I had been some wild animal, for all were so lost in amazement, that they never thought of shaking hands; and had any thing affectionate stirred within them, the scent of tar and bilge-water must have sent the feeling back whence it came" (118). It was only days later when he was well scrubbed and tailored, recalled Ely, that his family welcomed him home.

Sailor authors reproached their countrymen when they recounted such stories. They challenged Americans to justify the marginalizing of men who protected their nation's borders and facilitated its overseas commerce. Some of these writers also suggested that Jack Tar gravitated towards grog shops and other alleged dens of debauchery since these places were the only ones to welcome him. As Ely asserted, a sailor was "often reckless" since he was usually ostracized by genteel people. The latter "expect no good of him, and show him no civility." The results were predictable: "'Nobody cares for Old Joe; and therefore Old Joe cares for nobody'" (85–86).

At times a sailor author tried to reassure his readers that there was nothing to fear from mariners. William Whitecar Jr. was one such writer. Like Ely, he went on only one whaling voyage, lasting four years. His extensive vocabulary and dedication of his book to his father for encouraging his writing suggests that Whitecar came from an educated, middle-class family.[31] Perhaps this background made

---

[31] See Whitecar's *Four Years Aboard the Whaleship*. For his book dedication see viii. He came from Philadelphia and said that in June 1855 he joined the *Bark Pacific* leaving from New Bedford under Captain John W. Sherman (13). For confirmation, see "List of Persons Composing the Crew of the *Bark Pacific* ...," NARA. Two

him especially sensitive to slights that sailors suffered at the hands of "respectable" people. Like Ely, Whitecar asserted that such people "assist[ed]" in Jack Tar's "demoralization" by shunning him (384–85). He pleaded with genteel families, especially their ladies, to welcome sailors into their homes. Such men, asserted Whitecar, would not act like "a rude, uncouth being – half fish, half man" or "a boorish clown." More importantly, a seaman would never abuse the hospitality offered him by "corrupt[ing]" a family's daughter or "entic[ing]" their son to ship out to sea. Instead Jack Tar would quickly learn to "revere the ties and restraints of home and society" (386–87).

Whitecar's pleading tone suggests that he recognized how unlikely genteel Americans were to socialize with seamen. The narratives of many ex-mariners highlight how difficult it was for these men to establish themselves on land, especially if they had been at sea for many years. Their anguish was evident as they recounted how their countrymen and even members of their immediate family failed to welcome them back, let alone offer any badly needed help. Even those who eventually established themselves as relatively prosperous, well regarded citizens still had bitter memories of the numerous rebuffs they suffered when they tried to forge a new life on land.[32]

Although they articulated resentment against mainstream American society for often marginalizing, demeaning, mariners, sailor authors still sought to belong to this society. Through their dramatic stories of conversion to Christianity and temperance these writers hoped to convince even the most skeptical of their readers that they had in fact reformed. The act of autobiographical writing, therefore, was ultimately a strategy used by former mariners to become part of the dominant culture that often viewed Jack Tar with hostility.

Yet seamen authors also challenged the evangelical churches that were a mainstay of this culture. Like so many antebellum Americans, especially working-class people, these writers participated in a populist revolt against traditional church authority. They refused to be

William B. Whitecars appear in *Mc Elroy's Philadelphia Directory for 1855* ... 18th ed. (Philadelphia: Edward C. & John Biddle, 1855), 596. One was a druggist and the other was a real estate broker. Whitecar's father could well have been one of these men.

[32] Leech, *A Voice from the Main Deck*, 179–80; Nordhoff, *Whaling and Fishing*, 382–83.

pigeonholed into one denomination or be hemmed in by allegiance to particular sectarian dogma. They also insisted they had the right to interpret Christian teachings for themselves. As Nathan Hatch and other scholars have noted, these developments illustrated the democratization of evangelical Protestantism and the profound impact this process had on the lives of ordinary people in the early republic.[33]

Horace Lane highlighted these points. Despite his briefly joining the Methodist church after his conversion, Lane disavowed ties to any specific Christian denomination. He stressed that he sampled a variety of churches, adhering to none. Defiantly Lane asserted:

> I feel under no obligation as it regards tenets, to any society; for I got my knowledge from the bible, and my wisdom, be it little or much, from the same fountain from whence all Christians profess to obtain theirs.... I feel free to enter...every house or place of Christian devotion.... By this freedom, I have a chance to judge for myself, and not take a hearsay to judge my fellows with, striving to live by no law, but the law of faith and good works. (215)

Myers's approach to religion was similar to Lane's. Although baptized as an infant into the Episcopal Church, Myers was indifferent to which particular sect or denomination he belonged. "Sects have little weight with me," he stressed, "the heart being the main-stay, under God's grace." Convinced that there was "no difference" among the sects, Myers noted that he still occasionally attended Episcopalian services even though he had joined the Dutch Reformed Church because he liked one of its ministers (275).

Unlike Lane and Myers, Nicholas Peter Isaacs did not casually sample different churches. He joined the Methodist Episcopal Church, attracted by its revivalist measures, especially camp meetings which filled him with tremendous joy (179–81). Yet Isaacs also condemned churches, claiming that too many of them substituted a sterile, sectarian orthodoxy for genuine Christianity. To dramatize this point Isaacs

---

[33] Nathan O. Hatch, *The Democratization of American Christianity* (New Haven, CT: Yale University Press, 1989). See also the following works: Sutton, *Journeymen for Jesus*; Jama Lazerow, *Religion and the Working Class in Antebellum America* (Washington, DC: Smithsonian Institution Press, 1995); Ronald Schultz, "God and Workingmen: Popular Religion and the Formation of Philadelphia's Working Class, 1790–1830," in Ronald Hoffman and Peter J. Albert, eds., *Religion in a Revolutionary Age* (Charlottesville: University of Virginia Press, 1994), 125–55.

recounted a dream he had shortly after his religious conversion. Like the main character in John Bunyan's classic work *Pilgrim's Progress*, Isaacs described how in his dream he had to undergo all sorts of trials before achieving salvation. One of the obstacles he faced was a man who had only one large eye in the middle of his forehead and who preached the doctrine of predestination. When Isaacs rejected the man's Calvinist determinism, the latter marched away and he continued his journey toward God. According to Isaacs, "the one-eyed man may represent bigotry, which has an eye only for *theory* and creeds, and whether found in a Methodist or Presbyterian cares more for the letter than for the Spirit; more for the modes of faith than for a right state of the heart" (175, 178).

Stressing the importance of "a right state of the heart" was a leitmotif in numerous antebellum conversion narratives, including those by former mariners. Even ex-sailors who criticized orthodox churches and sectarian dogma stressed the importance of having a heartfelt faith in Jesus Christ. Only this faith, they asserted, could give downtrodden men the strength to manfully face numerous misfortunes and to forge better lives for themselves.

This theme was evident in the 1860 memoir of former merchant seaman James Caswell. He stressed that conversion to Christianity enabled him to overcome despair after his seafaring life ended in 1859. By then he was an impoverished, one armed man living in New Bedford, bereft of family and friends.[34] As Caswell ruefully noted in his narrative, he was "sick at heart." Conversion to Christianity, however, made him determined to "do right in the sight of God and man" (67).

Roland Gould perhaps offered the most poignant example of how Christian faith enabled a retired mariner to endure adversity. By 1846 Gould was an unemployed carpenter in Winchester, New Hampshire whose pretty young wife had left him. During a July 4th celebration an explosion of gunfire permanently blinded Gould. It also broke his

---

[34] Caswell's name appears on the crew lists of various whaling ships leaving New Bedford during the 1840s and 1850s. See "Crewmen Search Results," New Bedford Free Public Library, http://www.ci.new-bedford.ma.us/SERVICES/LIBRARY/whaling-project/crewlist.asp. Caswell, *Sketch of the Adventures*, 64–65, stated he lost his left arm after being wounded while fighting with Chilean rebels against their government at the Battle of Concepción, February 1859.

upper jaw, knocked out all his upper teeth, and mangled his right
arm. It was only during his prolonged convalescence that Gould felt
he experienced God's grace. At a time when he was badly crippled
and forlorn, Gould felt tremendously empowered, liberated, by allegedly hearing God's voice: "I felt as though a great burden had been
removed from my heart and that I could rely upon Jesus as my Savior"
(213–17).[35]

Gould's account underscored the piety that characterized the life
narratives of former mariners. These men asserted that manly independence, freedom, and success ultimately depended on embracing
Christian values. But this belief did not prevent them from often
challenging the authority of ministers who tried to enforce religious
orthodoxy or rebuking churches for treating seafaring men as pari-
ahs. Most of these writers also agreed on one point: reformers were
all too often naïve, meddlesome, and patronizing toward mariners,
understanding little about the hardships they endured.

These criticisms illuminate how democratic and populist Protestant
Christianity had become in the antebellum United States. Religion and
reform, seamen authors repeatedly insisted, should not be imposed on
the mass of Americans by evangelical elites. Instead ordinary working-class people should have the right to interpret these developments
in ways that empowered, nurtured, them. As they made this argument, sailor memoirists and autobiographers asserted their right to
shape the nation's culture as free, proud American men.

[35] The United States Federal Census for 1850 for the town of Winchester, Cheshire
County, New Hampshire, http://www.gale.ancestry.com, 22 of 79, lists Gould as a
thirty-three-year-old carpenter and notes that he is blind. Significantly, the census
listed nothing of value in the column under "value of estate."

Afterword

> There is an Indian story – at least I heard it as an Indian story – about an Englishman who, having been told that the world rested on a platform which rested on the back of an elephant which rested in turn on the back of a turtle, asked (perhaps he was an ethnographer; it is the way they behave), what did the turtle rest on? Another turtle. And that turtle? "Ah, Sahib, after that it is turtles all the way down."[1]

The anthropologist Clifford Geertz tells the above anecdote to illustrate a crucial point: past events and the stories constructed about them are so complex that it is ultimately impossible to get to the bottom of their multiple meanings. There are always more turtles to uncover as one engages in the process of analysis, interpretation. Yet if definitive interpretations elude historians that does not absolve them from trying to make sense of the past as best they can by subjecting extant texts to analysis.

Jack Tar's Story has done this with the life narratives of antebellum American sailors. These memoirs and autobiographies were deceptive. On the surface, they seemed like straightforward recollections of what these men experienced during their seafaring years. But, as this book has shown, these narratives actually offered richly detailed, multilayered stories about their authors' experiences, including impressment, combat, incarceration, flogging, roistering, and religious conversion.

---

[1] Clifford Geertz, *The Interpretation of Cultures: Selected Essays* (New York: Basic Books, Inc., Publisher, 1973), 28–29.

The entwined themes of manliness and nationalism permeated discussions of these seemingly disparate issues. Repeatedly, seamen authors stressed how they and their shipmates defended their manhood while upholding the liberty and honor of the United States. As they fleshed out this argument, these writers forged a public persona of American mariners as manly men who played a pivotal role in transforming a fledgling republic into a powerful nation.

Sailor memoirists and autobiographers were very ambivalent about mainstream American culture. Even as they sought to be a part of this culture, they stood apart from it. These writers tempered paeans to American nationalism by chiding their countrymen for not doing more to protect Jack Tar from foreign enemies and abusive officers in the United States' naval and commercial fleet. Although most sailor authors espoused evangelical Protestantism, they often did so in ways that challenged the authority of both established churches and reformers. Ultimately, these former mariners walked a fine line between professing allegiance to dominant American values while also challenging them.

The fact that they at times misremembered or misrepresented significant events from their seafaring past has complicated yet also enriched study of their autobiographical works. Analysis of sailors' actual experiences at sea and how these men later depicted these experiences in their narratives has highlighted what makes the study of such texts so challenging for the historian. In the end, autobiographies and memoirs are not necessarily accurate descriptions of the narrator/subject's past life. Instead they are carefully constructed interpretations of this past.

One of the goals of *Jack Tar's Story* has been to prod historians to focus more critically on the life narratives of antebellum sailors. More particularly, this book has urged scholars to recognize that such works are an important source for understanding the construction of historical public memory about war, masculinity, nationalism, captivity, punishment, and other crucial issues. This book has also explored a development that warrants further investigation by both literary and historical scholars – the process by which seemingly ordinary, often obscure, working-class men in antebellum America crafted stories about their lives.

It is often a frustrating and daunting task to study self narratives. One must determine how factually accurate these accounts were. The student of autobiographical works must also analyze the multiple concerns that shaped how a narrator/subject recounted his past. But investigation of such texts ultimately offers rich dividends when it illuminates the values of the authors who produced them and the world in which they lived.

Appendix

The following list contains the autobiographies and memoirs of antebellum sailors especially used in this study (I note the first editions of texts but relied on the expanded or revised editions):

1. Ames, Nathaniel. *A Mariner's Sketches, Originally Published in the Manufacturers and Farmers Journal* ... Providence, RI: Cory, Marshall & Hammond, 1830.

2. ——*Nautical Reminiscences*. Providence, RI: William Marshall, 1832; and Hartford, CT: W. Marshall & Co., 1832.

3. Browne, J. Ross. *Etchings of a Whaling Cruise, with Notes of a Sojourn on the Island of Zanzibar* ... New York: Harpers & Brothers, Pub., 1846.

4. Bunnell, David C. *The Travels and Adventures of David C. Bunnell, During Twenty-Three Years of a Sea-faring Life* ... Palmyra, NY: J.H. Bortles, 1831.

5. Caswell, James. *A Sketch of the Adventures of James Caswell, During Fifteen Years on the Ocean* ... New Bedford, MA: privately printed for author, 1860.

6. Clarke, Cyrene M. *Glances at Life upon the Sea, or Journal of a Voyage to the Antarctic Ocean* ... Middletown, CT: Charles H. Pelton, Printer, 1854.

7. [Cobb, Josiah], *A Green Hand's First Cruise, Roughed Out from the Log-Book of Memory* ... 2 vols. Boston: Otis, Broaders, and Company, 1841.

8. Dana, Jr., Richard Henry. *Two Years Before the Mast. A Personal Narrative of Life at Sea.* 1840. Reprinted with introduction, notes, and appendices by Thomas Philbrick. New York: Penguin Books, 1981.

9. Delano, Reuben, *The Wanderings and Adventures of Reuben Delano, Being A Narrative of Twelve Years' Life in a Whale Ship* ... New York: H. Long & Brother, 1846; and Worcester, MA: J. Grout, Jr., 1846.

10. Durand, James R. *The Life and Adventures of James R. Durand During a Period of Fifteen Years From 1801 to 1816* ... 1817. Revised and enlarged ed. 1820. Reprint of 1820 edition with introduction and notes by George S. Brooks. New Haven, CT: Yale University Press, 1926. This 1820 edition was reprinted by Chapman Billies Incorporated, Sandwich, MA, 1995. Pages in this book refer to this last edition.

11. Ely, Ben-Ezra Stiles. *"There She Blows": A Narrative of a Whaling Voyage* ... 1849. Reprint with introduction and notes by Curtis Dahl. Middletown, CT: Wesleyan University Press, 1971.

12. Roland F. Gould. *The Life of Gould, an Ex-Man-of-War's Man* ... Claremont, NH: Claremont Manufacturing Co., 1867.

13. Hazen, Jacob A. *Five Years Before the Mast, or Life in the Forecastle Aboard of a Whaler and Man-of-War.* Philadelphia, PA: Willis P. Hazard, 1854.

14. Holbrook, Samuel F. *Threeescore Years: An Autobiography, Containing Incidents of Voyages and Travels, Including Six Years in a Man-of-War* ... Boston: James French & Co., 1857.

15. Isaacs, Nicholas Peter. *Twenty Years Before the Mast, or Life in the Forecastle* ... New York: J.P. Beckwith, 1845.

16. Lane, Horace. *The Wandering Boy, Careless Sailor, and Result of Inconsideration. A True Narrative.* Skaneateles, NY: Luther A. Pratt, 1839.

17. Leech, Samuel. *A Voice from the Main Deck: Being a Record of the Thirty Years' Adventures of Samuel Leech* (originally published in 1843 as *Thirty Years from Home, or A Voice from the Main Deck* ...). 1857 (16th ed.). Reprinted with introduction and notes by Michael J. Crawford. Annapolis, MD: Naval Institute Press, 1999. This edition reproduces the text of the 1857 edition.

18. M'Lean, James. *Seventeen Years' History, of the Life and Sufferings of James M'Lean, an Impressed American Citizen and Seaman* ... 1814. Reprinted with introduction and notes in Daniel E. Williams, ed., *Liberty's Captives: Narratives of Confinement in the Print Culture of the Early Republic.* Athens: The University of Georgia Press, 2006, 164–79.

19. Murrell, William Meacham. *Cruise of the Frigate Columbia Around the World, Under the Command of Commodore George C. Read, in 1838, 1839, and 1840.* Boston: Benjamin B. Mussey, 1840.

20. Myers, Ned. *Ned Myers; or, A Life Before the Mast.* Edited by J. Fenimore Cooper. 1843. Reprinted with introduction and notes by William S. Dudley. Annapolis, MD: Naval Institute Press, 1989.

21. Nordhoff, Charles. *Man-of-War Life. A Boy's Experience in the United States Navy, During a Voyage Around the World in a Ship-of-the-Line.* 1855. Reprinted with introductions and notes and appendices by John B. Hattendorf. Annapolis, MD: Naval Institute Press, 1985.

22. ———*Whaling and Fishing.* In *Nine Years a Sailor: Being Sketches of Personal Experience in the United States Naval Service, The American and British Merchant Marine, and the Whaling Service.* Cincinnati, OH: Moore, Wilstach, Keys & Co., 1857.

23. Penny, Joshua. *The Life and Adventures of Joshua Penny, ... Who Was Impressed into the British Service ...* 1815. Reprinted in Williams, ed. *Liberty's Captives,* 197 – 238.

24. Smith, Moses. *Naval Scenes in the Last War; or, Three Years on Board the Frigate Constitution ...* Boston: Gleason's Publishing Hall, 1846.

25. Whitecar, Jr., William B. *Four Years Aboard the Whaleship ...* Philadelphia, PA: J.B. Lippincott & Co, 1860; and London: Trubner & Co., 1860.

26. Wordon, James M. *The Life and Adventures of James M. Wordon ...* 1854. Revised and enlarged ed. New London, CT: Starr & Farnaam, Printers, 1855.

Index

abolitionism, 62, 94, 114, 126
abuse of sailors by officers,
    47–8, 118, 119, 127, 128,
    See also flogging
African Americans
    Cuffe's account, 15, 93–7, 93 n14
    Equiano's slave narrative, 10, 14
    Haitian Revolution and, 93–7
    impressment as enslavement
        and, 60
    paucity of autobiographies from
        sailors, 14–15, 15 n34
    protest of abusive treatment at
        sea, 142
alcoholism
    Delano's struggle with, 160, 162
    as enslavement, 61, 165
    J. H. Garrison's, 144
    Lane's battle with, 35, 161–2
    Myers's struggle with, 159, 162
    social isolation and shame of, 160
    temperance movement against,
        61, 146–51, 165–7
Alert (merchant vessel), 45
Alligator, HMS, 64
America. *See* United States
American Revolution, 51–3, 57,
    92–3, 96

American Seamen's Friend
    Society, 150
Ames, Nathaniel, 31–3, 100–5,
    100 n27, 167
Anderson, Benedict, 4, 56
Anglo-Americans. *See also* race and
    racism
    book's focus on writings of,
        14–15
    disillusionment with Latin
        American independence
        movements, 100
    ethnic prejudice against
        Portuguese sailors, 124,
        139, 141
    slaveholder fears of black
        uprising inspired by Haiti,
        90, 96
audience. *See* reading public
authenticity of autobiographical
    writing
    book's purpose and, 23
    editorial intrusion, 18–21
    issues and analysis, 6–11, 8 n19,
        176
    official records as verification, 74
    Penny's and Durand's story
        discrepancies, 65–7